Slow Harms and Citizen Action

STUDIES IN COMPARATIVE ENERGY AND
ENVIRONMENTAL POLITICS

Series editors: Todd A. Eisenstadt, American University, and Joanna I. Lewis,
Georgetown University

*The Roots of Engagement: Understanding Opposition and Support for
Resource Extraction*
Moisés Arce, Michael S. Hendricks, and Marc S. Polizzi

*Fueling State Capitalism: How Domestic Politics Shapes Foreign Investments of
National Oil Companies*
Andrew Cheon

*Who Speaks for Nature? Indigenous Movements, Public Opinion, and
the Petro-State in Ecuador*
Todd A. Eisenstadt and Karleen Jones West

A Good Life on a Finite Earth: The Political Economy of Green Growth
Daniel J. Fiorino

*Slow Harms and Citizen Action: Environmental Degradation and Policy Change
in Latin American Cities*
Veronica Herrera

*The Politics of Extraction: Territorial Rights, Participatory Institutions, and
Conflict in Latin America*
Maiah Jaskoski

*Democracy in the Woods: Environmental Conservation and Social Justice in India,
Tanzania, and Mexico*
Prakash Kashwan

Breaking Ground: From Extraction Booms to Mining Bans in Latin America
Rose J. Spalding

Slow Harms and Citizen Action

Environmental Degradation and Policy Change in Latin American Cities

VERONICA HERRERA

OXFORD
UNIVERSITY PRESS

Oxford University Press is a department of the University of Oxford. It furthers the University's objective of excellence in research, scholarship, and education by publishing worldwide. Oxford is a registered trade mark of Oxford University Press in the UK and certain other countries.

Published in the United States of America by Oxford University Press
198 Madison Avenue, New York, NY 10016, United States of America.

© Oxford University Press 2024

All rights reserved. No part of this publication may be reproduced, stored in a retrieval system, or transmitted, in any form or by any means, without the prior permission in writing of Oxford University Press, or as expressly permitted by law, by license, or under terms agreed with the appropriate reproduction rights organization. Inquiries concerning reproduction outside the scope of the above should be sent to the Rights Department, Oxford University Press, at the address above.

You must not circulate this work in any other form
and you must impose this same condition on any acquirer.

CIP data is on file at the Library of Congress

ISBN 978-0-19-766903-7 (pbk.)
ISBN 978-0-19-766902-0 (hbk.)

DOI: 10.1093/oso/9780197669020.001.0001

Paperback printed by Marquis Book Printing, Canada
Hardback printed by Bridgeport National Bindery, Inc., United States of America

For Sebastián Ignacio

Contents

Acknowledgments   ix

1. The Politics of Slow Harms in the Latin American City   1
2. Slow Harms: Ubiquity and Invisibility in the Global South   33
3. Expansive Policy Shifts in Argentina: The Power of Strong Bonds with Strong Bridges   70
4. Stagnated Policy Shifts in Colombia: On Strong Bonds with Weak Bridges   113
5. Uninitiated Policy Shifts in Peru: The Challenge of Weak Bonds with No Bridges   157
6. Cities, Pollution, and Democracy   198

Appendix: Methodological Narrative   213
References   221
Index   247

Acknowledgments

We live in an era of rapidly unfolding environmental threats. Fracking and floods bring about complex challenges for policymakers and those whose lives are upended by environmental disasters. But not all threats barge in. This book examines a slice of environmental degradation—wastewater pollution—that, like many environmental problems, is ever present and yet invisible. Many harms become part of the everyday landscape through years of habituation. This book explores the politics of everyday toxic exposure and how the specific temporal dimensions of different environmental problems can impact whether collective action forms to address them.

Slow Harms and Citizen Action centers around the long-duration events of urbanization and industrialization in three South American capitals where rivers became, over time, the public urinal of the city. The book documents diverse forms of environmental activism in unexpected places and under hostile conditions. I also show how postconflict legacies matter for environmentalism, linking histories of political violence to today's pursuit of environmental justice. I was able to write this book due to the immense support I received from the nearly 200 people who sat for interviews, invited me into their workplaces and homes, and shared with me their perspectives on our changing planet. Several people were especially critical in opening doors for me. I am immensely grateful to Marina Aizen, Andres Napoli, Mora Arauz, Javier Garcia Silva, Javier Garcia Elorrio, Celia Frutos, Pepe Mateos, Medardo Galindo, Marta Luque, Jose Luis Vasquez Vega, and two individuals who wish to remain anonymous.

I received extended periods of institutional support to research and draft portions of the manuscript, from the Ford Foundation Postdoctoral Fellowship, the American Association of University Women Postdoctoral Fellowship, the Career Enhancement Fellowship from the Institute for Citizen & Scholars, and the Visiting Scholar Program at the David Rockefeller Center for Latin American Studies at Harvard University.

Numerous colleagues have provided invaluable feedback and encouragement at different stages of the manuscript's development, particularly in its very early iterations, including Matt Amengual, Taylor Boas, Ruth Berins

Collier, Kent Eaton, Todd Eisenstadt, Tulia Falleti, Gustavo Flores-Macías, Lorenza Fontana, Candelaria Garay, Ricardo Gutiérrez, Kathryn Hochstetler, Alisha Holland, Maiah Jaskoski, Scott Mainwaring, Lindsay Mayka, Eduardo Moncada, Megan Mullin, Jami Nunez, Evan Perkoski, Alison Post, Meg Rithmire, Timmons Roberts, Ben Ross-Schneider, Sylvia Sellers-Garcia, Rachel Stern, Mariela Szwarcberg Daby, Brian Wampler, and Erika Weinthal.

I benefited tremendously from questions and feedback I received in seminars and presentations of my work at American University, Brown University, Harvard University, MIT, University of Pennsylvania, UC Berkeley, University of New Mexico, Pomona College, and George Washington University. I am grateful to the Center for Innovation at UCLA and J. R. DeShazo for sponsoring a book conference to workshop the manuscript, and generous and incisive comments from Isabella Alcañiz, Aseem Prakash, Michael Ross, and Hillel Soifer. I finished this project after becoming an associate professor at UCLA; I thank my colleagues at the Luskin School of Public Affairs for welcoming me to a new environment during a global pandemic. I am also indebted to former colleagues at the University of Connecticut for their kindness, especially Evelyn Simien, Evan Perkoski, and David Yalof.

Many research assistants helped me over a long period of time, and I want to thank Diana Alcocer, Stephanie Andrade, Isabel Blank, Cheyenne Holliday, Josh Hooper, Nicole Lac, Shannon Magni, Stephanie Mercado-Irizarry, Renato Muguerza, Ashley Ortiz, Emily Steck, Delaruelle Tarpeh, and Yara Zoccarato. At the University of Connecticut, I was fortunate to receive the Competitive Large Grant in the Research Excellence Program for the Office of the Vice President, and support from El Instituto: Institute of Latina/o, Caribbean, and Latin American Studies, especially in connecting me with research assistants.

Thank you to Todd Eisenstadt and Joanna Lewis for inviting the manuscript to be part of the Studies in Comparative Energy and Environmental Politics series, and my editor Angela Chapnko at Oxford University Press for her encouragement and responsiveness. Many thanks to Pepe Mateos for the photography, Dennis Bolt for creating maps, and Deborah Patton for making the index. Some of the material from this book first appeared in a 2020 *Journal of Development Studies* article coauthored with Lindsay Mayka titled "How Do Legal Strategies Advance Social Accountability? Evaluating Mechanisms in Colombia."

I dedicate this book to my brother, Sebastián Ignacio Herrera. I will always carry with me his enthusiasm and interest in this project, especially from a long conversation in 2016, when the project was still finding its feet. The drafting of this book survived a cross-country move, a global pandemic, and the birth of a beautiful baby boy. In the past few years, I have been reminded of the importance of family like never before and how, when someone is engraved in our heart, we are blessed to have them with us forever.

1
The Politics of Slow Harms in the Latin American City

Harms as Everyday Landscape

In the outskirts of Buenos Aires, Argentina, neighbors young and old sat around a small office table in the municipality of González Catán, La Matanza. An elderly couple recalled what their neighborhood had been like when they arrived in the 1960s: "We had the Matanza River, where we would go every weekend and swim, have picnics, we would spend the day there because the water was crystalline. Back then, we could plant anything... corn, vegetables.... It was all green fields."[1] The younger neighbors listened on in disbelief, not recognizing the neighborhood being described.

For the past several decades, the community had watched as approximately 2,000 trucks a day meander through their residential street on their way to a nearby regional, open-air landfill. Nearby, children have grown up around the liquid toxins that seep into their yards before finding the Matanza Riachuelo River in Buenos Aires, and picked at squash and tomato plants born from a soil bed of dirty diapers, car parts, and organic waste. During an interview I conducted, residents described how in the early 2000s, an epidemiological survey organized by local elementary schools revealed a community sick with autoimmune disorders, skin diseases, and cancer. The pollution crisis in the river basin has many sources: open-air landfills dot the riverbanks, 65% of the city lacks residential sewage connections, thousands of industries dump untreated manufacturing waste into the river, and a Shell petrochemical processing plant transmits soil, water, and air toxins (World Bank 2009b, 1–3).[2]

---

[1] Interview with Domingo Martinez, Vecinos Autoconvocados de González Catán contra CEAMSE, March 11, 2017.

[2] Figure 1.1 is a photograph of open-air waste dumping outside of the González Catán landfill, and Figure 1.2 is a photograph of the wastewater lagoons that result from residents' autoconstruction of wastewater systems in their backyards in Villa Inflamable. The photograph in Figure 1.3 shows an

Figure 1.1 Waste dumping, González Catán, Buenos Aires.
Source: Photograph by Pepe Mateos, 2017.

Similar dynamics surfaced on the other side of the continent. Residents I interviewed in Bogotá, Colombia, described how, when they moved into a newly built apartment complex in the 1990s in the Suba neighborhood, nearby waterways connected to the Bogotá River were filling up with construction debris and untreated industrial and residential sewage. As neighbors began to document the unique flora and fauna native to what they determined to be a wetland, they noticed skin lesions and pulmonary disorders in their children.

Further south along the Bogotá River Basin, residents are exposed to polluted water daily as it is sprayed during electricity generation from the operation of the Muña Dam in the municipality of Sibaté. This process emits sulfuric gas and toxins that sicken livestock that drink from polluted streams and generates health impacts from close exposure, such as gastrointestinal, respiratory, and skin infections.[3] A 1996 Colombian newspaper article captures the essence of the problem: "The contamination can be felt,

example of the types of precarious housing that residents self-build on the shores of urban rivers in Latin America.

[3] Figure 1.4 is a photograph of livestock grazing on contaminated water in the Bogotá River.

Figure 1.2 Wastewater lagoons in Villa Inflamable, Buenos Aires.
Source: Photograph by Pepe Mateos, 2017.

Figure 1.3 Informal settlements on Matanza Riachuelo River, Buenos Aires.
Source: Photograph by Veronica Herrera, 2016.

Figure 1.4 Livestock grazing around the Bogotá River, Bogotá.
Source: Photograph by Veronica Herrera, 2016.

touched, smelled; in what was several decades ago a temple for flora and fauna, today it is a deathbed."[4]

Environmental degradation is not new, yet the impact of pollution on human health and well-being is growing. According to the World Health Organization, 12.6 million people die annually from living or working near toxic pollution, amounting to one-quarter of global deaths (Prüss-Ustün et al. 2016, 86). In the past decade, noncommunicable diseases have become a larger component of the global disease burden as more regions now have higher rates of noncommunicable diseases attributable to the environment. Diseases with the largest environmental component include stroke, heart disease, diarrhea, respiratory infections, and cancers, where factors such as ambient and household air pollution and water, sanitation, and hygiene are the main environmental drivers (Prüss-Ustün et al. 2016, xix, xx). Ninety-two percent of these deaths occur in middle- or low-income countries, where most of the global population lives. A Lancet Commission report

---

[4] "Embalse del Muña asfixia a Sibaté," *El Tiempo*, January 15, 1996.

estimated that welfare losses due to pollution were over US$4.6 trillion per year, which is equivalent to 6.2% of global economic output (Landrigan et al. 2017, 462).

While the global disease burden is rising, the markers of pollution—whether in our backyards or on our bodies—can be difficult to detect. Many environmental harms grow slowly enough to be invisible to those they affect. For the millions of communities around the world where pollution is a slow-moving, long-standing problem, residents born into toxic exposure often perceive pollution as part of the everyday landscape. Misinformation about the degree of harm inflicted and its origin can create "toxic waiting," or prolonged periods of confusion and biding time for low-income communities with limited resources (Auyero and Swistun 2009, 6; Auyero 2014, 238). Local communities may also be both victims of pollution and complicit in perpetrating it themselves (Lora-Wainwright 2017, 5). Some types of slow-moving harms are so physically difficult to detect—because they are invisible, nonodorous, and linked to everyday practices—that they may escape the notice of even highly resourced communities. The "invisibility" of certain types of pollution can impact both residents and policymakers. Rather than mobilize, "it is much more common for victims of pollution not to fight back" (Lora-Wainwright 2017, 11). Complacency or resignation regarding slow-moving harms feed cycles of citizen inaction. Because political influence requires collective action, citizen inaction lowers the possibility for policy change.

Argument in Brief

When and how do people mobilize around slow harms? This book examines how citizen action around slow harms forms and unlocks policy change. I investigate how citizen-driven efforts can push the state to implement environmental rights protections, and how ideas about pollution as a policy problem become institutionalized. Slow-moving harms are typically ignored or accepted parts of everyday life, particularly in the types of low-resource settings that characterize most cities in the Global South. Yet new environmental norms are emerging in settings that have historically viewed pollution as an acceptable practice. This book sheds new light on why and how.

I analyze the puzzle of slow-harms mobilization in the capital cities of Argentina, Colombia, and Peru, three cities that house historically contaminated rivers with high levels of toxic pollution that impacts millions. Despite decades of inattention to river pollution as a policy problem, by the mid-2000s the three rivers were receiving distinctly different levels of policy responses. In Buenos Aires, a relatively higher policy response emerged in terms of funds expended, infrastructure developed, institutional innovation, and regulatory capacity. In contrast, in Bogotá, governments enacted partial and fragmented policies with limited institutional innovation, and low regulatory capacity. And in Lima, public officials refused to tackle slow-harms pollution and continued to view it as an intractable problem for which they were not responsible.

This book argues that "bridging activism," the presence of resourced actors that can aggregate claims and connect them to the state, is critical for attending to slow-moving environmental harms. Grassroots activism lends initial visibility and legitimacy to slow-moving harms, but alone is often insufficient. Instead, bridging activism allows for local claims to move beyond singular, fragmented petitions into collective, high-visibility claims that can change the policy agenda. Strong bridges possess both material resources and shared prior collaborations. In South America, the most effective bridges advocating for remediation of slow-moving environmental harms were paradoxically not rooted in environmental organizing but rather in human rights movements.

In all three countries, guerrilla armed conflict and repressive military responses created periods of political violence that gave rise to human rights movements. This book examines the extent to which these historic human rights movements became connected to new environmental justice problems. In Buenos Aires, strong bridges for slow-harms river pollution were enabled by human rights mobilization and national-level supportive administrations from the center-left. There, center-left political administrations helped facilitate the development of strong human rights actors and institutions that credibly reframed environmental harms as human rights injustices to which the state was obligated to attend. Strong bridges were absent in Bogotá and Lima due to weaker human rights mobilization and the presence of conservative political administrations, and thus reform agendas were either stagnated or nonexistent in these cases. Conservative political administrations aligned with legacies of unresolved political violence and the interests of extractivist actors, which resulted in narrower spaces for institutionalized citizen participation.

This book makes three central contributions. First, this book theorizes about the social impacts of environmental degradation by developing the concept of slow-moving harms as a temporally and geographically situated phenomenon that increasingly impacts Global South cities. Second, the cases show how slow harms are infrequently attended, and when they are, environmental regulation in Latin American cities is increasingly driven by societal forces or not at all. Both grassroots pressure and bridging activism represent critical components of environmental governance in weak institutional settings, pressing for accountability and building an ad hoc citizen-led regulatory apparatus. Here environmental regulations are driven by societal bottom-up processes rather than Weberian bureaucratic capacity, in many instances citizen-led pressures are increasingly the environmental regulatory institution of last resort in Global South cities. Finally, I examine a slice of environmentalism in countries with histories of political violence and military rule, and thus connect democratization struggles with the rise of environmental institution building. By unpacking human rights movements as thoroughfares for environmental activism, these cases shed new light on the struggles for environmental justice in the Global South.

Toxicity and Invisibility: Slow Harms in the Global South City

The Urban Question

A major demographic shift in the Global South is reshaping much of the world's cities. By 2050, Asia and Africa will be majority urban, with Latin America reaching nearly 90% (United Nations 2018a, xix, 26). Urbanization is fueled by economically oriented migration from rural areas, natural population growth within cities, and increasingly migration due to conflict, both internal and international. These demographic changes suggest that the politics of urban development in Global South cities underpins the lived experience of much of the globe.

Research on the politics of urban development in the Global South has expanded in recent decades and has become a growing area for political scientists engaged in comparative analysis (Post 2018, 116, 119–25; Finkel, Lawrence, and Mertha 2019, 2–4; Auerbach et al. 2018, 262–64). Scholars have focused on, for example, questions of informal vending and markets

(Hummel 2021, 1–7; Grossman 2020, 47–49; Holland 2017, ch. 3), taxation (Bodea and LeBas 2016, 215–17), land use changes and redevelopment (Rithmire 2015, 1–5; Pasotti 2020, 5–9), housing (Donaghy 2015, 77–82; Paller 2015, 36–38; Zhang 2021, 1407–9), public services (Herrera 2017, 1–8; Auerbach 2019, 1–7; Herrera 2014, 16–18; Herrera and Post 2014, 621–28), and urban violence and public security (Moncada 2016, 3–4; Lessing 2021, 854–56; Mayka 2021, 8–17). In the post-decentralized setting in which most Global South countries find themselves (Cities and Governments 2008), understanding how urban land, public services, and labor are governed is more pressing than ever.

Urban settlements in the Global South are home to fast-paced migration, industrial activity, and land-use conflicts that have generated intense environmental degradation. While urban environmental hazards have been a focus of interdisciplinary research, the politics of urban environmental degradation has been relatively underdeveloped. Research on environmental politics—or how environmental issues are mediated by state decisions and citizen-state interactions—has grown dramatically in recent years in Latin America (Isabella Alcañiz and Gutiérrez 2022, ch. 1). Yet this research has frequently underscored environmental institution building in rural settings where high-visibility social conflicts undergird multinational megadevelopment projects. These important works chronicle a wide range of state and society responses to environmental harms over mineral and oil extraction (Jaskoski 2022, 3–6; Arce 2014, 45–65; Riofrancos 2020, 1–6; Eisenstadt and West 2019, 1–7; Svampa 2019, 1–19), deforestation (Alcañiz and Gutiérrez 2020, 38–42; Kashwan 2017, 1–6; Milmanda and Garay 2020, 4–5; Oliveira and Hecht 2016, 251–57), pesticide drift (Leguizamón 2020, 1–6), and megadams (Fearnside 2006, 16–19; Klein 2022, ch. 1). Unlike intense socioenvironmental conflicts in the countryside, urban environmental degradation is frequently slower moving and more dispersed, and thus its impacts especially difficult to measure.

This book's focus on the politics of urban environmental hazards on the urban fringe thus breaks new ground, generating new empirical evidence of a widespread and understudied phenomenon. The book also takes on important issues central to the peri-urban fringe (Allen 2003, 136–38; Rauws and de Roo 2011, 269–70), which are physical territories between the urban and rural divide where industrial and commercial activity, agriculture, and residential expansion meet. Due to the nature of urbanization in many Global South centers, peri-urban territories are amorphous and multijurisdictional and often have contested political and legal boundaries. It is here where conflicts over siting of hazards and downstream environmental bads from urban centers collide (Simon 2008, 176), and yet problematically where the state is often least present.

Environmental Justice and Brown Bodies in Urban Latin America

Who lives in the urban and peri-urban spaces in Latin American cities? Historically rural migrants have built homes in the urban peripheries on untitled land and petitioned the government for public services. The 1930s–1970s were characterized by rural-to-urban migration, when an accelerated influx toward a few receiving centers reshaped cities that were also political capitals, where elite economic classes lived, and which were the preferred location of most industry. Many elites then moved to remote suburban locations which received infrastructure services, and the poor settled in peri-urban locations that were often little more than barren fields, creating a spatial separation of social classes (Portes 1989, 7–8; Rodríguez-Vignoli and Rowe 2018, 254–55). The 1980s economic crisis and shift toward economic restructuring decreased urban primacy and helped facilitate the growth of other cities, but also increased underemployment and class polarization within cities (Portes 1989, 37).

It was not uncommon for internal migration patterns to exacerbate ethnic disparities, whereby migrants with indigenous backgrounds (such as Argentines from the Andean northern provinces or Quechua-speaking Peruvians from the Andes) settled cities in the urban fringes—and to different degrees were distanced from mestizo or white communities in more established neighborhoods. Furthermore, in recent decades political unrest and internal conflicts have accelerated migration patterns and reshaped the urban periphery. For example, Argentine slums saw an increase in Bolivian and later Venezuelan migrants, and Peruvian and Colombian slums became home to internally displaced persons from diverse ethnic and racial backgrounds.

Thus, while many cities developed with socioeconomic spatial segregation, this disparity also matched a racial/ethnic inequality, with concentrations of "Brown bodies," or residents with indigenous backgrounds, seeking economic opportunities or fleeing from social and political unrest. Viewing toxic hazards through environmental justice framing associated with the U.S. context of environmental racism (Bullard 1993, 17–19; D. E. Taylor 2000, 533–39) is rare in these urban marginalized communities. Yet the phenomenon itself is present—of a disproportionate amount of toxic exposure concentrated in "othered" communities in urban centers.[5]

Indigenous communities face some of the most pronounced environmental inequities in the region (Carruthers 2008, 5). While mobilization around indigenous claims have been pronounced in Latin America (Yashar 2005, 3–5; Van Cott 2008), ethnic claims making has been more concentrated in rural areas where there is more homogeneity than in the urban peripheries studied here. Perhaps because of the vast heterogeneity born of political, economic, and social crisis (the mix of new and old migrants, foreign-born and native-born, darker and lighter bodies), the identification of new environmental injustice claims, when they occur at all, have not been centered on a coherent frame of ethnic or racial exclusion, as understood by the U.S.-based environmental justice literature.

Nevertheless, the cases examined in this book of collective responses to toxic exposure in the urban fringe—or the lack thereof—are ones where ethnic disparities are overlaid on top of economic disparities—even if they are rarely understood as such. While observers may note that these "forgotten" communities are such because they represent the most economically marginalized sectors in society, we may probe whether they are also forgotten due to their ethnic or racial standing in the mestizo or white centers of political decision-making and social influence. Thus, the production and reproduction of environmental hazards are intimately entangled not only in the economic and social disparities that govern Latin American cities but also in the ethnic and racial difference of many impacted communities.

---

[5] Carruthers (2008, 6) argues that environmental hazards in Latin American cities are concentrated in industrial parks and impact neighborhoods of all social classes, yet evidence in this book suggests that hazards disproportionately impact low-income residents, many of which are indigenous and non-white. While industrial plant and hazards siting often predates establishment of surrounding neighborhoods—suggesting that racist siting policy did not create the disparities—the lack of attention from policymakers to the resulting adverse health impacts can be seen as a form of purposeful neglect due to the marginalized (ethnic/racial) status of these low-income communities. Thus, environmental justice issues are at play, even as they have not been framed as such by scholars.

Complex Risk Perceptions and Collective Issue Identification

Political scientists influenced by the Pluralist school assume that grievances are clearly visible, recognized, and subsequently acted upon. Nelson Polsby (1958, 235) notes, "[P]eople participate in those areas they care about the most. . . . [I]t is, therefore, expected that decisions affecting groups marginally will attract only marginal attention, and decisions affecting groups directly will attract their direct attention."[6] Yet various studies have shown that nonaction—or acquiescence—is a common form of nonparticipation influenced by unequal power relations. Aggrieved communities may self-withdraw because of a history of powerlessness in settings characterized by highly unequal power relationships (Gaventa 1982, 18). Aggrieved communities may also be subject to forceful coercion, for example, by being economically beholden to the forces that harm them through factory employment that endangers their health (Lora-Wainwright 2017, ch. 1). Following James Scott (1985, 29), communities may instead engage in "small acts of resistance," such as foot-dragging or sabotage, rather than more visible and risky forms of collective action. Aggrieved communities may fail to act because they suffer from uncertainty, confusion, and mixed signals about the source and degree of danger to which they are exposed. Auyero and Swistun (2009, 4, 6) dub this phenomenon "toxic uncertainty" and show how people's "confusion, mistakes and/or blindness" about the dangers that surround them can lead to silent habituation and inaction.

Many factors influence how people understand risk and assess hazards and whether they act. Rather than being objective "facts," hazardous environments are subjectively interpreted and experienced. Much literature on risk perception concludes that risk frames are molded by factors such as trust in the source of information about hazards, as well as degree of trust in power-holding institutions. The level of trust people have in expert systems, institutions that are responsible for protecting them, producers of hazards, and the state all shape risk perceptions (Beamish 2001, 6–8; Perrow 1997; Auyero and Swistun 2009, 8–9; Freudenburg 1993, 916–17; Lora-Wainwright 2017, 82).[7] Risk is a "collective construction" (Douglas and Wildavsky 1983, 186).

---

[6] See also Dahl (1961) and further discussion in Gaventa (1982, 6–7).

[7] See Freudenburg's (1993, 916–17) discussion on *recreancy*, or "behaviors of persons and/or of institutions that hold positions of trust, agency, responsibility or fiduciary or other forms of broadly expected obligations to the collectivity, but that behaves in a manner that fails to fulfill the obligations or merit the trust."

Collective risk identification is likely a matter of local, socially constructed awareness building. The popular epidemiology literature (Brown and Mikkelsen 1997, 7–15; Clapp 2002, 38–44) follows a familiar pattern of discovery by residents that begins when "everyday life is disrupted." An uncovering of a toxic hazard leads to more information gathered over time, and "residents turned activists" help mobilize others around discovered harms. Activists in Love Canal, New York, led by Lois Gibbs, fought against chemical waste poisoning and received redress and relocation (Levine 1982, 205–20), although similar stories abound in places like Woburn, Massachusetts, and Yellow Creek, Kentucky, and have become legend (Auyero and Swistun 2009, 7). In these cases, gatekeepers in the mass media also played an important role in amplifying residents' claims. Organizational skills and leadership were further critical ingredients to activists' success.

Much of this literature is developed in the U.S. context, where government institutions are relatively stronger and feature predominantly middle-class communities. They involve cases where communities are compensated or relocated following a formed consensus about the best course of action to take once pollution is discovered. The few studies of these phenomena in the Global South emphasize the propensity for a lack of shared consensus, the pervasiveness of inaction, and the various forms of nonpolitical environmental engagement (such as picketing at the factory gate) that is rarely organized beyond the neighborhood level (Auyero and Swistun 2009; Lora-Wainwright 2017).

Unlike the pioneering ethnographies that center on discovering action or documenting inaction in a singular point of contamination within one community, this book takes a multiscale and cross-national approach. I examine multiple sites of contamination within three Global South cities where impacted communities have varied responses to the toxins they face. In most instances, residents are resigned to pollution, view it as part of the everyday landscape, and, due to their low position within urban power structures, are unlikely to act. For those aware of the pollution, there is also often disagreement about what course of action is best and whether relocation is favorable to remaining within existing ties and networks. Yet for others, pockets of resistance emerge and coalesce and form both small- and medium-scale action. These pockets infrequently, if ever, collaborate across the long territories that divide them. Although environmental activism over slow harms in the Global South urban fringe is not widely pervasive, this theory-building book shows why and how it can unfold.

The Argument of the Book

Reform Process: Bonding and Bridging Mobilization

Why and how do communities mobilize around slow harms? This section advances a framework for understanding the process of slow harms mobilization via bonding and bridging mobilization, drawing on network theory and social capital scholarship. In cases with strong bonding mobilization, local grassroots leadership tends to lean on community ties to help build awareness about slow harms. When local impacted communities can effectively organize, they generate fire-alarm monitoring that sends visible smoke signals beyond their neighborhood. In cases with strong bridging mobilization, outsiders—within both civil society and the state—are brought into local mobilization efforts and use their external resources to aggregate grievances across large territories and scale up claims to make them more legible to the state. In these cases, collective issue identification is complex and multiscalar, and risks are assessed and navigated by actors at local, state, and national levels. The findings here show that both bonding mobilization and bridging mobilization were necessary to induce a policy shift. This book illustrates how a broad repertoire of citizen collective action such as protests, marches, roadblocks, litigation, referendums, and the filing of claims in agencies, ministries, and administrative courts is critical for igniting slow-harms remediation.

Bonding Mobilization: Constructing Visibility and Smoke Signals

Because of their opacity and the complex risk perceptions surrounding them, slow harms challenge traditional notions of collective action and grievance articulation. Thus, unlike more readily visible harms, grievances surrounding these issues must be actively constructed around problems that long went unnoticed or were accepted as part of the everyday landscape. For slow harms to be addressed, they must first be made visible to the communities they impact; and a local-level understanding of the grievance emerge. While some scholars argue that grievances are activated when they have immediate material or cultural impact (Simmons 2016, 1–4), opaque harms require a high level of active awareness building, or priming, through social interaction.[8]

Individuals impacted by slow harms are more likely to form small-scale collective grievances and begin collective smoke signaling when they both experience personal acute harm *and* have resources to engage in local organizing. Local-level mobilization around slow harms is highly variable, as stressed by the prior discussion of complex risk perceptions. Nevertheless, residents who become local leaders around toxic exposure tend to be ones who have experienced personal acute harm and have some amount of material resources (e.g., time, money, or education) that make them better poised to take on noncompensated grassroots organizing. Individuals choose to get involved for diverse reasons, yet they typically experience firsthand the consequences of invisible harms before mobilizing others to join them.

Impacted communities that are most likely to raise awareness over slow harms are ones that have strong ties with one another due to factors such as geographic immobility and lifelong friendships, similar familial or ethnic ties, or prior shared problem-solving experiences.[9] Similar to Granovetter's (1973, 1361–63) strong ties concept, bonding social capital—the connections between people who know each other—became an influential concept in the study of collective action.[10] Embedded, place-based ties are important for slow-harms mobilization because they are more likely to generate trust and information, key ingredients in seeing familiar surroundings in new ways. Place-based ties, as opposed to external ties or resources, are also more likely to generate interest in a common, locally oriented goal.

---

[8] For a discussion of the social construction of legal grievances through social interaction and priming by legal advocates, see W.E. Taylor (2020, 1330–33).

[9] Granovetter (1973) theorized that place-based grievance holders are often marked by "geographic immobility and lifelong friendships," which help them excel in local problem solving but make it difficult to create broad-based collective action outside of the communities that they do not already know (1375). In his work on strong vs. weak ties, Granovetter characterized "strong ties" as those with more frequent interactions, more emotional affect, more trust, and more information shared (1361).

[10] Bourdieu (1985) and Coleman (1988) popularized the concept of social capital. Bourdieu (1985, 248–49) defines social capital as "the aggregate of the actual or potential resources which are linked to possession of a durable network of more or less institutionalized relationships of mutual acquaintance and recognition—or in other words, to membership in a group." Coleman (1988, 102–3) argued that the presence of social capital was seen in trust, information, norms, and effective sanctions and the extent of obligations in a group. Putnam, Leonardi, and Nanetti's (1993) presented networks of civic engagement as determinant of regional government performance and economic development. According to Putnam et al., norms of social trust develop from networks of civic engagement, underpin the development of social capital, and lead to a range of development outcomes as well as better government (1993, 171–76). Their treatment of social capital has been critiqued, for example, as weakly linked to good government and for underestimating the potential downside of social capital (Levi 1996, 41–52) and for circular reasoning Portes (1998, 18–21).

The first step for slow harms attenuation is what I term "bonding mobilization," which is collective action from communities with strong, affective ties that provide social support and in-group solidarity. In these spaces, local leaders help organize grassroots pressure and initial visibility for slow harms, first for some members of the local community and then potentially more widely when activists can organize events that raise awareness outside of the community. Bonding mobilization can be aided by outside forces to raise initial awareness, but one of its key characteristics is that it relies on the embedded ties in communities that already enjoy in-group solidarity and social trust. Grassroots pressure is necessary to create initial visibility, or "firealarm monitoring," and local activists do this by engaging in activities that draw more eyes to the problem via marches, rallies, and other high-profile events that gain media attention and bring the problem out of the neighborhood. Grassroots pressure increases the visibility of slow harms to those outside of the community and provides legitimacy to environmental justice claims in the eyes of politicians, the courts, and journalists. Bonding mobilization helps create a local understanding of pollution as an unacceptable problem, but alone is insufficient.

Bridging Mobilization: Aggregating and Scaling Up

While local bonding mobilization is important, alone it is insufficient because impacted communities are often underresourced and claims are frequently fragmented across large territories. Due to the place-based nature of slow harms, what is needed are opportunities to bring geographically disparate grievances together. Various scholarly traditions have developed the notion of bridging ties. Granovetter (1973) argued that weak ties—between people who have spent less time together and have less emotional affect—can better transmit information and ideas across clustered communities that are composed of people who know each other well (and share "strong ties") (1373). Similarly, Putnam (2000, 22) argued that bridging social capital can connect people or groups that are different from one another, allowing them to acquire new resources, information, and opportunities. Therefore, what I term "bridging mobilization" is the presence of actors outside of impacted communities that can aggregate disparate local grievances across territories and connect them to the state.

What qualities do effective bridges for slow harms share? Importantly, effective bridges bring new resources to bear on the problem at hand. These resources may include new sources of information, expertise, relevant contacts, organizational experience, or money. These qualities allow bridging actors to connect claims from communities battling location-specific issues to an overarching problem with a broader, interconnected root. This is especially important in slow-harms advocacy networks that are fighting against nonpoint source pollution.

The most effective bridging actors have prior experience with one another. Bridging actors with shared common pasts have a history of working together and share informal or formal ties with one another, and thus have some measure of solidarity and trust. Particularly in the Latin American context, shared common pasts have undergirded new collective mobilization. For example, activists working toward the right for same-sex unions (Díez 2015, 9–10), women's political representation-quota laws (Krook 2010), indigenous rights (Paredes 2019, 189–93), and environmental networks (Hochstetler and Keck 2007, 75–83, 95–96) were undergirded by shared common pasts fighting old injustices that allowed them to build solidarity. Informal and formal networks of prior work experiences facilitate within-group and across-group bridging on new issues.

Bridges in Society: Bridging actors can arise from both within society and the state. For example, in society bridges may be nongovernmental organizations (NGOs), which are a type of civil society organization that is more likely to be issue-oriented than place-based. Such organizations, particularly national or international NGOs, are more likely to have greater resources to aggregate information across diverse actors. While NGOs are varied in form across different countries, key characteristics tend to distinguish them from grassroots activism. NGOs are typically characterized by having paid staff as opposed to volunteers, higher levels of human capital in terms of education and job training, and a legal charter recognized by the state. They may be service-oriented NGOs, advocacy NGOs, or regulatory (watchdog) NGOs (Beer, Bartley, and Roberts 2012, 326; Brass et al. 2018, 137–38, 143).

NGOs typically count on material resources such as expertise, education, and funding, or might draw on organizational resources such as prior experience and contacts working in diverse issue areas and territories. In some contexts, foundations, think tanks, professional associations, universities, and other organized, resourced institutions within civil society could potentially fill this bridging role. Frequently, experts associated with one form (e.g., an NGO) may also work within another (e.g., a university or professional association).

Bridges in the State: Alternatively, bridges may consist of state-level actors. For example, lower-level bureaucrats within horizontal accountability institutions such as an ombudsman's or comptroller's office or activist judges can be bridges for slow harms. While most studies of social mobilization distinguish between civil society networks and the state, with the former making claims on the latter, the state is a much more fragmented and multi-interested institutional form that may have sympathetic activists working from within. Jessica Rich (2019, 40–44) has outlined how AIDS activist networks in Brazil were assisted by activist public officials who created resources and opportunities that supported grassroots associations, leading to "state-sponsored activism." Studies of participatory governance in Brazilian water management relied on activists "inside the state" (Abers and Keck 2009, 303–4); in the Litoral Norte Basin of Brazil, "the state employees, not civil society groups, are the predominant activists" (Keck 2002, 192). In China, "disgruntled officials" were important allies for activists in their fight against hydroelectric dam projects (Mertha 2008, 8–9).[11] While bureaucrats may share personal affinities with activists or the issue area in question through prior work experiences or personal ties, they are unlikely to ally with grassroots groups advocating policy goals that are unrelated to their institutional mandate.

Enabling Conditions: Strength of Human Rights Mobilization and Presidential Partisanship

What enabling conditions allowed strong bridges to flourish? Enabling conditions are the factors that increase the likelihood of a change in an outcome of interest. Enabling conditions do not alone cause action; for example, when an airplane crashes we say it is because of a factor such as a mechanical malfunction (cause), not gravity (an enabling condition).[12] Social movement

---

[11] Similarly, a literature on public services provision underscores the pervasiveness of *co-production* (e.g., Mitlin 2008, 347–52; Ostrom 1996, 1078–82) which is defined as " the provision of public services (broadly defined to include regulation) through regular, long-term relations between state agencies and organized groups of citizens, who both make substantial resource contributions" (Joshi and Moore 2004, 40).

[12] For a discussion of causes vs. enabling conditions and their relationship to necessary vs. sufficient conditions, see Cheng and Novick (1991, 83–91).

scholars have emphasized the explanatory role of political opportunities, such as the role of supportive institutions, political systems, political alignments, or state propensity for repression.[13] I view political opportunities as a type of enabling condition that does not cause action but must be perceived and seized by actors in order to generate outcomes. Therefore, the term "enabling conditions" refers to political opportunities but also potentially other factors such as economic, geographic, or historical conditions.

Human Rights Movements: Two enabling conditions—and their interaction—undergirded the emergence of effective bridges in the South American cases examined here. The first is the presence, consolidation, and development of human rights movements. In the Southern Cone, periods of military rule or civil war ignited struggles for human rights recognition as activists formed collectives and NGOs and mounted resistance to state-sponsored violence. The democratization period for Argentina, Colombia, and Peru was characterized by the development of different trajectories for human rights mobilization; later periods of electoral transition further solidified human rights actors and institutions as politically protected, or further repressed them.

Human rights strength and messaging proved to be important for environmental claims making. Effective bridges were able to reframe the grievances of communities impacted by river pollution in terms of human rights violations. Reframing prior grievances that had hinged on NIMBY or class-based inequities into human rights violations increased their visibility, and previously unseen or underappreciated grievances were thus imbued with a broader, more culturally resonant appeal. Social movement scholars have argued that effective framing resonates due to its cultural salience as well as who is doing the messaging (Benford and Snow 2000, 619–22). For example, in Argentina, human rights messaging gave pollution claims greater resonance because of the cultural salience of human rights as well as the high credibility that human rights messengers in Argentina enjoyed. In the U.S. context, the environmental justice movement developed a broadly appealing "master frame" which linked racism to environmental outcomes and was "explicit, public, and potent" (D. E. Taylor 2000, 514–16, 533–36).

---

[13] Political opportunity theory has been criticized for conceptual stretching (connoting too many different phenomena within the same concept) and overly emphasizing institutional opportunities (see, e.g., Meyer and Minkoff 2004, 1458–61; Giugni 2011, 272–77). More recent treatments have stressed processes and mechanisms rather than structures and conditions (e.g., Tilly and Tarrow 2015).

Effective linking of human rights to environmental claims was possible in places where there was a preexisting human rights movement that was older, stronger, and more institutionalized. In spaces with more established human rights movements, there was no widespread violence against activists, and there was a government willing to engage with human rights actors. Human rights groups had social legitimacy. Human rights institutions also formed in these spaces and became linked to diverse governing institutions.

Presidential Partisanship: A second enabling condition for slow-harms bridging was the partisan orientation of the presidential party in power. Political parties' impact slow-harms mobilization, but not because major political parties adopt environmental issues as meaningful parts of their party platform. The postmaterial thesis suggested that postmaterial value changes would be reflected in Green parties (Tranter and Western 2009, 146–50; Inglehart 1977, 173), but few party platforms in the Global South represent that prediction. Green political parties in Latin America did not acquire electoral strength, and major political parties with electoral clout rarely championed environmental issues, nor did they become involved in river cleanup efforts. Yet presidential partisan orientation was an enabling condition for slow-harms bridging because human rights movements and participatory civil society spaces were more prevalent during left-of-center administrations. In conservative presidential administrations during the periods under study, support for civil society organizing was more limited, and human rights actors had fewer resources and political influence.

Presidential administrations and the support they showed for civil society organizations reflected both the legacies of political violence and the strength of economic actors. Historic armed conflicts had pitted socialist leftist guerrilla projects against government forces that were increasingly willing to violate human rights in the name of law and order. These dynamics cast a long shadow after democratization. When left-of-center administrations came to power, they aligned with human rights groups, but when right-of-center administrations came to power, they aligned with the military, the primary opponent of human rights groups. Conservative presidential administrations were also more likely to be hospitable to neoliberal development strategies with multinational firms playing a large role in the economy. In conservative administrations, presidents and their cabinets were more likely to be composed of military officers who had been accused of human rights violations or former business leaders who viewed civil society organizing as a leftist project aligned with guerrilla terrorism. In cases where presidential administrations were themselves composed of military officers *and* development strategies were most predatory and tied to a sizable extractives-export economy, such as the unregulated mining economy of Peru, civil society organizing was the most perilous and environmental activists have had good reason to fear for their lives.[14]

While involving distinct actors and logics, these two enabling conditions were themselves linked. Human rights mobilization was more likely under center-left presidential administrations, particularly if the latter consisted of multiple, sequential leftist administrations that allowed human rights organizing to not only develop but consolidate. In turn, human rights actors, to the extent that they were politically active, tended to support leftist administrations and could become key constituents of their electoral support.

Outcome under Study: Slow-Harms Remediation

This book examines three variant outcomes in policy shifts toward slow-harms remediation—in Lima, Bogotá, and Buenos Aires. Nonpoint-source pollution is a challenging issue that can be considered a "wicked" policy problem (Head and Alford 2015, 712), with both culpable private- and public sector actors, various public officials at multiple scales responsible for overseeing adherence to regulatory standards, and myriad impacts on human health. Thus, policy solutions are complex and multijurisdictional and require long-term policy horizons. It is not possible to measure a definitive resolution of the problem—that is, whether the river is definitively "clean"; such changes require longer time horizons than the decades examined here. Rather, the outcome in question is a policy shift away from invisibility and apathy and toward public sector recognition of pollution as a policy problem to which the state is obligated to attend. Put another way, policy shifts mean institutionalizing claims over pollution and increasing public sector accountability over the policy arena. Reforms are rarely linear; they can entail circular progress or backsliding and may result in pollution abatement in some respects but not others. Nevertheless, the initial "tipping point" toward changing the status quo begins with institutionalizing claims

---

[14] On the complex relationship between different forms of natural resource wealth (e.g., minerals vs. agricultural) and armed conflict, see Ross (2004, 37–38).

and accountability mechanisms in a given policy arena. It is with these types of changes that the book is concerned.

In the three cases, I measure policy shifts via three dimensions: institutional changes, financial commitments, and changes in regulatory monitoring capacity. Improvements (or lack thereof) within these three dimensions of reform are also examined with an eye toward whether they included greater accountability measures, for example, via participatory institutions or other mechanisms of citizen oversight. Improvements along these three dimensions help facilitate reforms, though they do not alone guarantee absolute and definitive resolution of the policy problem. Institutional changes may involve creating new institutions to oversee reforms and imbuing them with the financial resources and authority they require to make substantive changes. These may entail improving existing environmental standards or creating new ones; in most cases policy shifts require creating regulatory organizations or reforming existing ones that can coordinate across multiple political jurisdictions and that are backed by the political will to enforce contentious regulations on powerful actors. These institutions require financial investments, human resources, and some measure of insulation from partisan interference. Taken together, these three types of reform can generate visible changes to pollution abatement; in the wastewater pollution cases examined in this book these changes can result in increased oxygen levels for river basins, the return of flora and fauna, and clearing of visible debris on the river's mirror.

Financial commitments to the infrastructural changes necessary to remediate slow harms are an important ingredient to policy change. Historically many countries that continue to struggle with pollution—particularly river pollution—have invested financial resources yet seen little results due to misspending, corruption, or the inability of infrastructure development to keep pace with the rate of entry of new pollution points. Nevertheless, renewed financial investments for infrastructure development—such as in the case of wastewater pollution, residential wastewater treatment plants, and residential sewage connections—is a necessary, if alone insufficient, pollution abatement policy change.

Regulatory monitoring capacity—backed by political will—is perhaps the most difficult to achieve. Making legal or technical changes to pollution abatement policies are much less politically fraught than enforcing them. Regulators and inspectors need to contend with powerful interests, such as industrialists who are important sources of employment and mayors who are loath to lose jobs in their jurisdictions. Furthermore, elected officials receive political credit from being associated with the provision of particularistic goods (or private goods which are rival and excludable), such as residential tap water or sanitation service, and all else being equal are less likely to invest political capital in championing services that are public or common. Clean water in multijurisdictional rivers are common pool resources (nonexcludable and rivalrous), and sanitation treatment plants have public goods qualities (nonexcludable and nonrivalrous). Therefore the nonrivalrous benefits that accrue from environmental upgrades in the wastewater sector are dispersed and long term and thus easier for elected officials to ignore (Winters, Karim, and Martawardaya 2014, 32–33).

The cases examined in this book show variation across these three dimensions of policy shift toward pollution remediation, as seen in Table 1.1. In Buenos Aires after the social mobilization examined in this book, new institutions and financial investments have been relatively high, with regulatory capacity that, although imperfect, is considerably improved as compared to the other two cases. In Bogotá, institutions have been established but with less authority and accountability, and financial investments have been considerable but more limited than in Buenos Aires. Regulatory capacity remains weak. There have been no policy shifts in Lima; the new institutions that have been created have focused on protecting polluters and have generated no financial investments or regulatory capacity. In conceptualizing policy shifts of slow-harms remediation along these three dimensions, I differentiate among three potential outcomes (expansive, stagnated, or uninitiated) by averaging the sum of the three dimensions based on extensive field research and qualitative and quantitative sources cited in the empirical chapters (see appendix). Two or more high scores are labeled "expansive policy shifts"; two or more medium scores are labeled "stagnated policy shifts"; and two or more low scores are considered "uninitiated policy shifts."

Table 1.1 Comparing Policy Shifts in Slow-Harms Remediation

	Buenos Aires	Bogotá	Lima
New Institutions	High	Medium	Low
Financial Investments	High	Medium	Low
Regulatory Capacity	Medium	Low	Low
= Policy Shift	Expansive	Stagnated	Uninitiated

Table 1.2 Comparing Slow-Harms Mobilization in Three Cities

		Strength of Bridges	
		Low	High
Strength of Bonds	Low	Uninitiated Policy Shift Lima	(No Observed Case)
	High	Stagnated Policy Shift Bogotá	Expansive Policy Shift Buenos Aires

Previewing the Cases: Variation in Bonding and Bridging Mobilization around Slow Harms

The book illustrates the process through which slow harms can emerge as a policymaking focus after years of living in the shadows. This occurrence is not widespread in the Global South, a topic that is taken up in Chapter 2. Indeed, acquiescence and policy paralysis are more prevalent. Nevertheless, the cases examined here illustrate how civil society mobilization can enable these changes, as well as the factors that limit progress. Chapters 3–5 show how differences in bonding and bridging mobilization led to variation in policy shifts across the three polluted river basins, illustrating the role that organized grassroots activists, activist public officials, and professional NGOs with shared common histories play in holding recalcitrant states accountable. The enabling conditions of human rights mobilization and partisan presidential administrations are also instructive in understanding the strength of bridging mobilization. Table 1.2 shows how these three cases interact across the two dimensions of bonding and bridging mobilization relative to one another.

The Matanza Riachuelo River of Buenos Aires, once deeply polluted, saw the greatest amount of policy shifts toward slow-harms remediation, an expansive policy shift. Here grassroots organizing and pressure—bonding mobilization—was strong throughout multiple points on the river basin. Grassroots leadership emerged to rally for divergent issues such as urban renewal, access to toilets and sanitation services, and against open-air landfills and wetlands contamination. Grassroots activism was initially fragmented across the river basin but exhibited deep, entrenched ties within the localities where groups were most active. Ignored but determined, several local groups found allies in the capital city, where seasoned human rights NGOs were also working to take up the mantle of slow harms as a human rights violation. Bridging mobilization, or the participation of resourced allies, was strong in both state and society and included human rights NGOs, foundations, universities, the Ombudsman's Office, and legal institutions. Beginning in the late 1990s, human rights NGOs began working with the Ombudsman's Office to draw attention to the pollution crisis; later, grassroots activists generated litigation that achieved a historic victory in the Supreme Court.

Extensive advocacy work on behalf of bridging activists—including in support of litigation—helped to increase the visibility of slow harms and reframe the river's pollution as a grave human rights injustice. Bridges in society—namely professional NGOs that have a history of working together on prior human rights issues—were well connected to bridges in the state. Many activist officials in the Ombudsman's Office, urban environmental offices, or the city's Housing Development Office had previously worked or studied with those in the NGO field. Argentina's human rights movement has been particularly robust following democratization in the mid-1980s and has grown stronger under multiple supportive leftist presidential administrations that amplified their message by enacting accountability-seeking measures from the military following the Dirty War. The left-of-center presidential administrations of the Kirchners were economically insular, nationalist, and not politically linked to either military officials or multinational extractivist interests. Critically, a selection of human rights NGOs, imbued with strong social legitimacy and a united message, became involved in the river pollution issue, and were selected by the Supreme Court to oversee implementation with the ruling on a citizen oversight committee. Activist bridges have worked to ensure that the relatively expansive policy shift that has resulted continues and stressed the need for impacted communities to be centered in the remediation process.

In Bogotá, slow-harms remediation has progressed, but much more slowly and unevenly than in Buenos Aires, resulting in a stagnated policy shift. Bonding mobilization around the Bogotá River, as in Buenos Aires, was high, with strong local construction of grievances around several issues, including wetlands conservation, the right to water, and demands for mitigation of flooding impacts and infrastructure deficits. Yet the process of aggregating and scaling up grievances, or bridging mobilization, has been much more muted compared to the

Buenos Aires case. As in Buenos Aires, bridges emerged within the state in Bogotá, in the form of activist public officials within the judiciary and the Comptroller's Office, and these were much better positioned to be effective aggregators of grievances and to scale up the problem than the societal bridges. The societal-level bridges were weak compared to their Argentine counterparts. NGOs and experts that championed slow-harms remediation in Bogotá did not have shared common pasts and enjoyed little political muscle; they were not high profile or well known and lacked connections to the state. Neither the state-level nor societal-level bridges interpreted the slow-harms crisis as one of equity or social rights violations, but rather focused on environmental conservation claims that failed to attract broader societal support outside of environmental advocacy circles. Human rights mobilization in Colombia has been undermined by ongoing armed conflict and sequential conservative presidential administrations that have been hostile towards human rights activists, accusing them of being linked to guerrilla combatants. These dynamics are enabled by Colombia's political economy, including a larger export share of the extractives market than Argentina and a strong neoliberal orientation toward multinational firms and export-oriented development. In Colombia, human rights defenders have struggled for protection and consolidation, and thus human rights NGOs, and NGOs more broadly, are relatively weaker and underresourced.

Grassroots groups helped initiate a judicial process for the Bogotá River, which led to a legal ruling mandating river cleanup in the 2000s. Yet the ruling has yet to ricochet into an expansive policy shift. Despite strong bonding mobilization, the Bogotá case showcased weak bridging mobilization, where societal NGOs had little connection to other actors in the executive or judiciary branch and had few work experiences with each other prior to serving on the judicial advisory committee overseeing implementation of the ruling. Progress toward institutionalizing slow-harms remediation in Colombia is thus more fragile and subject to reversal, and industrial polluters have yet to be dismantled.

In Lima, mobilization around slow harms has failed to materialize, and policy shifts toward remediation were uninitiated. Bonding mobilization for slow harms has so far been weak: impacted communities in the city center face extreme poverty and toxic uncertainty. With a long tradition of self-help networks and low trust of government institutions, communities exposed to toxins in Lima have yet to turn their attention to slow harms, and rural communities impacted by mining tailings have organized but had limited success. Potential bridges are also weak. Potential activists within the judiciary or the public prosecutor or ombudsman's offices have not taken up the cause of decontaminating the Rímac River. Chapter 5 examines why environmental institutions are weak and human rights agendas have been stalled in Peru. Peru has the largest export share of mineral extractives of the three countries under study and an unregulated export-oriented development strategy. The Peruvian state, dependent on royalties from mining, has created a hostile setting for NGO mobilization around environmental harms, and multiple consecutive conservative political administrations have further tightened controls over NGOs and civil society activism to protect economic interests. Human rights mobilization, in the wake of the internal armed conflict, continues to be viewed with suspicion by government authorities, and activists struggle for resources and protection.

Thus, societal bridges are also weak for the Rímac River; both national and international NGOs are loath to help aggregate grievances against slow harms when doing so puts them in direct conflict with state bureaucrats who are charged with protecting mining interests. With both bonding and bridging mobilization being weak, Lima's Rímac River continues to be consumed by toxic slow harms, and no policy shifts have been initiated. Table 1.3 illustrates the variation between the cases with respect to bonding mobilization, bridging mobilization, and the enabling conditions that helped shape the strength of bridging mobilization.

Evaluating Competing Explanations

I argue that pollution remediation policies were the result of mobilization of both impacted communities (bonding mobilization) and resourced allies (bridging mobilization) and that resourced allies, or bridges, were strongest when they had material resources and shared common pasts. This occurred in countries with strong human rights movements and center-left presidential administrations that were unaligned with extractivist industries. This section examines other competing theories that could plausibly explain this variation, which appear in studies of social and environmental mobilization in other cases. These alternative explanations are then evaluated across the case material presented in Chapters 3–5.

Table 1.3 Variation in Explanatory Variables, Their Indicators, and Enabling Conditions across Cases

	Argentina	Colombia	Peru
Bonding Mobilization (number of nodes, numbers within nodes, number of campaigns)	High	High	Low
Bridging Mobilization: NGO Strength (number of groups, resources, influence)	High	Low	None
Bridging Mobilization: Activist Public Officials (number of groups, resources, influence)	High	High	None
Bridging Mobilization (issue reframing: united, resonant)	High	Low	None
Bridging Mobilization (collaborative work histories)	High	Low	None
Enabling Conditions: Presidential Partisanship	Left	Center-Right	Right
Enabling Conditions: Presidential Partisanship (ties to military)	Weak	Moderate	Strong
Enabling Conditions: Presidential Partisanship (ties to market-oriented/extractives)	Weak	Moderate	Strong
Enabling Conditions: Historic Human Rights Mobilization (level of consolidation vs. persecution)	Consolidated—Persecution Low	Fractured—Persecution Moderate	Weak—Persecution High
Outcomes: Slow Harms Policy Shift	Expansive	Stagnated	Uninitiated

Prevailing explanations have centered, for example, on the role of precipitating events that can serve as a flashpoint or "social cognitive trigger" for collective action, such as a riot, an instance of police brutality, or an assassination (Owens 2013, 1; Waddington, Jones, and Critcher 1989). Similar to sectoral crisis like an electricity blackout (Murillo and Foulon 2006, 1584–88) or economic crisis (Hall 1993, 284–87; Haggard and Kaufman 1995, 199–201), external shocks can serve as precipitating events that discredit prevailing policy ideas and reorganize public attention toward a new policy prescription or previously unattended problem. London was famously spurred into policy action in the mid-1850s after a heat wave caused an unbearable stench (the "Great Stink") from the deeply polluted Thames River to waft through the chambers of Parliament. Yet while periodic flooding of the polluted rivers examined here, worsening due to climate change variability, has generated media attention and occasional disaster relief, precipitating events have failed to generate comprehensive reforms. To the extent that precipitating events surrounding water pollution continue to impact only targeted communities and only occasionally grassroots mobilization, they alone do little to change the status quo. Great upheavals can bring change only when reformers have the plan and power to influence policy (Berman 2020).

Another prevailing explanation—that class is the primary determinant of whether people organize around environmental harms—is also incomplete. Inglehart's (1990, 56, 380–88) influential thesis stated that environmental concern stems from "postmaterial" values held by those whose economic needs have been met. Inglehart based this theory on evidence from Western Europe and argued that these beliefs manifest in Green ecological parties (Inglehart 1977, 173; Tranter and Western 2009, 148). Evidence from this book suggests that environmental concern does not manifest through ecological parties in the context of weak institutions, clientelism, and weak party discipline, and that environmental movements and machine politics do not mix.

Here class has partial explanatory power; for example, the low-income communities of Lima were much less mobilized against slow harms than those in Bogotá or Buenos Aires, likely due to their more pronounced struggle for livelihood alongside histories of state neglect and repression. Yet even within Bogotá and Buenos Aires, in low-income neighborhoods where grassroots organizing was relatively stronger there was considerable class variation in which communities took up the mantle of environmental mobilization. Indeed, higher income shantytown dwellers (shopkeepers, drivers, etc.) frequently did not do so. As such, the cases show that class alone cannot explain grassroots organizing, but that other key factors mediate between class and environmental collective action, such as individual risk assessment, preexisting social capital, and the macro-level enabling conditions that strengthen spaces for citizen claims-making that this book emphasizes.

The "environmentalism of the poor" thesis posited that Global South environmentalism arises from poor communities that use environmental resources as a source of livelihood ("ecosystem people"), such as those dependent on forests or farming (Wilson 2009, 61; Helmke and Rosenbluth 2009; Hilbink 2012). Variation in environmental mobilization in the urban context problematizes prior understanding of the economic valuation of environmental resources. Here, grassroots mobilization over environmental harms is intense in highly urban centers with no ecosystem resource use (e.g., Buenos Aires), and yet mobilization is relatively weaker in the peri-urban and agricultural areas where farmers engage in subsistence farming and one might expect a greater outcry (e.g., Bogotá's rural communities or Lima's outskirts). Other factors—such as legacies of conservative political rule and armed conflict, and how these interact with natural resource extraction—may further illuminate why grassroots mobilization over resource-dependent threats varies across cases. The cases suggest that for impacted communities, mobilization is more likely to occur not due to economic valuation but rather due to a combination of level of physical vulnerability and available tools for collective action (e.g., local leadership, limited state repression, internal cohesion of local community). It may also be the case that cities provide fertile ground for environmental mobilization for low-visibility environmental problems, a point that I take up in Chapter 6.

Explanations that center on the strength of institutions in prompting reforms also fail to fully explain the outcomes under study. Studies emphasizing the strength of legal institutions, open legal opportunity structures (Wilson 2009, 61; Helmke and Rosenbluth 2009; Hilbink 2012), or "judicial assertiveness" (Kapiszewski 2012, 11–12) stress that difficult reforms (e.g., controversial economic reforms or rights-based reforms) are more likely to be feasible in settings with a strong and independent judicial system and opportunities for citizens to access the courts. The presence of environmental laws did not make a difference in the cases under study; despite variation in policy shifts toward slow harms, all three countries had environmental laws that guaranteed the protection of environmental rights and legal mechanisms to bring lawsuits against violations of environmental rights. At first glance, judicial assertiveness and judicial autonomy seemed causally significant; they were present in the Argentina case, which also had a relatively higher case of policy shift toward slow-harms remediation. Yet these same conditions failed to generate broader reform in Colombia, suggesting that the strength of legal institutions is likely important for environmental rights claims making when accompanied by other supportive factors, such as the presence of resourced, high-profile, and autonomous civil society groups and no state repression.

Methodological Approach and Organization of the Book

In order to build a theory of slow harms, I chose to focus on one environmental policy arena rather than several. A "one-sector, many places" approach (e.g., Bates 1999, 3–4; Karl 1997, 17–22) allows me to hold institutional and sector-specific characteristics of policymaking more constant than comparing across multiple types of environmental harms. Wastewater pollution is an emblematic example of slow-moving harms, for even the most toxic wastewater—including industrial or chemical discharge—can be nonodorous and clear. Wastewater pollution is a multijurisdictional and complex policy problem. Wastewater is coproduced by industries, residents, and the state, the last of which is problematically both a producer of pollution and charged with regulating it. It is also a policy arena that has low political and cultural appeal. Global sanitation is a "silent crisis," due to the taboo associated with human excrement and toilets, subjects few want to discuss publicly. Therefore, it represents a "crucial case," a policy arena that is least likely to exhibit propitious conditions for change, and as such, if change does occur, it lends more weight to the proposed theory. Finally, wastewater policy is an understudied yet increasingly critical policy arena for both environmental and human health: approximately 20% of global wastewater receives treatment (UNESCO 2017, 2). Thus, by examining the social and political production of wastewater pollution, this book illuminates a key policy arena of environmental and humanitarian concern.

This theory-building study employs a two-tiered strategy of causal inference. The first is to analyze the cases comparatively through the "most similar" comparative method, which asks whether explanatory factors and outcomes are correlated with the theory among cases that share many initial conditions hypothesized to be relevant, except the explanatory variable of interest (Lijphart 1975, 163–65; Seawright and Gerring 2008, 304–6). The empirical chapters therefore present evidence relevant to these associations—namely, if the conditions hypothesized to be necessary were indeed present in the cases examined, and if they were absent, did the predicted outcomes fail to occur.

This book compares three cases to examine variation in institutional and political change surrounding slow-moving harms. The research sites are three river basins that cross the capital cities of Argentina, Colombia, and Peru. These three cities and countries share similar characteristics: they are middle-income countries with electoral democracies, and they all have histories of military and armed conflict. The country capitals are decidedly primate cities, housing a large share of the nation's urban population as well as generating over a quarter of national GDP through concentrated regional industrialization. Each country's high rate of urbanization (over 80%) has unfolded through weak and disorganized urban planning that has brought extreme environmental pollution. The result has been three river basins deemed biologically dead due to extensive wastewater pollution.

These are three industrializing countries that share similar patterns of slow-moving harms production. As capital cities they also house the seat of political power, with the greatest probability of policy attention to this key problem. Also, the three rivers cross not only capital cities but also many adjacent municipalities which are governed by different political parties and factions. While residents of these three cities share different traditions, histories, and cultures, they are all Spanish-speaking South American urbanites with similar legacies of political and economic development as compared to cities in other regions. Comparing similar conditions of historically embedded slow harms in these three settings is therefore a fitting strategy for identifying the factors that lead to the outcome under study.

This comparative case (small-n) approach is also premised on careful attention to causal mechanisms through within-case analysis, or process tracing. Process tracing is an analytic tool for drawing descriptive and causal inferences from diagnostic evidence (Collier 2011, 824). Some evidence provides higher inferential value than others, a key Bayesian insight (Bennett and Checkel 2015, 16). Process tracing requires careful attention to sources that clarify the deliberation, information, and reasoning patterns that shaped actors' ideas, beliefs, and decision-making processes. Process tracing therefore uses diagnostic evidence chosen through careful attention to context and background knowledge to establish the causal mechanism. Importantly, this same approach also evaluates and disconfirms alternative explanations. Process tracing—through causal process observations—is particularly well suited for understanding change over time.

In conducting process tracing, the study gains analytic leverage from a wide range of primary and secondary sources. I draw on nearly 180 in-depth interviews in Argentina, Colombia, and Peru with grassroots organizations, NGOs, government officials, industry leaders, industrial associations, lawyers, judges, reporters, and academics, as well as participant observations in Argentina and Colombia. I also conducted an original questionnaire with 31 civil society organizations, which included qualitative network-mapping exercises. I triangulated between different sources to identify the relevant actors in the slow-harms networks and the relational dynamics between them. I relied on diverse text-based sources, including government documents, legal rulings, newspaper articles, civil society organizations' self-produced materials such as social media communications, YouTube videos, radio interviews, pollution assessment reports, posters, pamphlets, and scholarly sources. More information about the data collection and analysis strategies can be found in the appendix.

In what follows I introduce the concept of slow harms, discuss how wastewater river pollution is a key example of slow, targeted harms, and then trace the historical production of slow harms in the three cities under study. Chapters 3–5 illustrate the theory through an examination of the Argentina case (expansive policy shift), the Colombia case (stagnated policy shift), and the Peru case (uninitiated policy shift). Chapter 6 revisits the framework I developed regarding slow-harms advocacy centered around bridging mobilization, and then unpacks the role of cities as unique sites of disruption and bridging. Increased attention to legacies of political violence and civil society organizing can help explain the challenges cities face in pollution remediation, and environmental governance more broadly. If the right to dissent underlies environmental regulation building, then democracy and environmentalism are inextricably linked. I explore the relationship between democracy and environmental regulation through reviews of environmental policymaking under authoritarian regimes in post-Soviet countries and China. The book concludes by emphasizing the role of citizen collective action in Global South environmental institution building.

2
Slow Harms
Ubiquity and Invisibility in the Global South

Danger can pounce, or creep up slowly. This chapter unpacks the concept of a particular type of harms—slow-moving harms—which accumulate in a gradual and layered manner over a long period of time. In contrast to forest fires or flash floods, slow harms often escape scrutiny for years. Dangerous toxins spread throughout communities and become part of the everyday landscape. Generations are born into these settings, and the associated risks are often obscured. The activities that give rise to the harms, whether from residential waste dumping or industrial effluent discharge, also become familiar, a given. Residents may not remember a time when things were different. Despite the ubiquity of this type of environmental hazard, it is largely invisible.

River pollution makes up a type of slow harm that is a growing global problem. Many rivers throughout the world have become sewage canals as more than two million tons of human waste are dumped in freshwater bodies, thus deteriorating the drinking water supply, the aquatic habitat, and many associated economic activities such as fisheries and tourism (Nelson and Murray 2008, 120). Only approximately 20% of global wastewater—including residential, industrial, and agricultural—receives any form of treatment. Global estimates suggest that middle-income countries treat between 28% and 38% of municipal and industrial wastewater; this figure falls to 8% in low-income countries (UNESCO 2017, 2).[1] The remainder is deposited into open bodies of water. Wastewater pollution is spreading against a backdrop of high rates of urbanization and concentrated spatial segregation in the Global South. The result is a widespread problem of toxic

---

[1] The wastewater coverage situation may be worse than these numbers suggest, as only 55 out of 181 countries had available information on the generation, treatment, and use of wastewater in 2017 (UNESCO 2017, v).

river contamination and deeply unequal impacts between those who suffer its consequences and those who produce it.

This chapter examines two key dimensions of environmental harms: geographical and temporal proximity to bodily harm. After establishing how slow, targeted harms compare to other types of environmental harms with distinct temporalities, I discuss wastewater river pollution as a key exemplar of slow, targeted harms. I then trace the development of 20th-century slow harms along three urban river fronts: Buenos Aires, Bogotá, and Lima. Slow-harms river pollution developed in similar ways throughout the three capital cities and reflects common patterns of urban social and economic development. By tracing the histories of urban waterfront pollution in these capital cities, the chapter provides descriptive baseline measures against which the variation in policy shifts can be assessed.

Defining Slow Harms for Environmentalism

Not all environmental harms are created equal. Rob Nixon (2013, 2) coined the term "slow violence" to refer to a wide range of environmental bads, such as climate change, toxic drift, and deforestation, whose gradual nature, devoid of "sensational visibility," dampens efforts to decisively take action. Yet the concept of slow violence masks important differences between diverse types of environmental harms and the resulting propensity—or barriers—for collective action.

Environmental harms present numerous impediments to organized citizen action, but how and of what kind? I propose that environmental issues vary in terms of both temporal and geographic proximity to bodily harm. The ways in which these two dimensions interact create distinct barriers to citizen organizing on environmental issues. Because each environmental problem has unique characteristics with respect to its time horizon and the geographic dispersion of threats, not all environmental issues will be perceived as equally slow or equally violent by impacted communities. Thus, some environmental harms will be more difficult to generate citizen action around than others.

Social processes—and crucially, politics—unfold in time (Pierson 2004, 5). A burgeoning literature has explored different aspects of temporality—including sequential ordering of events, temporality in path dependence, and the analytic length of causal chains and critical antecedents (Abbott

Table 2.1 A Typology of Environmental Harms

		Temporal Proximity to Bodily Harm	
		Imminent	Gradual
Geographic Proximity to Bodily Harm	Concentrated	Rapid Targeted Harms incoming siting: landfills & incinerators, mines, hydrodams	Slow Targeted Harms established siting: landfills & incinerators, mines, wastewater pollution
	Dispersed	Rapid Diluted Harms metropolitan air pollution, coastal flooding, regional wildfires	Slow Diluted Harms fisheries depletion, ocean plastics pollution, biodiversity loss

2001, 209–239; Buthe 2002, 484–9; Falleti and Mahoney 2015, 215–225; Page 2006, 89). Focusing on duration—or the temporal length of an event—illuminates key social behaviors surrounding environmental harms.[2] The production and siting of environmental harms entail complex social processes with different temporal dimensions. I find that distinct environmental harms generate temporally differentiated threats to bodily harm that can influence patterns of citizen action. By "bodily harm" I refer to immediate physical danger as it relates to human security and health, as well as other related threats, such as material threats through loss of income or livelihood, or threats to social or cultural traditions from forced relocation. As Table 2.1 indicates, temporal proximity to bodily harm moves along a spectrum from imminent to gradual. Threats to bodily harm that are imminent come from development projects that have not yet occurred or have only recently occurred. Their duration is short, and it may be the perceived threat (which has not yet occurred) or the newness of the event that shapes action. Perceptions of temporality shape action. Actors will adjust their strategies based on their anticipated time horizons, reacting to, for example, whether an event is unfolding quickly, or how much time is left (Grzymala-Busse 2011, 1273).

In contrast, long-duration events produce a slow accumulation of effects. The most basic type of slow-moving causal process is incremental

---

[2] Gryzmala-Busse (2011, 1269–70) identifies four key aspects of temporality: duration, tempo, acceleration, and timing. Duration measures how much time elapses between the start and end of an event; tempo is change over time of an event's duration; acceleration is a measure of the rate of change; and timing consists of the placement of a given event on a timeline.

or "cumulative"; some examples are migration, suburbanization, and long-term shifts in electorates (Pierson 2004, 82). When threats to bodily harm are gradual, they represent long-standing environmental harms that have unfolded slowly over time. In the case of slow-moving environmental degradation, harms become familiar parts of the daily landscape, embedded into the spaces where communities live and work, and thus may not even be perceived as problems by impacted communities. Toxic exposure from long-standing landfills and impacts of biodiversity loss are often experienced as slow-moving, subtle, gradual processes. A long temporal duration breeds familiarity and complacency, which can generate the perception of inevitability and resignation. Thus, environmental harms that evolve slowly over time can easily become low priorities for citizen action. Long-standing, pre-existing arrangements, in contrast to new or imminent threats, may make it difficult for groups to identify a root cause and assign blame.

Geographical proximity to bodily harms adds an additional dimension to explain how harms are perceived and acted on by impacted communities. I conceive of geographic proximity to bodily harm as on a spectrum that ranges from being geographically concentrated in distinct and identifiable communities to being dispersed across large populations and territories. When harms are concentrated, they impact a specific geographic location and thus a smaller, predefined group. Geographic concentration of harms creates a bounded target of potential grievance holders; this is likely to have higher salience to impacted communities than harms occurring further away. Concentration of environmental harms has been associated with low-income communities and communities of color in the United States (Commission for Racial Justice 1987, xiii–xvi). Environmental bads are also disproportionately concentrated in low-income communities in the Global South, creating "environmental inequality." Vulnerability, "or the susceptibility to be harmed" (Adger 2006, 269), is a complex social-ecological phenomenon, but one that is centered on exposure to physical harm. Physical proximity to environmental hazards is emerging as a key determinant to environmental concern in developing countries. For example, survey research from Ecuador shows proximity to oil drilling and mining sites increases environmental concern from impacted communities because it reduces their ability to make a living from these resources (Eisenstadt and West 2019, 3–7). Scholarship on the environmentalism of the poor also relates to actions and concerns over environmental damage from those who depend on environmental services for their livelihood, or "resource deprivation" (Guha and Alier 1997, 6). Thus, the geographic concentration of harms on impacted communities generates a set of concerns or conflicts that are distinct from those where exposure to environmental harms is more dispersed and diluted.

Slow, diluted harms, as seen in the lower right quadrant of Table 2.1, often represent the greatest challenge for organized citizen action. Here harms are dispersed across large territories and populations, and as such their impacts are diluted. Compounding the geographic dispersion of harms, these types of harm occur gradually, over time. Some examples include fisheries depletion, ocean plastics pollution, and biodiversity loss. Outside of committed activists and academic specialists, slow, diluted harms can appear abstract because the negative consequences are unlikely to directly impact specific communities in the near term as these involve slow-moving processes. While ocean plastic pollution and glacier melt can have far-reaching consequences, they are experienced in such a dispersed, long-term manner that it can be difficult to generate broad-based urgency surrounding these issues. Furthermore, these types of harm have been layered over time and have multiple production points. They typically involve diverse institutions (both private and public) and actors across multiple jurisdictions; therefore, coordination can be extremely difficult. Creating policy change for these types of harm involves ending existing path-dependent arrangements as opposed to the negation of incoming action. It is true that committed activists and specialists have historically created environmental change around issues such as forest and animal protection, particularly in advanced industrial nations. For example, U.S.-based conservation movements created the American national parks system, helped push for the 1969 EPA Act, and were mirrored in European countries that developed parallel organizations and institutions (Guha 2014). Global NGOs such as Greenpeace, World Wildlife Fund, Friends of the Earth, and Conservation International are well-resourced and networked actors that can influence policy change (Wapner 1995, 315), but their advocacy work in Global South countries is frequently on less politically contentious issues, such as the establishment of a natural reserve. All else being equal, slow, diluted harms often remain under the purview of a limited number of committed activists.

Accelerating the time horizon of dispersed harms can elevate the visibility of an environmental issue and improve the possibility for social mobilization, as shown in the lower left quadrant of Table 2.1. Rapidly occurring diluted harms may thus be more likely to prompt action due to the creation of a punctuated equilibrium: threats are imminent or have recently occurred, which makes harms more highly visible and urgent. Rapid, diluted harms are dispersed across larger territories, which, under certain conditions, can generate broad-based support. Metropolitan air pollution, coastal flooding, and regional wildfires are some examples of environmental problems that have a broad geographic reach. Broad geographic reach is more likely to cut across class; here middle- and upper-class groups are unable to shield themselves from environmental bads, raising the probability of their involvement in demand making. For example, when air pollution becomes extreme, it is difficult to breathe, at times even see, and residents of all income levels are exposed. Public administration studies have shown that the middle class, whether due to connections, education, or resources, has an advantage when it comes to making demands about policy and public services (Matthews and Hastings 2013, 76–77). Urban middle-class residents are often leaders in urban clean air campaigns, mobilizing policy attention toward the problem and demanding answers (Cao and Prakash 2012, 67; Véron 2006, 2095). In addition, when harms cross larger regions, becoming citywide or statewide, they may be more likely to intersect with the locus of power in capital cities, where key decisions about financing and policy prioritization are made. For example, after years of abandonment, a major impetus for the 19th-century construction of London's citywide sewers and Thames River remediation came from a summer-long heat wave that wafted intense odors into the windows of the recently built Houses of Parliament (Solomon 2011, 250–51). Similarly, scholars have suggested that when political leaders address extreme smog, they are responding to a highly visible problem to which they are likely to receive political credit, as China's current "war on air pollution" campaign illustrates (Ahlers and Shen 2018, 302–5).

Rapid, targeted harms stand in sharp contrast, as seen in the upper left quadrant of Table 2.1. These imminent, concentrated threats are most likely to generate local, organized citizen action. NIMBY (not in my backyard) movements around the world embody the idea that physical proximity of imminent threats is likely to generate protest and obstruction (Hager 2015, 3–4). Many communities tend to rally against incoming siting of, for example, landfills, sludge facilities, or incinerators. In the Global South, rapid, targeted harms frequently pertain to proposed megadevelopment projects, such as a hydrodam, and natural resource extraction, such as a mine. These types of conflicts are more visible, often involve contentious environmental impact assessment processes, and generate conflicts related to relocation, compensation, pollution of land and water, loss of livelihood, and cultural ties to homeland. These socioenvironmental conflicts produce myriad societal responses, such as contentious mobilization through protest, sit-ins, and marches (Mertha 2008, 78–83; Ponce and McClintock 2014, 118–120; Arce 2014; Hochstetler 2020, 175–220); participatory spaces such as roundtables, working groups, and prior consultation (Jaskoski 2022, 6; Falleti and Riofrancos 2018, 88–89); or demand making over distributive rents or compensation (Amengual 2018, 33; Mertha 2008, 69–73). Stopping a threat to imminent harm involves successfully forcing action to discontinue harm before it has occurred. Imminent harm mobilization is the negation of incoming action, such as, for example, anticipated water scarcity from a proposed mining project (Jaskoski 2014a, 878); this stands in sharp contrast to mobilizing to remediate prior action. Conflicts over imminent threats arise because these threats represent a punctuated equilibrium; they are unfamiliar and not yet part of the everyday landscape. Communities are not yet resigned because the harms are not yet embedded and invisible. Furthermore, the initial planning and design phase may be the only space within which communities can negotiate material distributive outcomes (compensation, relocation patterns) or procedural justice (ability to influence and participate in deliberative processes). Under propitious conditions these characteristics can create more opportunities for contention, counteraction, and organized strategies for policy reversal.

This book is about the politics of slow, targeted harms, referred to throughout the book as simply "slow harms." As Table 2.1's upper-right-hand quadrant illustrates, these harms are both slow moving and concentrated in specific communities; they include, for example, established sludge facilities, mines, landfills, and wastewater pollution. These types of harms are some of the most difficult around which to organize citizen action. They involve harms with long time horizons—both long duration and largely steady tempos. These harms have developed gradually over time, often through multiple generations, and thus have become embedded into the landscape and may be difficult for impacted communities to identify. These harms tend to also be geographically concentrated in marginalized populations that have the fewest resources with which to mount resistance; environmental bads are commonly sited on low-value land. In Latin America, urbanization patterns often produce inexpensive informal housing settlements near factories (Kopinak and Barajas 2002, 227–34). Established environmental bads are typically "distanced" from higher-income residents. If conflicts once arose around the original siting of environmental hazards, such as a landfill or mine, the battle was long lost by impacted communities who over multiple generations have become resigned to the associated hazards. In the case of urban slums, resourced residents may have moved away, and other low-resourced residents—often immigrants—may have moved in; thus, what frequently remain are communities with low levels of education, income, and access to the state. Guha and Martinez-Alier's (1997, xxi) focus on environmental activism ignores the temporal dimension of environmental harms. "Environmentalism of the poor" movements emerge in poor communities in developing countries when environmental conflicts threaten economic livelihoods and tend to feature environmental threats that manifest as rapid, targeted harms. But when the duration and tempo of environmental issues are considered, we can observe an impact on subsequent citizen action. Slow-moving harms tend to lead to protracted, yet silent "environmental suffering" (Auyero and Swistun 2009, 16–18) and inaction as opposed to vibrant environmental activism.

Once accustomed to pollution, the probability of mounting resistance decreases. A local leader in the Ecuadorian rainforest opposing incoming oil drilling says, "[T]hose whose lands have been polluted are in favor of more extraction. They live in that reality. Those who are opposed are those of us whose lands have not yet been contaminated" (quoted in Eisenstadt and Jones West 2017, 246). Similarly, Lora-Wainwright (2017, 10–15) shows how Chinese villagers living with the effects of phosphorous mining, fertilizer production, lead and zinc mining, and electronic waste processing occasionally engage in low-level resistance, such as picketing at the factory gate, but their protests are most often tempered by resignation.

Similar challenges are evident in highly polluted urban slums in Latin America that, rather than sites of engaged activism, are often filled with quiet and resigned acquiescence. Resignation can result from uncertainty, as it can be difficult for low-resourced actors to assess risk and act decisively. Thus, slow-moving, targeted harms generate long-term social processes that inhibit collective citizen action. The long duration of these events as well as their slow tempo generate perceptions of low risk, like the proverbial frog in the slowly boiling pot of water. The geographic proximity of slow-moving harms frequently concentrates onto low-resourced populations who may have the least resources—time, money, education, allies—with which to effectively organize sustained action. Thus, slow, targeted harms create complex social arrangements that disfavor citizen collective action. The following section examines how slow targeted harms (referred to simply as "slow harms") have unfolded in the wastewater sector, before turning to an examination of slow-harms accumulation in three urban river basins in 20th-century South America.

The Slow Harms of Wastewater River Pollution

"The sewer is the conscience of the city. Everything there converges and confronts everything else. . . . [A] sewer is a cynic. It tells everything" (Hugo 1862, book 2, ch. 2). The disposal of wastewater reflects societal and cultural traditions and underlying political economies of consumption across societies. Historians have studied, for example, the technical and political contexts that have historically undergirded wastewater management (Melosi 2008; Solomon 2011, 249–65) and the evolution of wastewater technologies (Lofrano and Brown 2010; Tarr 1996, 111–58). Development scholars have stressed wastewater's importance in economic and social development (McGranahan 2015, 242–45; Rosenqvist, Mitchell, and Willetts 2016, 300–305), and urban planners have emphasized the role of adequate sanitation for healthy cities in the Global South (Pastore 2015, 484–87; McFarlane 2008, 422–28). Studies have also documented the political economy of sludge workers and caste-based discrimination (Murungi and van Dijk 2014, 69–73; Human Rights Watch 2014).

Building on these prior studies, a focus on the politics of wastewater policy in the Global South illuminates a key development problem with massive environmental consequences. Water pollution due to poor wastewater management has worsened dramatically since the 1990s and affects the majority of rivers in Latin America, Africa, and Asia (UNEP 2016, xxx). One study shows that 30 of the 47 largest rivers, which together discharge half of global runoff to oceans, show moderate threats, with eight of those rivers showing high threat for human water security (Vörösmarty et al. 2010, 555).

The relationship between ecosystem degradation and human health is inextricable. Unmanaged wastewater is a "vector for disease" (Corcoran et al. 2010, 40); wastewater-related diseases include typhoid, paratyphoid, dysentery, gastroenteritis, and cholera. Over half of the global population that is hospitalized suffers from water-related diseases, and diarrheal diseases make up over 4% of the global disease burden (Corcoran et al. 2010, 11). The World Health Organization estimates that approximately 58% of all cases of diarrhea in low- and middle-income countries are attributable to the environment and cause 20% of global deaths of children under the age of five (Pruss-Ustun et al. 2016, 16–17; Corcoran et al. 2010, 11). Figures on wastewater contamination are even more startling when they incorporate the effects of toxic exposure from heavy metals, chemicals, and persistent organic pollutants, which are increasingly combined with residential wastewater near urban communities. These adverse health impacts are likely to be most dramatic in cities, which globally tend to be disproportionately located near rivers and shorelines (Grimm et al. 2008, 757; Kummu et al. 2011).

Many early cities in Latin America developed around rivers because they helped sustain the city by providing, for example, drinking water, habitats for plants and animals, and cooling temperatures. Rivers also facilitated navigation, helped connect communities through recreation, and over time became focal points for commerce and industry. As cities grew, so did the pollutant load of their river basins and the health impacts on riparian communities. This section examines the role of three rivers in shaping the social and economic development of the capital cities of Argentina, Colombia, and Peru, and their subsequent deterioration.

Slow-harms accumulation for river pollution follows a similar pattern in the three cases. City officials in all three cases failed to keep up with the costs of urbanization on waterways in the second half of the 20th century. The mounting pollution derived from liquid effluents at the residential level, as well as industrial contamination (including in some cases mining), and was further exacerbated by inadequate solid waste management. Human settlements continued to expand, landing at the water's edge in increasingly high numbers during economic crises or other forms of displacement via social or political conflicts. Toxins accumulated over time. Government officials vacillated between denial and empty promises to clean up. Harms spread as slowly as the widespread habituation toward them. Periodic punctuation of equilibria occurred via flooding events but ultimately did little to transform the state's approach to the policy problem. While these cities have different histories, political economies, and ecosystem services, their rivers shared strikingly similar trajectories of slow-harms accumulation.

Slow Harms on the Matanza Riachuelo River in Buenos Aires

As with many political capitals, Buenos Aires developed as the engine of Argentina's economic growth. Located on the western shore of the estuary of the Plata River (Río de la Plata), the city's port facilitated early trade of cereals, cattle hides, and dried beef to the interior of South America during Spanish crown rule. When Argentina became one of the world's principal exporters of agricultural products in the 19th century, the port connected industrial production of cattle, beef, and wheat to maritime trade. The Matanza Riachuelo River (El Río Matanza Riachuelo), through a 64-kilometer-long trajectory that empties into the Plata River and defines the southern boundary of the city, also reflected the class divide that deepened as the city grew. As working-class immigrants settled close to the southern shore of the river near jobs in port facilities and slaughterhouses, middle-class residents moved up north across Avenida de Mayo. Despite economic and demographic expansion, by the early 20th century the Matanza Riachuelo River was still biologically alive. Figure 2.1 shows a newspaper headline heralding a museum exhibition documenting sunbathers gathering in the 1930s that reads, "Memories of a city in which the Riachuelo was a clean mirror." An NGO leader I interviewed remembered, "[W]e were from a generation that would swim in the Plata River, sunbathe on the beaches, where everyone would gather together and socialize."[3] Industrial and residential wastewater contamination accumulated slowly over time, deepening toward the end of the 20th century.

By the turn of the 21st century, unregulated, fast-paced industrial expansion and urbanization had turned the Matanza Riachuelo into the city's public toilet. This process did not happen overnight, and in some places the changes moved so slowly they were imperceptible to impacted communities. For example, in the Villa Inflamable neighborhood of Avellaneda, "contamination has been incubating. . . . [N]obody points to a moment in history where things made a turn for the worse" (Auyero and Swistun 2009, 5). The tempo of change differed across locations, accumulating more quickly or becoming more visible in some sections of the river than others. In a 1956 newspaper article shown in Figure 2.2, one resident likened a particularly contaminated section of the river to "a canon's mouth pointed at the health of the people."[4] By the 2010s, the river had gained international attention when it made a global list of the top 10 most polluted places (Blacksmith Institute 2013, 17). One city official remembered, "After those articles were

---

[3] Interview with Mora Arauz, founding member, Fundación Ciudad, April 18, 2016.
[4] "Una cloaca abierta en el Gran Buenos Aires," Congreso de Sociedades de Avellaneda, August 21, 1956, retrieved from *Clarín* Newspaper Archives, Buenos Aires, April 2016.

Figure 2.1 Eduardo Videla, "Recuerdos de una ciudad en que el Riachuelo era un espejo limpio," *Pagina 12*, March 23, 2000.
Source: Photograph by Veronica Herrera in Clarín Archives, 2016.

published, many tourists flocked here to take tours, wanting to see the most contaminated place in the world."[5] The international press was then privy to what had long been evident to millions of Argentines: the contamination of the river had become a dire public health threat yet was also part of the everyday landscape.

Approximately 4.57 million lived in the river basin in 2020, with over 1.2 million below the poverty line and 10% living in informal settlements

---

[5] Interview with Javier Garcia Elorrio, Buenos Aires City Government, DGLM Riachuelo, April 15, 2016.

Figure 2.2 "Una cloaca abierta en el Gran Buenos Aires," *Congreso de Sociedades de Avellaneda.* August 21, 1956.
Source: Photograph by Veronica Herrera in Clarín Archives, 2016.

(World Bank 2009b, 1; ACUMAR n.d.). The toxic contamination is dispersed unevenly throughout the territory, concentrated downstream in the middle and lower basin and in poor communities that live most proximate to the river in low-value flood-prone zones. Many of these residents are migrants. By 2001, Argentina was home to over half of South America's migrant populations, largely from Paraguay, Bolivia, Uruguay, and Peru, with Paraguayans and Bolivians settling at the highest rates in Buenos Aires (Jachimowicz 2006). By 2019, nearly 650,000 Venezuelans had migrated to Buenos Aires.[6] These working-class immigrant communities frequently settled in urban shantytowns. In one survey, 40% of native-born Argentines favored restrictive immigration policies due to many factors, including prejudice.[7] The environmental impact is intensely concentrated in a relatively small area where 65% of the population lacks residential sewage connections (World Bank 2009b, 12). Throughout the basin, approximately 10,000 tons of solid waste is produced daily, resulting in a sharp increase in open-air landfills (ACUMAR n.d.). Thus, the victims of pollution are also its unwitting perpetrators.

Yet most toxic pollutants are industrial. A history of import substitution industrialization (ISI) policymaking midcentury concentrated industry in the capital city region, adding to the historic accumulation of manufacturing activity already in place at the river's shore through tanneries built by Italian and Spanish immigrants in the early 1900s. Thousands of industries dump untreated manufacturing waste directly or indirectly; heavy metals are discharged from tanneries, meat processing plants, and electroplating processes in the middle and lower basin.[8] The river contains levels of lead, zinc, and chrome 50 times higher than the legal limit in Argentina, with 25% of the contamination stemming from industrial sewage and waste and the remaining 75% originating from residential wastewater (Engel et al. 2011, 29). A petrochemical refinery compound in Avellaneda, Dock Sud, has been in operation since 1931 and stores chemical products, a chemical factory, and a thermoelectric power plant. The companies include Shell, Solvay Indupa, and Petrobas, among many others and have developed decades of political connections and historically created thousands of jobs.[9]

Most of the people affected by pollution are those living in shantytowns or villas on the riverbanks over garbage dumps and low-value land too polluted for commercial development. The river floods frequently during the rainy season, and the flooding spreads highly polluted water into informal settlements (World Bank 2009b, 1). Residents suffer from diarrhea,

[6] Cassandra Garrison, "Venezuelans in Argentina Get Sense of Déjà Vu as Crisis Builds," *Reuters*, September 5, 2019.
[7] "Amid Economic Woes, Argentina Reconsiders Its Immigrant-Friendly Stance." *World Politics Review*. December 12, 2018.
[8] Using a voluntary industrial census, the environmental regulatory agency as of 2014 has identified the presence of 13,388 industries in the river basin, although not all of these generated liquid effluents (ACUMAR 2014). For a journalistic account of these industries, see Aizen (2014, 52–89).
[9] For more on the petrochemical processing plant, see Greenpeace (2015) and Defensor del Pueblo de la Nación (2003).

Figure 2.3 Woman dumping waste into Matanza Riachuelo River.
Source: Clarín Archives. Photo by Clarín, January 28, 1976.

respiratory problems, anemia, neurological disorders, skin diseases, lead poisoning, and cancer.[10] The class divide, spatially distributed between the north and the south, has further contributed to the development of slow harms.[11] As one government official noted, the city adopted a development strategy that allowed environmental harms to concentrate in the south, and "the rest of us turned our backs to the river."[12]

For centuries, the river's contamination has grown alongside empty government promises to clean it up.[13] In 1811, the first independent Argentine

---

[10] See Defensor del Pueblo de la Nación (2003, 73–106, 211–12); JICA (2003, 117–33); Fundación Ciudad (2002, 30–37). For an ethnographic account of living among toxins in Villa Inflammable, see Auyero and Swistun (2009).

[11] Figure 2.3 is a photograph of a woman using the river to discard household waste, a historically common practice for communities who lack solid waste collection services.

[12] Antolin Magallanes, former ACUMAR director, April 11, 2016. See also Merlinksy (2013, 57–62).

[13] The historic transporter bridge in Avellaneda is seen in Figure 2.4. The bridge operated from 1914 to 1960 and continues to serve as a symbol of the region's industrial past.

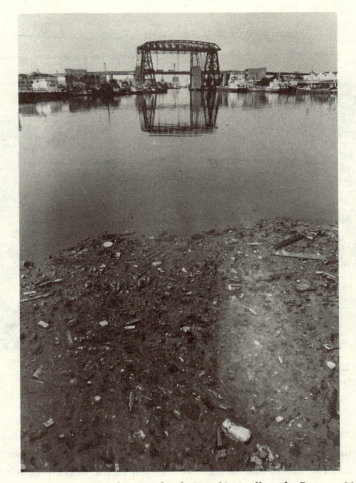

Figure 2.4 Transporter Bridge, Riachuelo Nicolás Avellaneda, Buenos Aires
Source: Clarín Archives. Photo by Clarín, Undated.

government pledged to clean the river as tanneries and slaughterhouses settled on the waterfront and animal waste routinely reddened the waters. Nineteenth- and 20th-century governments vacillated between promising cleanup efforts (e.g., in 1811, 1871), passing decrees prohibiting industries along the waterfront (e.g., 1822), and beginning infrastructure projects to revitalize the river that were rarely completed (e.g., 1913 but not finished even

Figure 2.5 "Prometen que el Riachuelo estará limpio antes de las elecciones del '95," *Clarín*, February 20, 1993.
Source: Photograph by Veronica Herrera in Clarín Archives, 2016.

by 1982).[14] Most notably, as seen in Figure 2.5, in 1993 Secretary of Natural Resources María Julia Alsogaray promised that the Riachuelo would be clean in 1,000 days, declaring that, "[I]n 1995, we will be boating, drinking mate, bathing, and fishing."[15] For financing, Argentina accepted a US$250 million loan from the Inter-American Development Bank, of which only US$1 million was spent on infrastructure works, most was misused or stolen, and

---

[14] Laura Rocha, "El Riachuelo, sucio desde 1811," *La Nación*, June 21, 2005, retrieved from *Clarín* Archives, April 2016.
[15] Comentarios, "Medio ambiente: Antecedente: Los mil días de María Julia," *Clarín*, August 25, 2006.

US$150 million was redirected toward social assistance during the Argentine 2001–2 economic crisis.[16] An engineer who headed the office created to execute these public works in the 1990s revealed that they "didn't have the conditions to expediate the works" and that they were held back in part by cumbersome coordination between multiple jurisdictions that had other priorities.[17] Journalist and environmentalist Sergio Federovisky summed up the problem: these were more "electoral slogans rather than real efforts against the contamination."[18] A 1995 headline concluded that "the 1,000 days of the official promise to clean the Matanza Riachuelo river are over, and you would have to be crazy . . . to swim or fish."[19]

The first documentation of public health risks was conducted by the Japanese Development Agency (JICA) in 2003 in Villa Inflamable, a shantytown that borders Dock Sud and the Shell Petrochemical processing plant. Two definitive independent reports from JICA confirmed that 45% of children under five had elevated lead levels in Villa Inflamable and that these children had incidents of lead poisoning three times higher than other nearby shantytowns (JICA I and JICA II) (see JICA 2003).[20] A local government official revealed in an interview that the federal government attempted to stop the media from reporting these findings.[21] Government records regarding public health risks have historically been incomplete and closely guarded.[22] Efforts by officials to cast a veil over the environmental crisis exacerbated a general public ambivalence about the inevitability of the polluted area that, for the most part, was perceived as impacting only "invisible communities." Newspaper headlines seen, shown in Figure 2.6, summed up the temporal nature of the problem: "The Riachuelo, dirty since 1811."

---

[16] Dante Marín, "Denuncian desvío de fondos del Riachuelo para planes sociales," *Ámbito Financiero*, January 29, 2003; Romina Ryan, "Sólo invirtieron $US1 millón en la limpieza del Riachuelo," *Clarín*, May 7, 2006.
[17] Interview with Javier Urbiztondo, former director of Obras Publicas de Gran Buenos Aires (2000–2005), April 4, 2016.
[18] Sergio Federovisky, "Prometen que el Riachuelo estará limpio antes de las elecciones del '95," *Clarín*, February 20, 1993.
[19] "Se cumplen los mil días de la promesa oficial de recuperar la Cuenca Matanza Riachuelo, y hay que ser loco o aventurero para nadar o pescar," *Diario Popular*, September 27, 1995.
[20] "La tragedia ambiental de la Villa Inflamable," episode 21 of *Ambiente & Medio*, 2019, http://www.ambienteymedio.tv/portfolio_item/la-tragedia-ambiental-de-villa-inflamable/.
[21] Interview with city official, April 2016.
[22] Doctors and healthcare centers have aided in disseminating the narrative that health risks of Inflamable shantytown residents were a result of poverty rather than pollution from chemical and toxic exposure (Auyero and Swistun 2009, 101–5).

Figure 2.6 Laura Rocha, "El Riachuelo, sucio desde 1811," *La Nación*, June 21, 2005.
Source: Photograph by Veronica Herrera in Clarín Archives, 2016.

Slow Harms on the Bogotá River in Cundinamarca

Since the founding of Bogotá in the 16th century, the river that crosses it has played an important economic and social role in the development of the region. Much longer and more voluminous than its Argentine counterpart, the Bogotá River is 347 kilometers long, crossing the region from the northeast to southwest and traversing 46 municipalities in the department of Cundinamarca and the western limits of the capital city of over 10 million people. Legend has it that the indigenous people of the savanna, the Chibchas (or Muiscas) developed a deep bond with the river, "speaking to it, praying to it, and respecting it,"[23] but this connection to nature eroded with the arrival

---

[23] The founding of the Bogotá River follows a similar pattern of other well-known flood origin myths. The legend "Chibcha of the Funza River" tells the story of ancient tribes that fell into

of the Spanish. In 1701, 7,000 people died of a "mysterious illness," and from then on, the river's trajectory mirrored the economic development patterns of first colonialism and later postindependence Colombia.

The death of the Bogotá River followed a slow-paced development pattern that began in the 19th century. The change from indigenous respect for the river to the Spanish crown's utilization of it as a wasteland was not just common practice but was inscribed in law. An 1872 law (Acuerdo 10) permitted using the river to discard human excrement "between the hours of 11 p.m. and 4 a.m."[24] Over time, the river became a primary dumping ground for families and businesses. One interviewee in the upper-basin municipality of Villapinzón described growing up as a young girl in the 1950s: "My mother would have me clean the house and then throw the trash in the river. That was just where we put things we didn't want. On order of the mayor supposedly."[25] As shown in Figure 2.7, the communal practice of laundering along the riverside, where women cultivated community and earned needed income, is emblematic of the social and economic role of the river that was not without its environmental impact.

Slow harms developed over time, and perceptions of contamination were not widespread prior to the 1950s. During this time the river was used primarily for recreation, the generation of electric energy in the middle basin, and potable water. As seen in Figure 2.8, the Tequendama Waterfalls, with its dramatic 150 meters drop, attracted so many visitors from the capital region and around the world, that a luxury hotel was built to service the burgeoning tourism. Other riverside areas in the region, such as Apulo and Girardot, were also frequent spaces for wildlife sighting and recreation, such as the boat race featured on the Muña dam in Figure 2.9 (Vélez Pardo 2015, 12). One

---

corruption and murderous activities, moving away from their cultivation of the earth and stewardship of the river. As punishment, the gods father Xué and mother Chía unleashed torrential rain that flooded the valleys and made the savanna uninhabitable. The tribes prayed for the Sun, and the god Bochica came to dry the rains, revealed a rainbow, and created the Tequendama Waterfalls, giving birth to the River Fuza (or the Bogotá River). The native Colombians of the Cundinamarca *sabana*, the Chibchas (or Muiscas), thus called the Bogotá River the "sacred river" (Caballero Calderón 1985, 29–31).

[24] Translated from Spanish: "No one is allowed to discard onto the streets, pipes, squares, public roads, any garbage, animal waste, or any kind of filth, other than in the places expressly noted in this accord, nor relieve themselves in the streets, but are only to do so in the public baths; however, those without this access in their homes are permitted to throw excrement into canals and rivers between 11 p.m. and 4 a.m." Acuerdo del 10 de febrero de 1872 (Rodríguez Gómez, n.d.).
[25] Interview with small-scale tannery owner, Villapinzón, August 4, 2016.

Figure 2.7 Luis Alberto Acuña, *Lavenderas*, 1910.
Source: Museo de Bogotá, Fondo Luis Alberto Acuña.

shopkeeper reminisced, "Our grandparents used to say that, about 80 years ago, this river was clear, even 40 years ago you could drink from the Bogotá River." An elderly man remembers bathing in the river: "The water was crystalline and freezing. If the day was sunny, one could see at the bottom of the river many fish. We also saw crabs on the shoreline."[26] An indigenous leader in the municipality of Cota recalled, "Near the river there were reeds, and many ducks, birds, and herons" (Vélez Pardo 2015, 15).

Post–World War II economic and population expansion due to ISI began to more noticeably muddy the waters.[27] Similar to their development in Buenos Aires, tanneries of all sizes were built near the mouth of the river in Villapinzón; by 1990 there were over 150 tanneries dumping toxic effluents and animal refuse directly into the river.[28] The expansion of floriculture and agriculture, and of their fertilizers, also began to have an impact. One study

---

[26] Carolay Morales, "La historia no recordada del río Bogotá," RCNRadio.com, April 23, 2019; Vélez Pardo (2015, 14). Figure 2.10 is a photograph of the Bogotá river in the early 20th century.

[27] A common response by engineers, adopted for the Bogotá River post-1950s, was to canalize the river and thus attempt to separate the growing toxicity of the river from the most dense urban communities (World Bank 2010, 4).

[28] "Aun se puede frenar una gran tragedia ecológica el Río Bogotá: Una amenaza," *El Tiempo*, November 4, 1990.

Figure 2.8 Gumersindo Cuéller Jiménez, *Salto de Tequendama*. Foto 9. Bogotá, Biblioteca Luis Ángel Arango, Biblioteca Virtual, Colección Gumersindo Cuéller Jiménez, Identificador del objeto digital rbbr3962_1561.

in 1990 by the Bogota water utility (Empresa de Acueducto y Alcantarillado de Bogotá, EAAB) found that of the 10,300 industries in the capital region, there was no regulatory oversight over the ones that most contaminated the river, which included approximately 600 industries producing chemicals, oils, metallurgy, beer and soft drinks, chicken slaughterhouses, and tanneries.[29]

Mining activities further exacerbated the pollutant load (Pérez Preciado 1993, 4, 6, 29). One study found that from 2000 to 2020, 95% of mining concession applications nationwide were approved or were in the process of approval by the Environment Ministry. (These do not include illegal small-scale mining.) As of 2020, 24 mining zones were active in the Bogotá savanna, largely mining construction materials such as sand, carbon, salt, and silica rather than heavy metals. Yet mining has occurred in protected areas for migratory bird species, as well as areas abutting human settlements, those adjacent to aquifer recharge zones, those next to forest reserves in the upper

---

[29] "Aun se puede frenar una gran tragedia ecológica el Río Bogotá."

Figure 2.9 Gumersindo Culler Jimenez, *Regatas en el lago del río Muña*.
Source: Biblioteca Luis Ángel Arango, Biblioteca Virtual, Colección Gumersindo Cuéller Jiménez, Ferencia FT1736 brblaa1042991-4.

basin of the river, and those impacting small-scale subsistence agriculture, particularly potatoes, strawberries, and milk production in Chocontá. All would carry toxic liquid effluents into the Bogotá River.[30]

Slow harms accumulated further as urbanization spread in the second half of the 20th century. Fifty years of armed conflict in Colombia created one of the world's largest documented populations of internally displaced people, as many as 7 million internal migrants (Camargo et al. 2020, 1–2). Forced displacement spurred rural-to-urban migration without a concomitant growth in capacity to manage the growing impact of residential wastewater in the capital region. Communities around three tributaries that feed into the Bogotá River (Salitre, Fucha, and Tunjuelo) also expanded and further diminished the river's oxygen levels.

---

[30] "Actividades mineras chocan con la recuperación del río Bogotá," *Semana Sostenible*, August 13, 2020; Angélica Lozano Correa, "Zonas de míneria en la sabana de Bogotá," *Angelicalozano.com*, March 9, 2017.

Figure 2.10 Gumersindo Cuéller Jiménez, *Paisaje del Río Bogotá*. Puente Grande, Bogotá.
Source: Biblioteca Luis Ángel Arango, Biblioteca Virtual, Colección Gumersindo Cuéller Jiménez, Foto 1. Identificador del objeto digital: rbbr3962_815.

By 2010 the situation was dire. Reports showed that only about 20% of the wastewater discharged into the river received primary treatment (World Bank 2010, 1). One of the few comprehensive available reports from the Cundinamarca Environmental Agency (CAR) prior to this period showed that the river had zero dissolved oxygen and ratios of Total Suspended Solids (TSS) to Biological Oxygen Demand (BOD5) that facilitated algal blooms. Contamination stems from residential sewage (76%), heavy metals from manufacturing (24%), and mining (46%), which contributes the largest pollutant of suspended particles (Pérez Preciado 1993, 29). The Bogotá River became classified as the largest open sewer in the country at the turn of the 21st century (Contraloría de Bogotá 2014, 4; World Bank 2010, 1).

Slow harms began to impact community health, although their pace moved imperceptibly for years and were not frequent topics in media or government reports. Within Bogotá, low-income neighborhoods adjacent to the river became the most vulnerable to toxic exposure, with toxic waters overflowing via flooding during rainy seasons (World Bank 2010, 4). A 1993 report by CAR stated that "the communities living near contaminated water suffer water-borne illness at a much higher rate than communities living far from the rivers" and estimated that 500,000 residents, mostly low-income, were impacted by toxic contamination (Pérez Preciado 1993, 6). A news article summarizing the findings of the CAR report stated that in 1990 88,000 residents suffered illnesses along the basin, most commonly bacterial infections, digestive problems, food poisoning, diarrhea, and gastritis.[31] These sources emphasized how livestock and agriculture which drew from the river's contaminated water further expanded the river's toxicity beyond immediate communities.[32] While the Bogotá River was less densely populated on the river's edge as compared to its counterparts in Buenos Aires and Lima, one source from 1990 suggests that over 1,500 riverine residents were impacted by contamination.[33]

One of the more accelerated forms of slow harms developed around the river's use as a hydroelectric power generator beginning in the 1940s in the south of Bogotá. Here the Hydroelectric Muña Dam straddles the municipality of Sibaté, where, as the river became more contaminated, residents became exposed to polluted water daily, sprayed in the process of generating electricity. The spraying resulted in emitted sulfuric gas and toxins that sickened livestock and generated parasites and gastrointestinal, respiratory, and skin infections.[34] A shopkeeper in Sibaté remembered the community in the late 1970s as having "bits of paradise," but by the early 1990s that had changed.[35] By then, Cundinamarca hospitals regularly treated patients for skin and respiratory infections. One nurse noted, "[T]he lives of our patients are jeopardized. . . . [T]he rat and mosquito plagues are uncontrollable."[36]

---

[31] "En 1990 hubo 88,000 enfermos," *El Tiempo*, December 9, 1993; "El Muña, otro enemigo del Julio Manrique," *El Tiempo*, November 2, 1996.

[32] "Aún se puede frenar una gran tragedia ecológica el Río Bogotá: Una Amenaza," *El Tiempo*, November 4, 1990; "En 1990 hubo 88,000 enfermos," *El Tiempo*, December 9, 1993; "Río Bogotá: En el Muña es cadáver," *El Tiempo*, May 22, 1994; Pérez Preciado (1993, 5, 8, 29).

[33] "Aun se puede frenar una gran tragedia ecológica el Río Bogotá: Una Amenaza," *El Tiempo*, November 4, 1990.

[34] "Temor por gases del Muña," *El Tiempo*, February 23, 2004.

[35] "Embalse del Muña asfixia a Sibaté," *El Tiempo*, January 15, 1996.

[36] "Embalse del Muña asfixia a Sibaté."

Slow harms have received slow responses from the state. Efforts to construct sanitation treatment plants and infrastructure to connect them across multiple jurisdictions have been stalled by corruption, a lack of political will, and failed technical solutions that cost millions (World Bank 2010, 2; Lamprea 2016, 295). The hydroelectric power company, owned by ever-changing concessionaires, has denied involvement in the environmental crisis. EAAB has historically dumped untreated residential wastewater directly into the river. CAR was charged with regulating unlawful discharge yet was historically ineffective at fining illegal industrial effluents or controlling the tons of garbage dumped daily from dozens of municipalities; little progress had been made by local authorities to do the same. In a 1990 article, reporters stated that some city council people opposed the fines imposed by EAAB that would force industries to pay for environmental damages.[37] In 1993, the environmental public prosecutor was quoted as "[questioning] practically all the authorities of the country and Bogotá, because they do not administer the appropriate resources or fail to use them, to protect the environment."[38] Another report cites the director of National Planning as telling the Bogotá water utility in 1990 that "the recuperation of the Bogota River is not a priority for the nation."[39] The comptroller's office summed up decades of mismanagement by noting that "investments and efforts have been so dispersed and disconnected that [they have failed] to solve the problem at its root" (Contraloría de Bogotá 2014, 4). Similar dynamics are evident in Peru's capital city.

[37] "Aún se puede frenar una gran tragedia ecológica el Río Bogotá: Una Amenaza," *El Tiempo*, November 4, 1990.
[38] "Cuestionan el manejo del medio ambiente," *El Tiempo*, November 10, 1993.
[39] "Surge polémica entre los gobiernos distrital y nacional recuperar el Río Bogotá no es prioritario: Planeación," *El Tiempo*, November 17, 1990.

Slow Harms on the Rímac River in Lima

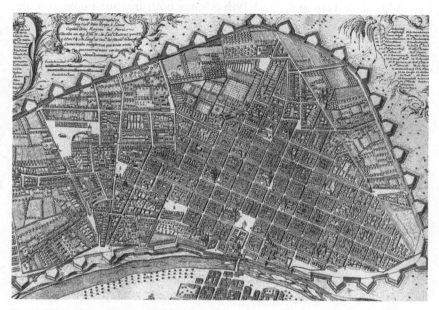

Figure 2.11 Lima, 1748, with a View of Rimac River, De Ulloa, Antonio y Jorge Juan. *Source:* Fondos Bibliográficos (Sección Siglo XVII o Etapa Colonial) del Archivo Histórico del Guayas, Guayauil, Ecuador. Wikipedia Commons, by J. Javier García A. Ecuador.

Nicknamed the Talking River (El Río Hablador), the Rímac River takes its name from Quechua, where *rimaq* means "to speak" (Colchado Lucio 1975). The Rímac follows a 145-kilometer course that begins in the eastern highlands of the Huarochirí Province at an altitude of 550 meters, traversing the Lima-Callao Metropolitan region before discharging into the Pacific Ocean. Located in the arid region of Western Pacific Peru, the Rímac has historically been the primary source of drinking water for the Lima-Callao Metropolitan region.

Old Lima was founded during the Spanish conquest in 1535 along the southern banks of the Rímac. Three centuries later the Lima district of Rímac would develop on the northern side of the river, connecting to old Lima by bridges.[40] Although Lima was the center of wealth and power as the

---

[40] The drawing in Figure 2.11 illustrates how the gridded city of Old Lima was designed around the Rímac during colonial rule. The illustration in Figure 2.12 shows the bridging structure of colonial Lima over the Rímac.

Viceroyalty of Peru given its coastal location, growth slowed after independence. From the 17th to the mid-19th century, both area and population size expanded slowly and in 1746 was devastated by an earthquake that destroyed the city.

By the turn of the 20th century, Lima was controlled by export-oriented oligarchs, whose trade markets in sugar, cotton, and minerals were based on economic power concentrated in rural enclaves (Collier 1976, 12). Unlike other countries where proletariat reforms began to dismantle oligarchic rule, Peru's capital remained a politically conservative and socially stratified city into the early 20th century. After the 1940s, urban migration would take off, particularly after new forms of transportation and related infrastructure developed in the metropolitan region and helped bring in rural migrants in greater numbers.

After the 1940s, the city's urbanization and industrialization patterns worked together, increasingly in closer physical proximity, to exacerbate water availability. The population of Lima rose from 3.9% in 1908 to 8.4% in 1940 (Collier 1976, 15). Migration from the provinces exploded after 1940, from 645,000 to over nine million in 2010 (Ioris 2012, 266), settling largely in the northern and southern parts of the city. New migrants occupied lands through "invasions," some receiving titles and basic services in what were called *pueblos jóvenes*.

Squatter settlements would form part of reformist political movements in Peru, threatening the long-standing power of oligarchs who ran the export sectors. Low rainfall and mild winters were conducive to the building of informal settlements with minimal materials, and these conditions helped fuel their proliferation: "The appearance of settlements in Lima has been accompanied by a pattern of urban growth in which the city is constantly catching up with surrounding settlements that are initially formed at the periphery of the city" (Collier 1976, 19). The major areas of settlement growth developed along both sides of the Rímac River in the late 1940s and early 1950s on the outskirts of the city. By the late 1950s, the entire left bank of the river was surrounded by commercial and industrial zones (Collier 1976, 20). By the 2010s, 81% of the basin's population was located in the municipalities (*distritos*) of Lima, Vitarte, Chaclacayo, Chosica, and Matucana (DIEGESA 2011, 1).

Peru was not as industrialized as Colombia and Argentina when it moved toward ISI at the end of the 1950s. Industrial growth accelerated to 9% a year from 1960 to 1965. The traditional ISI experiment did not last long, and Peru's military regime (1968–80) adopted a nationalist development strategy based

Figure 2.12 A late 19th-century illustration of Lima located in the valleys of the Chillón, Rímac, and Lurín Rivers, in the desert zone of the central coastal part of the country, overlooking the Pacific Ocean.
Source: De Luan/Alamy Stock Photo.

on agriculture, fishing, industry, and mining (Thorp 1977, 128–30). The post-1950s period thus saw increased urbanization, manufacturing, and mining under military and civilian rule that did not prioritize environmental concerns.

Basic services were also historically underdeveloped. As of 2018, Lima had developed only four landfills to service what would become nearly 10 million residents (Ministerio de Ambiente 2018). As one observer explains, "The problem is with municipal governance. . . . [R]esidents throw their trash into the river. Yet although many things pass by, the trash trucks never come. So if the trash trucks do not come, neighbors have nowhere to put their trash, and they see the river as a solution."[41] National estimates show that only

---

[41] "El origen del río Rimac," *Cuarto Poder*, July 4, 2008, reporting by Augusto Thorndike, featuring Jorge Luis Baca.

Figure 2.13 Rimac River in Lima, Peru, 2014.
Source: Klaus Ulrich Müller/Alamy Stock Photo.

70% of solid waste receives residential service pickup, and only 30% of that amount is deposited in landfills (Defensoría del Pueblo 2007). Additionally, the river has become an open sewer in a city where 90% to 98% of residential wastewater remains untreated as of the late 2010s (Ioris 2012, 266; Juárez Soto 2012, 9). Both solid waste dumping and residential wastewater have contributed to the river's deterioration, particularly after the 1950s urbanization wave.

Since its founding, the Rímac River has served multiple purposes, but the main one has been providing Lima's drinking water. Unlike Bogotá and Buenos Aires, which rely on other sources of potable water, the slow-moving contamination of the river in Peru's capital has represented a dire assault on its sole source of water for human consumption. Through the years, Lima developed extraordinary water security challenges as the second driest capital city in the world. Seventy percent of the country lives on the arid Pacific coast, where less than 2% of the country's water resources are located (Lubovich 2007, 2). The Rímac also generates electricity from four hydroelectric dams that help power the city. The melting Andean subtropical glaciers above Lima (already 25% reduced compared to 1980) decreases precipitation, and mining activities have further stressed water availability (World Bank 2014, 23).

Because the Rímac is the critical source of drinking water that feeds the city, there has been heavy investment in water potability treatment. A chemical engineer overseeing the Atarjea and Huachipa potable water treatment plants explains:

> When you design a plant, you choose a river that complies with the necessary standards to be treated in processes like the ones in our plant. But if you find that over time the river begins to deteriorate until it becomes a dead river, that has nothing, no fish, nothing alive, you cannot put that water directly into the water treatment processing plant. We have to now pretreat, which means adding chlorine, and sulfate because the water is full of algae, carbon to control odors, and coagulants so sediments settle and after all of that, the water can enter the plant.[42]

Like the Matanza Riachuelo and Bogotá rivers, the Rímac is deeply polluted from industrial growth. As the country's industrial center, Lima accounts for nearly half of the nation's industrial production and houses over 10,000 large and medium firms (INEI 2018, 1). The Ministry of Production's environmental agency listed 105 registered manufacturing firms in 2016–17 whose liquid effluents discharge into the river, mostly from paper, beer, dairy manufacturers, tanneries, laundromats, chemical companies, oils, and textiles production (PRODUCE, n.d., 9, 10). A 2015 government report lists

---

[42] Interview with Miriam Vasquez Osorio, SEDAPAL, May 5, 2017.

722 sources of contamination, including 50 agro-industrial, 6 agricultural, 7 mines and 14 mine tailings, and 221 landfills; a 2009 report shows that contamination comes from 44% residential wastewater, 40% industrial firms, and 16% mining (Ministerio de Ambiente, 2009, 1; ANA 2015, 5). As in the other two cases, there is no available data or estimates on the number of informal or unregistered manufacturing companies; thus these figures likely underestimate total polluting effluent discharge.

Much of the pollution in the River Rímac is a result of mining, a practice that dates back over 100 years. While the area does not house the majority of Peru's mining enclaves, there are several active mines operating near the Rímac riverbank as well as numerous abandoned mines. Concrete data about the quantity and quality of mining and industrial effluent discharge remain elusive. A new environmental agency from the Ministry of Production (PRODUCE) summed up the situation: "Most industrial liquid effluents are deposited directly in bodies of water and sewage. Information about these are insufficient, fragmented, dispersed and unreliable, making it impossible to understand the characteristics and volumes of industry's liquid effluent discharge and their water withdrawals" (PRODUCE, n.d., 3). Independent assessments of government water quality testing have found that agencies produce different, and conflicting, water-quality data (Juárez Soto 2012, 71).[43] Data from government sponsored observatories report figures in total volume discharge with no reference to offending polluters or individual effluent discharge locations ("Autoridad Nacional Del Agua" n.d.). Mining activity is most intense in the middle and upper basins of the Rímac. The mining tailing sites, some of which are located at the mouth of the river, result from the propensity of mining companies to shut down and leave tailings unremediated to leach into the river. Reports of the number of mining tailing sites conflict across agencies, for example, 14 (Autoridad Nacional del Agua), 17 (OEFA), 20 (Observatorio del Agua), and 40 (Ministry of Environment) (Observatorio del Agua Chillón Rímac Lurín 2019, 35; Ministerio de Ambiente, 2009, 2; ANA 2015, 5).[44]

---

[43] A SEDAPAL engineer is quoted as attributing 60% of the river's contamination to mining activities. Official figures vary across competing government agencies for many reasons, one of them being that officials tend to underestimate the toxic impact of the policy sector for which they are responsible; in this case SEDAPAL is responsible for wastewater provision and treatment, not mining regulation. "Relaves mineros component 60% de contaminación del río Rímac," *Andina*, October 3, 2012.

[44] Fernando Leyton, "El río Rímac en constante amenaza por 17 relaves mineros," *La Republica*, August 5, 2017.

Public officials debate and obscure the extent of the river's contamination and who is responsible. Authorities have been slow to analyze toxic effluent effects of mining activity or conduct epidemiological studies of most proximate populations; when water-quality samples are analyzed, they are found to be within permissible discharge limits.[45] A 2011 study by the regulatory agency DIGESA tested water quality of toxins such as fats and solids, hydrocarbons, cyanide, nitrates, chlorides, aluminum, arsenic, cadmium, copper, chrome, iron, lead, magnesium, and zinc and found only three heavy metals (aluminum, arsenic, and cadmium) to be beyond the permissible limits (DIEGESA 2011, 4–6). Yet independent studies have documented the presence of heavy metals such as lead, cadmium, and arsenic well above legal limits (Guillén et al. 1998, 7; Juárez Soto 2012, 72).

The most controversial mining tailing is located five meters away from the mouth of the river, the Tamboraque, which has been a constant source of conflict for decades in the upper basin. Medical evaluations near this Mayoc zone revealed high levels of chronic dermatitis and cognitive dysfunction in the population, and experts found lead, copper, zinc, cadmium, arsenic, and other toxic metals in the tailings. These tailings are just a landslide or heavy rain away from falling into the Rímac, and engineers worry about long-term toxic exposure as well as a catastrophic collapse of the mouth of the river that threatens lives and the city's drinking water. One engineer decried that if there was seismic activity, the Tamboraque could fall and cause a natural dam, containing the crisis only momentarily until the debris swept into the city and killed potentially thousands. "If it happens at night, there wouldn't be time to warn anyone."[46] Seismic activity would also ensure that the city would lose water for months or, according to one engineer, be left without a water source as the Tamboraque contains 638,000 tons of toxic tailings and "there wouldn't be the capacity to treat so much water."[47] The company, Nyrstar, has paid US$200,000 in fines, and other pending fines are tied up

---

[45] Interview with public official, MINAM, March 2017.
[46] Óscar Cáceres, civil engineer, interviewed in "Río Rímac amenazado: Relave minero al borde de la principal frente de agua que abastece Lima," Panorama Televisión, April 2, 2017, time stamp 10:50.
[47] Monica Untiveros, civil engineer and hydraulic resource specialist, interviewed on Documentary: Historias de Agua, produced by Red Muqui and KillaKuyay, December 13, 2017, time stamp begins 38:00.

in administrative judicial proceedings. When explaining why they have not moved more of the tailings away from the mouth of the river, one Nyrstar engineer said, "If the tailings are currently in a stable place, why touch them?"[48]

Public officials have a history of ignoring or obfuscating information related to the river's growing dangers. Communities in other extremely contaminated locations in Peru, such as Cerro de Pasco, Junín, and Oroya, report that when they have been found to have elevated lead in their blood by local doctors and mining company studies, officials have told them to "eat more iron" or "keep their houses cleaner," negating responsibility.[49] One Environment Ministry bureaucrat admitted that the nexus between environment and health is the "topic least addressed in our public policy."[50]

Table 2.2 provides an overview of key characteristics examined in this chapter across the three river basins. These include geographic dimensions such as river length, land cover, and population size along with the types of polluters and identified toxins reported in the sources consulted during and after field research in these three capital regions.

---

[48] "Río Rímac amenazado: Relave minero al borde de la principal frente de agua que abastece Lima," Panorama Television, April 2, 2017, time stamp 7:24, 12:26.

[49] *Documentary: Historias de Agua*, produced by Red Muqui and KillaKuyay, December 13, 2017, time stamp begins 38:00.

[50] Interview with Jose Luis Vasquez Vega, MINAM, Dirección General de Investigación, April 28, 2017.

Table 2.2 Comparative Characteristics across River Basins

	Matanza Riachuelo River, Argentina	Bogotá River, Colombia	Rímac River, Peru
Length	64 km (1)	347 km (10)	145 km (18)
Basin Size	2,047 km^2 (1)	5,400 km^2 (11)	3,240 km^2 (19)
Population Size of Metropolitan Area	15 million (2)	10.5 million (2)	10.3 million (2)
% of National Population	33.5 (2)	21.4 (2)	31.9 (2)
Population Size of River Basin	4.57 million (1)	1.29 million (12)	6.49 million (19)
No. of Residents on High-Risk Land	17,771 families (2010) (3)	N/A	196,978 individuals (20) (2019)
Municipalities	14 (+ Buenos Aires) (1)	46 (+ Bogotá) (10)	52 (+ Lima & Callao) (20)
Precipitation (mm/year)	1,146 (4)	800 (4)	9 (4)
Water Reserve per Capita (million m3)	43 (4)	117 (4)	37 (4)
% of National Industry	30 (5)	41 (12)	46 (21)
Industry Types	Chemicals, petrochemicals, food, tanneries, electroplating, meat processing, metallurgy (1)	Chemicals, oil, metallurgy, electroplating, beer, soda, slaughterhouses, tanneries, floriculture, agriculture (13)	Paper, beer, dairy, food, tanneries, laundries, chemicals, oils, textiles (22)
No. of Identified Contaminating Industrial Discharges	669 (6)	1,635 (13)	(105 registered manufacturing firms; incomplete data) (22)
Mining	No (1)	Yes (24 approved zones; 520 active, 120 inactive, 200 abandoned): sand, stone, carbon, silica (14) (15)	Yes (7 active, 20 abandoned tailing sites, over 3,000 informal miners) (19)

(continued)

Table 2.2 Continued

	Matanza Riachuelo River, Argentina	Bogotá River, Colombia	Rímac River, Peru
Identified Heavy Metals	Lead, chrome, mercury, cadmium, hydrocarbons (benzene, toluene, ethylbenzene, xilenium) (7)	Cadmium, chrome, mercury, zinc, arsenic, lead (16)	Lead, cadmium, arsenic, copper, zinc, hydrocarbons (benzene, toluene, ethylbenzene, xilenium) (22) (23) (24)
Identified Illness (Illustrative, Not Exhaustive)	Diarrhea, respiratory problems, anemia, neurological disorders, skin diseases, lead poisoning, cancer (7) (8) (9)	Diarrhea, gastritis, bacterial infections, food poisoning, respiratory and skin infections (16) (17)	Chronic dermatitis, neurological disorders, cancer (missing data) (23) (24)

Sources compiled by author: ACUMAR (n.d.), 2. United Nations (2018b), 3. Convenio (2010, 1), 4. OECD (2021, 176), 5. www.britannica.com/place/Buenos-Aires/Economy, 6. ACUMAR (2022). 7. Defensor del Pueblo de la Nación (2003, 84–106, 211–12), 8. JICA (2003, 117–33), 9. Fundación Ciudad (2002, 30–37), 10. CAR (2022), 11. World Bank (2010, 2), 12. Minambiente (2015), 13. Secretaría Distrital de Ambiente (2021, 35, 36), 14. CAR (2006, 10); 15. "Actividades mineras chocan con la recuperación del río Bogotá," *Semana Sostenible*, August 13, 2020, 16. Pérez Preciado (1993, 6), 17. "En 1990 hubo 88,000 enfermos," *El Tiempo*, December 9, 1993, 18. Minesterio de Ambiente (2009, 1).), 19. Observatorio del Agua Chillón Rímac Lurín (2019, 4, 32, 35), 20. Autoridad Nacional del Agua (2019, 7–9), 21. INEI (2018, 141, 143), 22. PRODUCE (n.d., 9–10), 22. DIEGESA (2011, 1–6), 23. Guillén et al. (1998, 7), 24. Juárez Soto (2012, 16).

The Common Trajectory of Slow Harms

Individuals adjust their strategies based on their anticipated time horizons, reacting to, for example, whether an event is unfolding quickly, or how much time is left. Temporalities of environmental dangers are rarely considered even though key differences across threat types impact the likelihood of collective action. Faster-moving harms are more likely to generate a sense of crisis and policy attention, while slower-moving harms may hide in the shadows for decades. This chapter has presented a framework for understanding environmental harms across two key dimensions: the time horizon and geographic dispersion of perceived threats. The typology presented here allows for a more fine-grained understanding of the barriers to collective action between different types of environmental harms. Slow targeted harm, the topic of this book, is one of many types of environmental harms. Slow harms are a long-duration event with steady tempos, producing a type of complex social process that makes them recede in the background and take a backseat to seemingly more urgent problems. When slow harms are geographically concentrated (or targeted) onto specific communities, the likelihood of collective action and policy attention decreases further.

Wastewater river pollution is a ubiquitous example of slow, targeted harms; its long historical trajectory reveals the social and economic development trajectories of the cities in which they were created. While the accumulation of slow harms in this chapter occurred in distinct countries with different histories and cultures, they share strikingly similar patterns. Cities developed along waterways well before industrialization because of the many social and economic benefits that rivers historically provided. As industrialization exploded in the 20th century in Global South countries, slow harms accumulated in capital regions with tributaries that fed into these same principal rivers, concentrating the toxic impacts of liquid effluents.

In Latin America, rural-to-urban migration led to spatially segregated cities where low-value riverine land with a propensity to flood became settling grounds for many low-income, migrant, immigrant, and brown communities. Where once communities bathed and consumed water freely along river shores, they later began to feel sick from darkening waters. Vegetation and livestock near contaminated water sickened nearby communities and those consuming contaminated products throughout the city. Mounting health concerns were often ignored or denied by government officials. Occasional flooding events did little to reverse public policy. The nature of polluters was similar across the cities studied here: residential, industrial, and, to varying degrees, mining. Multiple jurisdictions and political parties became charged with overseeing different aspects of this growing wicked problem, the most common outcome being policy paralysis.

Against this initial backdrop, diverse social and political coalitions mobilized to change the level of public policy attention to this forgotten problem in the three cities, which is taken up in the following chapters. The next chapter examines how expansive bonding mobilization within grassroots groups across Buenos Aires's Matanza Riachuelo River Basin, coupled with bridging mobilization between outsiders who had a shared common history of working together, helped alter the amount of policy attention toward the river and ignited a historic policy shift.

3
Expansive Policy Shifts in Argentina
The Power of Strong Bonds with Strong Bridges

After a period of military rule, the return to democracy in 1986 ushered in a wave of new environmental legislation and constitutional rights in Argentina, but institutional changes remained largely disconnected from change on the ground. As slow harms accumulated over time, they were largely ignored. Beatriz Mendoza, a healthcare worker in an informal settlement that bordered the Matanza Riachuelo River, told me in an interview, "Contamination didn't exist for us. It wasn't a topic we were concerned with."[1] Yet by 2020, slow harms on the Matanza Riachuelo River—and environmental rights more broadly—had become a more prominent and accepted part of the national conversation. Once invisible as a policy problem, slow harms on the Matanza Riachuelo River had been taken out of the shadows.

At first glance, a historic 2008 Argentine Supreme Court ruling mandating river remediation, the *Mendoza* case (CSJN 2008), seemed to have kickstarted policy changes. In contrast, this chapter illustrates how judicial activism was undergirded by a broad civil society network that worked with public officials before, during, and after the ruling to create an expansive policy shift. The civil society network was composed of strong bonding mobilization—impacted communities that were organized, vocal, and persistent in their claims about pollution. Strong bonds sent smoke signals about pollution and provided legitimacy for harms-based claims in the eyes of the media and public authorities, but they alone lacked the resources necessary to get the state to respond.

Strong bridges alleviated this impasse. Strong bridges—resourced external actors in both state and society—were able to utilize their material resources and prior collaborations to connect pollution-related grievances to the state. In Argentina, national-level NGOs became involved in the river pollution case and drew on prior collaborations in a vast human rights network

---

[1] Interview with Beatriz Mendoza, plaintiff in historic 2008 Supreme Court ruling, March 16, 2017.

Slow Harms and Citizen Action. Veronica Herrera, Oxford University Press. © Oxford University Press 2024.
DOI: 10.1093/oso/9780197669020.003.0003

as well as the discourse of human rights to credibly reframe river pollution as a human rights violation. NGOs were joined by state-level human rights institutions that were also steeped in a human rights legacy to further institutionalize progress on river cleanup. Multiple center-left presidential administrations that were champions of human rights accountability provided conditions for activists to be physically and politically protected and connected to public sector agencies. This political support occurred against a backdrop of insular, nationalist economic policymaking that did not depend heavily on mineral extractive export markets. These conditions, in the 1990s and 2000s, enabled bridges to strengthen and become more politically influential, positioning them to be effective advocates once NGOs and activist officials turned their attention to river pollution remediation in the 2010s.

This chapter argues that strong grassroots activism, or *bonding mobilization*, ignited across the large territory, but it was only when strong resourced outsiders engaged in *bridging mobilization* that expansive river remediation policies were adopted. Resourced bridges joined active bonds in an advocacy network that used litigation, participatory institutions in the judiciary, protests, marches, rallies, and media campaigns to demand and oversee a new era of policy reform for environmental regulations. The chapter reviews national-level environmental frameworks, traces the histories of strong bonds and strong bridges, illustrates the critical role bridges played in augmenting transparency and accountability for environmental harms, and concludes by evaluating alternative explanations. The Argentina case shows how environmental concern developed not due to the passage of a court ruling or a postmaterial concern about environmental conservation, but rather because of a reconceptualization of pollution as a human rights crisis.

Environmental Institutions: A Brief History

Argentina's early adoption of environmental institutions belies its historically low levels of regulatory capacity and political will to combat environmental degradation.[2] Similar to most countries in the region, international influences were key to initial adoption of environmental frameworks. During

---

[2] For a timeline of Argentina's environmental institutions and legislation, see Acuña (1999, 7–10) and Díaz (2009).

his third presidential term (1973–74), Juan Perón created the Secretariat of Natural Resources and Human Environment, inspired by similar environmental institutions being created in Europe while he was in exile in Spain in the early 1970s (Gutiérrez and Isuani 2014, 299; Díaz 2009, 45–66). After the Secretariat was dismantled by the military junta (1976–83) (Díaz 2009, 69–82), it was not until President Carlos Menem's administration (1989–1999) that a new National Environmental Secretariat was formed in 1991.

Menem's environmental policy reflected his neoliberal policymaking agenda. He created environmental institutions to appease his international audience and make Argentina a more attractive place to do business. Some authors stress that environmental institutions were a precondition for multilateral aid and loans; indeed a 1993 US$30 million Inter-American Development Bank (IDB) loan was disbursed to strengthen the country's environmental institutional framework. Menem's environmental secretary María Julia Alsogaray followed his agenda and created institutions designed to participate in an open economy with a small role for both the state and society (Gutiérrez and Isuani 2014, 303–5; Hochstetler 2003, 9–10). Despite Alsogaray's administration being discredited after she was arrested for misappropriating secretariat funds, Argentina's environmental institutional framework was strengthened during this time (Gutiérrez and Isuani 2014, 305).

Thus, environmental issues gained de jure priority in the 1990s. In a 1994 constitutional amendment, Article 41 established the right to a clean environment, allowing for both individual and collective litigation by those directly and indirectly impacted by contamination (the *amparo*, writ of protection for individual rights). The constitutional amendment spelled out numerous rights related to the environment, such as the right to information about environmental issues, to litigate to uphold environmental rights (both individual and class action), to reparations, and to citizen participation.[3] Although Menem's quest to amend the Constitution was driven by his extraconstitutional reelection ambition and was antidemocratic, it resulted in environmental protections attaining constitutional status and being imbued with human rights language from the posttransition democratic agenda (Gutiérrez and Isuani 2014, 305–6; Christel and Gutiérrez 2017,

---

[3] After the return to democracy, provincial governments adopted environmental legislation that created piecemeal environmental protections by province, but the 1994 constitutional clause for environmental rights gave the federal government more control over environmental laws that impact the whole nation, alongside permitting collective rights litigation. Interview with Nestor Cafferatta, secretario de justicia ambiental, CSJN, March 16, 2017.

3–6).[4] Financed in part by the IDB loan, new legal proposals were drafted for national environmental assessments, solid waste disposal, various sector laws, and, most important, the General Environmental Law (25.675) in 2002 (Hochstetler 2003, 10; Gutiérrez and Isuani 2014, 308). Observers estimate that Argentina has created 3,000 to 5,000 laws related to environmental preservation at three levels of government (Bertonatti and Corcuera 2000, 129).

Yet regulatory capacity and political will to enforce new environmental legislation remained weak. Two primary reasons blocked further development of de facto environmental protections. First, Menem was more interested in the economic benefits of the environment than in preserving it. His administration took on high-profile opportunities to court an international audience, even hosting one of the conferences of the parties of the Kyoto Protocol on Climate Change. But this fanfare only thinly camouflaged a low political will to keep environmental commitments at home (Hochstetler 2003, 10; Bueno 2012, 143–47). Thus no penalties related to the new environmental laws were applied from 1994 to 1999, and existing laws remained ineffective (Gutiérrez and Isuani 2014, 305, 307; Reboratti 2008, 103–4). Second, the 1994 constitutional amendment also strengthened the nation's federal framework in Article 124, giving the federal government responsibility for establishing norms and subnational governments for sanctioning. The result was stark variation in the implementation of environmental protections across regions. The decentralized nature of environmental management has led to weak coordination and exacerbated noncompliance (Milmanda and Garay 2019, 79; Amengual 2016, 157–59). One leading NGO summed up in 2000, "[T]here are few illicit actions against the environment that are investigated, and fewer still that are resolved. Sentences are light, and when penalties are applied, they tend to not demotivate the transgressor" (Bertonatti and Corcuera 2000, 129).

Against this backdrop, many of the nation's waterways became polluted over time. Despite the presence of institutions that suggested otherwise, environmental concern remained low for decades. As the slow death of the Matanza Riachuelo River in Chapter 2 illustrates, the government did not historically view environmental issues as a public policy problem to which it

---

[4] The environmental provisions in the Constitution were taken directly from the work of the CCD (Consejo para la Consolidación de la Democracia). The CCD was created by President Raúl Alfonsín (UCR) in 1986 upon the country's return to democracy and created background material for constitutional reform. The adoption of the CCD report into the 1994 constitutional amendment reflected a negotiation between Menem and the then opposition party leader in Congress, Alfonsín. See Gutiérrez and Isuani (2014, 305–7).

was obligated to attend, even, as the following section shows, when grassroots activists collectively drew attention to slow harms.

Strong Bonding Mobilization Sends Smoke Signals

Bonding mobilization is organized grassroots pressure from impacted communities about perceived harms. This section describes the grassroots organizing surrounding four issue areas in the Matanza Riachuelo River basin: urban renewal, wastewater services, landfill pollution, and wetland conservation. Table 3.1 provides a list of additional groups. Table 3.1 shows how the membership bases of local groups varied considerably, from groups with two to four members, to those whose activities attracted hundreds, and how groups used diverse strategies to further their goals. The locations of grassroots organizing documented in this section are listed on Map 3.1.

Claims about pollution emerged largely from low-income communities, providing evidence that environmental concern is not just for the wealthy or educated. Residents faced challenges as they pleaded with neighbors to join an uphill battle, documented mounting illness, and appealed to dismissive public officials. Grassroots pressure can resolve small-scale NIMBY claims, but the ability of local groups to address broader policy change of river remediation is often hampered by limited resources and a power imbalance that facilitates public officials' recalcitrance to change. Although bonding mobilization was high in the Matanza Riachuelo case, it alone was insufficient to drive policy change.

Urban Renewal in La Boca. The Boca Neighborhood Association (Asociación de Vecinos de la Boca) was led by a small handful of elderly working-class neighbors who rallied around remediating the Matanza Riachuelo River because the floating trash and extensive pollution disincentivized development of urban services. A local tourist destination for tango lovers, the Buenos Aires neighborhood of La Boca had become crime ridden and underserved, according to local activists. The Boca Association never had a large membership base; its president noted, "The extent of the problem, lack of trust, the neighbors would tell me, 'if [government] won't fix the potholes in front of my house, or fix the lamppost . . . and you want them to fix the Riachuelo?'"[5]

[5] Interview with Alfredo Alberti, Asociación de Vecinos de la Boca, April 1, 2016.

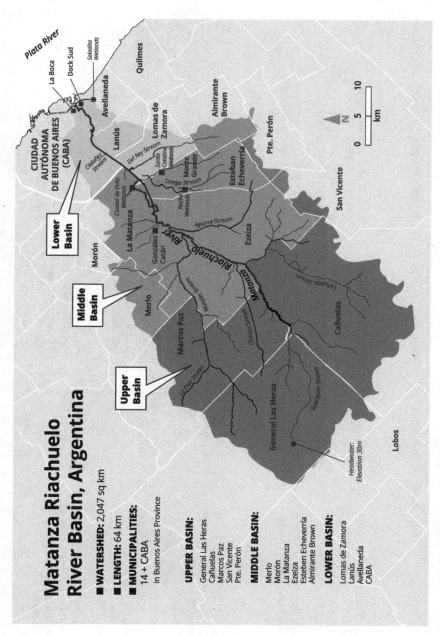

Map 3.1 Map of Matanza Riachuelo River
Source: Map by Dennis Bolt.

Table 3.1 Local Activist Groups involved in the Matanza Riachuelo River in Argentina (Actors in Bonding Mobilization)

Name	Dates Active	Number of Activists	Mission	Action Strategies	Judicial Advisory Committee
Boca Neighborhood Association (Asociación de Vecinos de la Boca)	1999–present	18 Directive Board; 3–5 active members (1,118 Facebook likes)	Reduce neighborhood crime, decontaminate the Matanza Riachuelo River	File official complaints, speak with public officials, document government incompliance, media interviews, blog updates	Yes
Hydraulic Forum (Foro Hídrico de Lomas de Zamora)	~2002–present	15 activists (684 Facebook likes)	Improve local conditions, e.g. sewage connections, potable water access, and public health	Alliance with Doctors without Borders for public health study, petition authorities for water, sewage connections, health services	No
Neighbors in Defense of Santa Catalina (Vecinos en Defensa de Santa Catalina)	2008–present	N/A (8,072 Facebook likes)	Protect wetlands, establish natural reserve for Santa Catalina wetlands, and promote its upkeep	Marches, demonstrations, political lobbying	No
Pilmayqueñ Environmental Organization (Organización Ambiental Pilmayqueñ)	~2008–present	15 activists (6,924 Facebook likes)	Protect wetlands, establish natural reserve for Santa Catalina wetlands, and promote its upkeep	Marches, demonstrations, create educational materials, litigation	No
Rocha Collective (Colectivo Ecológica Unidos para la Defensa de la Laguna de la Rocha)	2008–present	~40 activists (8,736 Facebook likes)	Protect wetlands, establish natural reserve for Rocha Wetlands, and promote its upkeep	Marches, rallies, social media campaigns, litigation, document government malfeasance	No

Hey Kids Foundation (Fundación Che Pibe)	~1990–present	N/A	Defend children's rights in Villa Fiorito, Lomas de Zamora	Provide food, clothes, healthcare, and education services to needy children	No
InterBasin Space RRR (Espacio Intercuenca RRR)	2007	>300 activists in 120 organizations (in 2007)	Generate participation, mobilize en masse, impact legal outcomes	Three mass mobilizations; confrontational strategies	No
Southern Ecologists Front (Frente Ecologista del Sur)*	~1990s–2010s	N/A	Remove petrochemical plant from Dock Sud; reduce air and water pollution, clandestine dumping	Media interviews, neighborhood organizing, legal petitions, demands on government agencies	No
Neighbors Organized against the CEAMSE in González Catán (Vecinos Autoconvocados contra la CEAMSE de González Catán)	~2003–present	12 Directive Board, 100 members	Close or better regulate municipal landfill, secure healthcare services for sick population	Assemblies, marches, documentation of illegal activity, lawsuits	No
Sowing Together (Sembrando Juntos)	~2015	2–4 members	Promote awareness of pollution and health problems in Villa Inflamable	Create educational campaigns, distribute water tankers	No

Source: Author compilation based on various sources, including interviews, groups' self-produced materials, and social media. See appendix for discussion of data collection strategies. Social media information taken from 2017.

* (also includes Sociedad de Fomento Dock Sud, Asociación Civil Ambiente Sur).

Yet the Boca Association was the first local organization to leave a paper trail for authorities that bore witness to the extent of the pollution.[6] Members filed hundreds of official complaints with numerous government agencies and created a lengthy paper record. One activist remembers,

> Whatever petition you made, you had to go to the place where the problem was. That is how we traveled to the province, talked to the water authorities there, with senators, with congressmen, with agencies. With the city and with the federal government, the same work. It was the work of ants... presentations, written petitions, hearings, meetings... [It was] endless. One day, an official told us, 'Please stop sending petitions.' We said we would as soon as they did their job.[7]

The Boca Association also joined forces with other nearby local groups. For example, the Boca Association was a founding member of the InterBasin Space RRR (Espacio Intercuenca, or RRR), an umbrella association that formed to combat contamination of three principal rivers, the Riachuelo, the Reconquista, and the Plata in 2007. After three large mass demonstrations, the movement disintegrated due to partisan takeover of its leadership. One activist explained, "We had one objective, but when that was lost, then it didn't work anymore."[8] Although the Boca Association's ability to build strong bonds with local residents was limited, they were aided by university professors and reporters who elevated their message, both within the neighborhood and across the city.[9] Numerous other activists organized around environmental problems in the south of the city, particularly those related to the Shell petrochemical processing plant, although their organizational strength and capacity for working together waxed and waned through the long period of time they were active.[10]

---

[6] Figure 3.1 is a photograph of some of the members of the Boca Association.

[7] Interview with Cristina Fins, Asociación de Vecinos de la Boca, April 6, 2016. "Hoy: Segunda marcha ambiental nacional," *Comunicación Ambiental*, December 12, 2007; "Segunda marcha nacional contra el saqueo y la contaminación," *Partido Comunista Revolucionario*, October 2, 2010.

[8] Interview with Cristina Fins, Asociación de Vecinos de la Boca, April 6, 2016.

[9] Interview with Alfredo Alberti, Asociación de Vecinos de la Boca, April 1, 3016.

[10] The Dock Sud Society (Sociedad de Fomento Dock Sud) led marches and petitions against the Shell petrochemical plant in Avellaneda, demanding epidemiological and impact studies. Their activism followed from a 1984 fire (el Buque Perito Moreno en el Canal Dock Sud), which alarmed residents living close to the plant. As the Dock Sud Society eventually disintegrated, the Civil Association of the South (Asociación Civil Ambiente Sur) emerged, and alongside other organizations formed the Southern Ecologists Front (Frente Ecologista del Sur), which grouped multiple organizations working on environmental issues in Buenos Aires's southern neighborhoods (Aizcorbe et al. 2007, 8, 12–14, 20, n18; Ryan 2004, 12–15). Interview with Cristina Fins, Asociación de Vecinos de la Boca, April 6, 2016; "Dock Sud no resiste más contaminación," *Inforegión.com.ar*, January 9, 2007.

Figure 3.1 Antonio Parodi, Manuel González, and Alfredo Alberti, members of the Asociación de Vecinos de la Boca.
Source: Photograph by Lucila Pellettieri, Global Press Journal Argentina, 2017.

Sewers Now! in Lomas de Zamora. A tight-knit group of activists emerged in 2000 in the municipality of Lomas de Zamora, calling themselves the Hydraulic Forum (Foro Hídrico de Lomas de Zamora), to demand sewage services and storm water drains. Their activism dates to the neighborhood assemblies that began after a devastating historic flood in 1976; they have been fighting against periodic flooding due to a high water-table ever since.[11] These shantytowns, located along the riverine path, are home to migrants from around the country whose daily battles for subsistence are compounded by exposure to toxic contamination. These informal settlements house low-income families with high rates of unemployment. One neighbor said, "My name is Marta, I've lived here for 40 years. [The flooding] continues, as more people move in. Unfortunately, the public works projects remain uncompleted. We went to the municipality, we did a working table [*mesa de trabajo*] with the neighbors. . . . Officials have come down here, they have informed

---

[11] Jorge Gómez, Foro Hídrico, *Asi Todo Noticias Zona Sur GBA*, video dated April 9, 2018. The water tables became even more unbalanced when the water utility, AYSA, became privatized and the private company Aguas Argentina changed their water source from underground aquifers that decreased the municipality's water tables to a different river, exacerbating the flooding problem.

Figure 3.2 Protest signs demand, "Sewers Now!"
Source: Foro Hídrico de Lomas de Zamora.

us that there is chrome, lead poisoning in the children, and no one does anything."[12] Activists, many of whom have lived in close quarters for decades, have been very successful in organizing neighbors to their cause and creating a horizontally organized leadership structure. Their street demonstrations have attracted hundreds of residents who embrace their simple rallying cry: "Sewers Now!" (*Cloacas Ya!*), as seen in Figure 3.2. They have been less able—despite connections with Doctors without Borders and university professors—to marshal a response to their problems from government officials.[13]

[12] "Inundaciones en Lomas de Zamora," *Barricada TV* video, November 13, 2014.
[13] The Forum has also teamed up with a children's services organization in nearby Villa Fiorito (the birthplace of soccer legend Diego Maradona), named Che Pibe, to provide healthcare services in the absence of government provision. Interview with Eva Koutsovitis, Foro Hídrico, April 10, 2016. *Informe Foro Hídrico de Lomas*, video by Siete Días en Lomas, March 25, 2016; "La muerte silenciosa de los niños en Lomas de Zamora: El plomo, para los caños," *Agencia de Noticias RedAcción*, September 24, 2014; Sabrina Gonzalez Flores. "Contaminación por falta de obras cloacales," *InfoRegión*, September 4, 2019.

Landfill Toxins in González Catán. Groups united against landfill pollution that leaked into the Matanza Riachuelo River and made residents sick. In the municipality of González Catán, La Matanza, the Neighbors Autonomously Organized against the CEAMSE (Vecinos Autoconvocados Contra CEAMSE de González Catán) rallied against a regional landfill in their neighborhood that had become open-air and received many more garbage trucks then legally permitted. Residents were acclimated to the trucks and noxious smells until an epidemiological study organized by local schoolteachers revealed the extent of the problem. An activist explained, "What caught our attention was the different types of illnesses we saw in the studies. . . . We were all getting sick. None of us were born green or were environmentalists, nothing of the sort. . . . Unfortunately as humans we don't act until we feel a direct impact."[14] A small group of resourced working-class residents (who owned their homes and small businesses) started organizing meetings in 2002, and others quickly joined them: "Neighbors started participating because they knew us. Maybe Martínez or Ana would go, and then several others would show up with them."[15] They also spread the word through photocopied pamphlets and door-to-door conversations to convince neighbors that their illness was due to their proximity to the landfill and to the spread of contaminants through creeks that circled their homes and fed into the river. Local activists eventually led rallies that gained media attention, attracting hundreds of participants in the months before local elections. Their legal claims and mass marches led authorities to close access to the landfill to dozens of Greater Buenos Aires municipalities and begin to accept waste only from González Catán. Despite this important victory, residents continue to monitor the landfill's poor maintenance practices as contaminants seeps into their backyards.

Wetlands Conservation in Esteban Echeverría and Lomas de Zamora. Groups also organized in protection of local wetlands. These were middle-class groups of teachers and university students. Several wetlands protection

---

[14] Interview with Celia Frutos, Vecinos Autoconvocados Contra CEAMSE de González Catán, March 11, 2017.
[15] Interview with Celia Frutos, Vecinos Autoconvocados Contra CEAMSE de González Catán, March 11, 2017. Figure 3.3 is a photograph of some of the members of Vecinos Autoconvocados holding up copies of the legal petitions they have filed regarding contamination in González Catán.

Figure 3.3 Vecinos Autoconvocados contra la CEAMSE de González Catán.
Source: Photograph by Pepe Mateos, 2017.

groups formed, for example the Neighbors in Defense of Santa Catalina (Vecinos en Defensa de Santa Catalina) in Lomas de Zamora and the Rocha Collective (Colectivo Ecológica Unidos por la Laguna de Rocha) in the municipality of Esteban Echeverría, the latter is seen in Figure 3.4. Activists stressed, "[W]e are going to keep organizing because each year we are greater in number. . . . [W]e are a group of neighbors that not only want greener spaces, but to defend our rights."[16] The Rocha Collective mobilized against the proposed sale of a 700-hectare portion of the Rocha wetland to build an industrial warehouse. Activists engaged in mass protests, "shaming and blaming" campaigns in the media, and community outreach through pamphleteering (Herrera 2022). Working with national-level environmental NGO Fundación Ambiente y Recursos Naturales (FARN, Environment and Natural Resources Foundation), Rocha activists were able to secure a provincial-level legislative victory to declare the Rocha wetland a protected mixed-use natural reserve by 2012, but wetlands groups continue to struggle

---

[16] These activists were from the group Neighbors in Defense of Santa Catalina, see Table 3.1. "Argentina: Santa Catalina: La defense de un bosque incredible y su laguna," *Biodiversidadla.org*, September 1, 2009.

Figure 3.4 Colectivo Ecológica Unidos por la Laguna de Rocha.
Source: Colectivo Ecológica Unidos por la Laguna de Rocha.

to defend these natural reserves against real estate speculation and unreliable local officials.[17]

Table 3.1 shows that at least 10 organized groups in the Matanza Riachuelo River basin were active in mobilizing around grievances related to the river's pollution. These local groups were dispersed across a vast territory and focused largely on remediation of specific claims; most groups only coordinated, if at all, with their most proximate partners. Despite hard-fought, animated battles for improved living conditions, territorial grievances surrounding the contaminated river basin remained fragmented, dispersed, and largely ignored in the 1990s. A neighborhood association leader captured the difficulty of making the polluted river more visible to the public in prior years: "The Riachuelo is a thing of folklore, every so often a newspaper prints

---

[17] Interview with Martin Farina, Colectivo Ecológica Unidos por la Laguna de Rocha, March 15, 2017.

something, and it remains a [story] that comes out once a year.... [T]he silence is total."[18]

Yet these claims accumulated over time, becoming a thorn in the side of bureaucrats who were tasked with attending to residents' petitions. Local claims also left a significant paper trail. Alone they were insufficient to prompt change, but they would later prove to be a necessary initial ingredient.

Strong Bridging Mobilization in Both State and Society

Local grievances about pollution were loud but remained at an impasse for years when public officials viewed them as NIMBY problems. This began to change when resourced bridges, or "outsiders," took an interest in the topic and helped to aggregate grievances, scale them up for maximum impact, and connect them to powerholders within the state. Strong bridges formed an advocacy coalition to bring slow harms to light and to begin a comprehensive policy shift that was unimaginable decades earlier.

Bridging mobilization was composed of state-level activists and national-level NGOs that took up the mantle of environmental injustice on the Matanza Riachuelo River due in part to a shared history that was rooted in the human rights movement that began during the military abuses of the 1970s. The next section examines how the human rights movement emerged, and the subsequent enabling political and economic conditions that strengthened it decades after the military junta left power. Eventually this movement would become central to bridging mobilization around slow harms.

Strong Enabling Conditions: Human Rights Protected Under Supportive Leftist Political Administrations

During the "Dirty War" (1976–83), a movement formed to denounce grave human rights abuses perpetrated by the military government, where guerrilla insurgents, leftist intellectuals, and union sympathizing members of the

---

[18] Alfredo Alberti, quoted in Pablo Policicchio, "El Riachuelo limpio sigue siendo una eterna utopía," unidentified newspaper, unlisted date, retrieved from *Clarín* Archives, April 2016.

Peronist Party were persecuted.[19] The movement was further strengthened by sequential presidential administrations from the center-left that supported military trials and increased the legitimacy of human rights claims through the creation of new institutions for accountability. These presidential administrations were oriented inward and not beholden to export-oriented mineral extraction markets, which, coupled with the subsuming of the military under civilian control, helped to strengthen the spaces for civil society claims-making over time.

During a period of active repression, human rights groups such as Las Madres de la Plaza de Mayo (Mothers of the Plaza de Mayo), a trailblazing movement known for wearing white handkerchiefs made from baby diapers to symbolize the forced disappearance of their grown children, and activists who formed the Center for Legal and Social Studies (CELS) risked their lives to organize against the junta and contributed to its demise.[20] CELS was formed by lawyers who sought to document state involvement in repression by analyzing data and establishing patterns of abuse, creating the most complete human rights archive in Argentina (Brysk 1994, 45–51). Human rights groups pushed for more accountability during the National Commission on the Disappearance of Persons (CONADEP), it's report *Never Again* (*Nunca Mas*), and the 1985 trials of military officers. The assistant prosecutor during the trials asserted that "without the human rights organizations, there wouldn't have been a trial" (Brysk 1994, 78).[21]

---

[19] The Process of National Reorganization (Proceso) was designed to eliminate "subversive" activity from Cuban-inspired Communist guerrilla groups such as the ERP and Montoneros (Lewis 2002, 46–47; Feitlowitz 2011, 6–7), as well as repress nonviolent political activists from the left, such as unionists (connected to the Peronist Party), artists, journalists, academics, lawyers, and psychiatrists, all of whom were seen as having the capacity to question the regime's ideological hegemony. President Jorge Videla told a foreign journalist, "[A] terrorist isn't just someone with a gun or bomb, but also someone who spreads ideas that are contrary to Western and Christian civilization" (Brysk 1994, 35, 40). Military tactics included clandestine kidnappings, torture at detention centers, sexual violation and rape, death flights where bodies were clandestinely thrown out of planes, and the kidnapping of hundreds of babies born in detention (Philip 1984, 627–29; Feierstein 2006, 149–53; Brysk 1994, 36–40). Official accounts say 20,000 were disappeared, but human rights group report the number at closer to 30,000.

[20] According to Brysk (1994, 45–51), 10 main organizations formed an initial human rights network, including civil society groups, family-based organizations, and religious movements. The first and most active family-based group was Las Madres de la Plaza de Mayo, mothers who sought information about their disappeared adult children during their weekly vigil in the capital's central square. Las Madres also organized petitions (one got 24,000 signatures) and newspaper advertisements. A related organization was the Abuelas de Plaza de Mayo (Grandmothers of the Plaza de Mayo), that focused especially on tracing their missing grandchildren, and groups that predated the junta, such as the Argentine League of Human Rights and the Permanent Assembly for Human Rights (Brysk 1994, 45–51).

[21] CONADEP brought 1,087 cases directly to the federal appeals courts, and its report, *Never Again*, sold 250,000 copies in Argentina alone, with an accompanying television broadcast viewed by

The 2003 presidential election of Néstor Kirchner, a member of the generation of the Peronist Party that had been brutally repressed, further expanded the power of the human rights movement. Néstor Kirchner was a vocal advocate of human rights. His human rights policy promoted the recuperation of former detention centers to construct memory spaces, vetted government officials linked to the dictatorship, purged the federal police, and forced dozens of military officials into retirement. Kirchner also supported international cooperation with extradition requests from abroad and reopened trials in Argentina.[22] The Day of Remembrance for Truth and Justice, March 24, was made a national holiday in 2006. As of 2017, 2,979 people had been tried for their role in the dictatorship, and another 593 cases remain in process.[23] "The implementation of 'memory, truth, and justice' policies of the Kirchner government . . . became the heart of a reformist wave in the state" (Guthmann 2017, 29).

The human rights movement introduced a powerful public narrative about citizenship and accountability, which influenced the reform of existing institutions and creations of new ones in the postdemocratic period. Demands for greater human rights accountability led to the creation of government institutions such as the Anti-Corruption Office, the Human Rights Commission, and a National Ombudsman (Defensor del Pueblo de la Nación) (Peruzzotti 2012).[24] To underscore civilian control over the military, Néstor Kirchner appointed Nilda Garré—a political prisoner during the Dirty War—as the country's first female minister of defense.

Accountability institutions were also established in the judiciary. In 2002, a group of rights-based NGOs, including CELS, FARN, and Citizen's Power (Poder Ciudadano) published "A Court for Democracy," a plan for Supreme Court reforms which would establish judicial autonomy after President Menem's court packing in 1990 (ADC et al. 2002). President Kirchner

over a million people. When the final volume of the report was published on September 20, it was met with a demonstration of 70,000 supporters (Brysk 1994, 70–71; Crenzel 2008, 181–89).

[22] See Kaiser (2015) on the military trials during the Néstor Kirchner administration. Kirchner ratified the Convention on the Non-Applicability of Statutory Limitations to War Crimes against Humanity and in 2004 completed the policy on reparations. Kirchner led the congressional annulment of amnesty laws in 2003, which were later declared unconstitutional by the Supreme Court in 2005. For more on Néstor Kirchner's human rights policy, see Lessa (2010).
[23] Rut Diamint, "Truth, Justice and Declassification: Secret Archives Show US Helped Argentine Military Wage 'Dirty War' That Killed 30,000," *The Conversation*, May 10, 2019.
[24] Although incomplete, according to some experts Argentina has made the most advances in the region in subsuming the military under civilian control, aided in part by Néstor Kirchner's human rights policy (Diamint 2008, 96).

adopted the document into Decree 222/03 in 2003, establishing measures to improve the selection of justices, remove Menem's packed appointments, and formalize *amicus curiae* (friend of the court), which allowed for entry of a third-party opinion and increased citizen participation. The new Supreme Court, in the words of one NGO leader, "was attempting to generate its proper legitimacy."[25] These reforms augmented constitutional guarantees, increased the scope of actors that could be involved in litigation, and strengthened judicial independence (Smulovitz 2010, 241–42). The human rights movement played a large role in prompting these changes. "The politics of human rights helped many in society visualize how the judiciary functions, the criminal justice system, court cases, and due process, and all that makes up a legal culture" (Guthmann 2017, 26).

Argentina's political economy provides further background for situating Néstor Kirchner's reforms and support of human rights mobilization. While the Menem years had presided over extensive market reforms where much of Argentina was "for sale," the 2001 economic crisis ushered in multiple Kirchner administrations (both Néstor and Cristina) that were more inward-oriented and nationalist and benefited from soaring commodity prices that boosted Argentina's export-oriented agricultural sector (Levitsky and Murillo 2008).[26] Néstor Kirchner sought to rebuild Argentina's industrial base, refused a structural adjustment program, and renationalized privatized public services including the water utility, AYSA. Argentina's economy is not highly dependent on extractives, which make up only 3.8% of total revenue, only 4.5% of exports, and only 4.6% of GDP (EITI 2018a). The Kirchner administrations in Argentina were oriented toward nationalist economic policy and more diplomatically isolated than those in Colombia and Peru. Combined with reforms to legal institutions and human rights tribunals, these protectionist policies helped to restore public trust after the political and economic crisis of 2001 (Levitsky and Murillo 2008, 21–22).

Under the Kirchner administrations, human rights organizations became more closely integrated into government. The Mothers of the Plaza de Mayo held their last rally in 2006, for the first time deeming a president to be their ally, and both Kirchner administrations publicly supported their accountability-seeking missions (Romanin 2012, 48–52). The Mothers

---

[25] Interview with Andres Napoli, FARN, March 31, 2016.
[26] When it suited his nationalist position, Néstor Kirchner supported environmental causes, such as the pulp-mill dispute on the Argentine-Uruguay border (Isabelle Alcañiz and Gutiérrez 2009, 112–17).

transformed from a resistance group into one that sought to work inside the government. Other groups, such as CELS, also became more closely linked with the Kirchner governments, and some human rights activists were given positions within government. A member of the human rights group Citizen Association for Human Rights (Asociacíon Ciudadana por los Derechos Humanos, ACDH) (formed in 2002) said in an interview that many members of the human rights groups were ideologically left of center, largely affiliated with the Frente para la Victoria front that had brought Kirchner to power, and went to work for the government during the Kirchner years.[27] "The increased proximity of the state implies an increase in the intensity of ties between the human rights groups and the institutional and bureaucratic policies of the state" (Romanin 2012, 52).

The Argentine human rights movement was a key protagonist that helped launch "a justice cascade" of human rights innovations globally (Sikkink 2008, 14–16), but they were also highly influential domestically in helping to reform the state. Despite the ongoing struggle for securing human rights and strengthening democratic institutions on many fronts, the power of the human rights network, a heterogeneous group of old and new organizations, continued to expand into the 2010s. These groups were buoyed by the supportive political environment that was comparatively much more oriented toward human rights than other cases examined in this book. Unlike in Colombia and Peru, in Argentina subsequent center-left presidential administrations did not stray far from alliances with rights-based actors that had developed during Néstor Kirchner's administration; these included the administrations of Peronists Christina Kirchner (2007–15) and Alberto Fernández (2019–). The enabling condition of left-of-center administrations friendly to human rights organizing helped the human rights narrative and discourse increase in stature rather than be persecuted. Human rights groups had strong legitimacy because organizations such as Las Madres, Las Abuelas, and CELS had been founded by leaders who had put their lives on the line. As the next section illustrates, in the mid-2000s, some of these same NGOs worked with state-level institutions to elevate the Matanza Riachuelo River pollution as a national problem that involved the violation of intrinsic rights.

---

[27] Interview with Carolina Ciancio, ACDH, April 19, 2016.

State-Level Bridges Aggregate and Scale Up Claims

Although many government agencies, ministries, and elected officials within the executive branch were either incompetent or complicit in the making of the ecological crisis, several public sector employees and public institutions played a critical role in bridging mobilization for slow harms. State-level—institutional—bridges such as the Ombudsman's Office, judges, public defenders, prosecutors, and specially appointed offices and commissions worked alongside civil society organizations to help reframe slow-moving harms as a human rights violation that could no longer be swept under the rug.

State Level Bridges: Ombudsman's Office. The most important institutional bridge to help unify claims around slow harms was the National Ombudsman's Office. This institution became enshrined in the 1994 Constitution—in the aftermath of the human rights crisis—with a dual mandate to protect human rights and monitor public administration (Reif 2004, 197). By the early 2000s, the Ombudsman's Office had received thousands of complaints about the Matanza Riachuelo River, "about the trash, smells, lack of waste facilities and potable water, flooding . . . etc."[28] The Ombudsman's Office decided to act, creating a Matanza Riachuelo working group in 2002 in response to a petition from the Boca Association, the neighborhood organization discussed earlier, and another from Maria Carmen Brite, resident of Villa Inflamable near the Shell plant in Dock Sud, who complained that her children were sick from pollution exposure.[29] The Ombudsman's working group produced two comprehensive diagnoses reports and proposed solutions to the ecological crisis (Defensor del Pueblo de la Nación 2003, 2005). The working group consisted of prominent civil society organizations such as the notable human rights organization CELS, FARN, Fundación Ciudad (City Foundation), and Poder Ciudadano (Citizen's Power). These were joined by the Boca Neighborhood Association, the City's Public Defender's Office, and the National Technological University (Universidad Tecnológica Nacional).[30] One NGO leader described how, despite differences in policy goals and ideological orientation among them, the Ombudsman Office was a unifying

---

[28] Interview with Leandro Garcia Silva, Ombudsman's Office, April 11, 2016.
[29] Interview with Alfredo Alberti, VDB, April 1, 2016; interview with Horacio Esber, Ombudsman's Office, April 11, 2016.
[30] The second report in 2005 also included the Matanza Popular Association (Asociación Popular La Matanza), the NGOs Fundación Metropolitana and Greenpeace, and the National University of Matanza (the Universidad Nacional de la Matanza).

force: "That is the strength that the Ombudsman gave us.... Our strength was to recognize that we were working together on this, no matter what."[31]

State-Level Bridge: Legal Institutions. The judiciary further helped aggregate and scale up claims about slow harms. Litigation around the Matanza Riachuelo River began in 2004 when 17 residents of La Boca, Dock Sud, Villa Inflamable, and Avellaneda led by Maria Carmen Brite and healthcare worker Beatriz Mendoza brought a collective lawsuit against the federal, provincial, and city governments, 14 municipalities, 44 industries, the AYSA water and sanitation utility, and CEAMSE, the waste management company.[32] The *Mendoza* case would be the most important instance of environmental litigation and the first collective action lawsuit in the country.[33] The lawsuit helped activate the collective nature of the right to a clean environment, which in 1994 had become a constitutional guarantee understood to be "an intergenerational human right... that... when violated, not only constitutes a problem for those [immediately] impacted but for society at large" (arts. 41 and 43) (Merlinsky 2013, 97).[34]

Two other legal institutions played a critical role in defending citizens' housing rights during riverine cleanup conflicts following the Supreme Court ruling. First, the city's Public Defender's Office (Defensoría del Pueblo de la Ciudad de Buenos Aires) was the primary point of contact for citizens who were impacted by the proposed relocations. Following the Supreme Court ruling, a federal judge ordered the relocation of thousands of families from the riverfront, which resulted in mass evictions. The Public Defender's Office was staffed by young, middle-class, and left-of-center attorneys. They sought to protect the rights of shantytown dwellers, many of whom had property titles and autoconstructed homes. This office also helped establish participatory working sessions (*mesas de trabajo*) between residents and city officials,

---

[31] Interview with Andres Napoli, FARN, March 31, 2016.

[32] The attorney representing the 17 residents described how the legal team was able to file a suit against only 44 industries despite the presence of thousands of industries, due to a declassification of an internal government document admitting culpability of the 44 industries. The legal team was able to unearth this declassified document and use it in their case. Interview with Daniel Sallaberry, attorney representing claimants for Mendoza litigation (*Causa Mendoza*), April 12, 2016.

[33] For more on the *Mendoza* ruling (CSJN 2008), see Merlinksy (2013, 97–121), Botero (2018, 174–80), and Sigal, Rossi, and Morales (2017, 145–46).

[34] The claimants based their case on the National Environmental Law (Ley General del Ambiente 25675), which was passed in 2002 and for the first time defined environmental damage and created a legal personality for the environment, apart from individuals or public patrimony. However, the Supreme Court refused individual compensation for claimants, passing decisionmaking over those to a secondary court, which had as of 2016 yet to rule in favor of claimants and seemed unlikely to do so. Interview with Daniel Sallaberry, attorney representing claimants Mendoza litigation (*Causa Mendoza*), April 12, 2016.

which were often frustrating efforts in accountability-seeking but were critical for, as one attorney said, "having their voices heard in the process."[35] The National Public Defender's Office (Defensoría General de la Nación) also created a Riachuelo working group to attend to residents' requests for increased participation, information, public services, and housing.[36]

The next section illustrates how, by the time the Supreme Court issued their historic ruling in 2008, a powerful advocacy network of national-level NGOs and activist public officials—influenced by Argentina's human rights movement—had developed to influence the public policy agenda on slow harms.

Powerful Bridges within Society: National-Level NGOs Aggregate and Scale Up Claims

Strong bridging mobilization relied on the combination of both state-level and societal allies. State-level bridges were effective in their work on slow harms because they were accompanied by a resourced group of national-level advocacy NGOs. By the early 2000s, diverse NGOs had begun to perceive the Matanza Riachuelo River as a complex social problem that resonated with their institutional mandates. Some NGOs became involved because they responded to petitions from local activists, while others began to participate when convened by the Ombudsman's Office or during the public hearings conducted by the Supreme Court. These included vertically structured NGOs such as CELS, FARN, and Greenpeace, as well as foundations such as City Foundation and Metropolitan Foundation. Table 3.2 provides an inventory of the eight formal, professionalized NGOs that became involved in the Matanza Riachuelo remediation case.

Extensive Staffing, Expertise, and Funding

National NGOs brought new resources to the problem that local activists had previously lacked. For example, Table 3.2 shows that FARN and Greenpeace

---

[35] Interview with Public Defender's Office of Buenos Aires, April 6, 2016.
[36] Interview with Mariano Gutierrez, Defensoría General de la Nación, Coordinador del Equipo de Abordaje Territorial de la Causa Riachuelo, March 14, 2007.

Table 3.2 NGOs involved in the Matanza Riachuelo River in Argentina (Societal Actors in Bridging Mobilization)

Name	Dates Active	Number of Employees or Activists	Mission	Action Strategies	Judicial Advisory Committee
Environment and Natural Resources Foundation (Fundación Ambiente y Recursos Naturales (FARN))	1985–	10 employees	Promote social justice through environmental conservation	Litigation, policy recommendations, access to information requests, research	Yes
Center for Legal and Social Studies (Centro de Estudios Legales y Sociales (CELS))	1979–	50 employees	Defense of human rights, including economic, social, and cultural rights	Litigation, policy recommendations, research	Yes
City Foundation (Fundación Ciudad)	1995–	4–5 employees	Promote citizen participation to impact urban policy	Organize participatory deliberative forums, debates, seminars	No
Citizen Human Rights Association (Asociación Ciudadana de Derechos Humanos (ACDH))	2003–	<5	Defense of human rights, "new rights" of LGBTQ, economic and social rights, reproductive rights, gender equality	Television show *Acción Urbana*, participate in public hearings, lobbying	Yes
Civil Association for Equality and Justice (Asociación Civil por la Igualdad y la Justicia (ACIJ))	2002–	25 employees, 10 volunteers	Defense of the most vulnerable citizens and strengthening democratic institutions	Litigation, access to information requests, research, clinics	No

Greenpeace Argentina (Greenpeace Argentina)	1987–	45 employees, 600 volunteers, 110,000 members, 1.2 million cyberactivists	Expose and confront global environmental problems	Nonviolent, confrontational strategies of public mobilization, lobbying, research	Yes
Citizen's Power (Poder Ciudadano)	2003–	N/A	Promote transparency, anticorruption, education, participation, and government accountability	Election monitoring, lobbying for congressional reforms and Independent Judiciary	No
Metropolitan Foundation (Fundación Metropolitana)	2000–	~9 employees	Shape urban public policy for a just, equal, and solidarity-driven city	Forums, seminars, and participatory meetings, consultant for municipalities, publications	No

Source: Author compilation based on various sources, including interviews, NGO websites and documents, and social media. See appendix for discussion of data collection strategies. Social media information taken from 2017.

are staffed by approximately 10 and 45 employees, respectively, most of whom are college-educated and conduct research supporting litigation, policy recommendations, and pollutant testing. CELS and Asociación Civil por la Igualdad y la Justicia (ACIJ) count on approximately 50 and 25 employees, respectively; many are researchers or attorneys working closely on the right to housing and land tenure issues. City Foundation and the Metropolitan Foundation, while smaller organizations, were staffed by experienced, educated personnel with relevant backgrounds on participatory deliberation and urban design. In addition, FARN, CELS, Greenpeace, and ACIJ are all supported by international financing, some of which makes up most of the funds they draw on.[37]

These NGOs used their resources to generate more data about the ecological crisis in order to influence policymakers. Since 2009, Greenpeace Argentina has published at least eight major reports on the Riachuelo, including taking samples and providing evidence of the levels of contamination in reports on toxics and tanneries (Greenpeace 2012, 2009). FARN has emphasized increasing transparency and participation in the cleanup process. FARN's website houses monthly progress reports and generates hundreds of online posts, notably publishing "Una política de Estado para el Riachuelo" in 2009 and dozens of others (Nápoli 2009). CELS (2015) produced reports on the right to housing in the Riachuelo cleanup process, and alongside ACIJ contributed to a foundational report by the Public Defender's Office on housing rights in the relocation of impacted communities (Defensa Pública 2014). Through these reports, these organizations have greatly increased access to information about the river contamination, underscoring the many areas of pending work and calling on government agencies to comply with their obligations.

NGO Framing Emphasizes Social Justice and Human Rights

These NGOs used rights and justice language to tackle a wide range of policy areas. They were inheritors of the human rights movement in

---

[37] For example, CELS's, FARN's, and ACIJ's budgets are almost exclusively derived from international sources, and Greenpeace Argentina had 110,000 dues-paying members in 2016 and is also financially backed by Greenpeace International. Interview with Andres Napoli, FARN, March 31, 2016; interview with Leonel Mingo, Greenpeace, April 8, 2016; interview with Noelia Garone, ACIJ, April 14, 2016; Gastón Chillier, "Financiamiento que proviene de las comunidades locales: ¿Qué es posible en América Latina?" Cels.org.ar, August 21.

Argentina, in terms of both their institutional mission as well as their ability to legitimately deploy the human rights frame. CELS was a first-generation human rights NGO; its founding members had been jailed and tortured during the military junta, and as noted earlier, CELS became a leader in the search for truth and reconciliation during the military trials. FARN was not just an environmental NGO; as their director explained in an interview, "Our focus is fundamentally on the defense of rights."[38] ACIJ worked in defense of vulnerable citizens and to strengthen democratic institutions; City Foundation focused on increasing urban citizen participation; Citizen's Power championed election monitoring, transparency, and anticorruption.

These rights-based NGOs were not primarily conservation oriented, such as being focused on forests or animal welfare, as other environmental movements that had gained limited traction had previously been. Restoring the river's ecosystem services was important, but more so was the need to hold government accountable for its role in what came to be seen as a human rights violation. With a focus on rights and participatory processes, the Matanza Riachuelo NGOs sought to strengthen democratic institutions and the rights of residents impacted by pollution. Rather than addressing NIMBY claims or promoting conservation, these NGOs sought to participate in a policy battle to realize the collective rights outlined in the Constitution. Each NGO had specific institutional mandates through which they filtered these broader social justice goals onto their Riachuelo work. For example, when asked what language they would use to encapsulate their most important mandate, FARN emphasized "environmental justice," CELS and ACIJ stressed the need for an "inclusive and socioeconomically just habitat" and "accessing housing rights," and Fundación Ciudad underscored "participatory deliberation" and "the right to the city."[39] An attorney in the Ombudsman's Office characterized the participation of the advocacy NGOs as transformative: "instead of treating the problem how it had always been treated, they tried to find a new way of understanding the problem, and generated a new dynamic," which called for social justice.[40] The language of social justice and human rights was imbued in their

---

[38] Interview with Andres Napoli, FARN, March 31, 2016.
[39] Interview with Andres Napoli, FARN, March 31, 2016; interview with Leandro Vera Belli, CELS, March 30, 2016; interview with Noelia Garone, ACIJ, April 14, 2016; interview with Mora Arauz, Fundación Ciudad, April 18, 2016.
[40] Interview with Horacio Esber, Ombudsman's Office, April 11, 2016.

policy memos, educational materials, and dialogues with public officials.[41] New framing around slow harms as a human rights violation helped to elevate the problem of slow harms and make it more visible and resonant to the media and organs of the state. The Supreme Court ruling initially increased media attention on the Riachuelo, and subsequent monitoring activities in which rights-based NGOs were active helped to keep the river pollution issue in the national media (Botero 2018, 179).

Prior Shared Experiences

The rights-based NGOs were effective bridges due largely to their past experiences of working together prior to the Ombudsman's Matanza Riachuelo group in 2003. NGO leaders knew each other and could easily get on the phone and consult and resolve problems directly without needing the Ombudsman as an intermediary. Histories of prior shared work predated the Supreme Court reforms. CELS, FARN, and Citizen's Power had collaborated on the pathbreaking report published in 2002, "A Court for Democracy," to reform the Supreme Court, which was later adopted by President Néstor Kirchner to transform the High Court, as discussed earlier. In 1999, the rights-based organization City Foundation had created focus groups throughout the entire river basin to develop deliberative participation with residents and other stakeholders, including FARN and the Boca Association (Fundación Ciudad 2016). The information gathered on residents' experiences throughout the basin and the practice of deliberative consultation was brought into the Ombudsman's working group on the Matanza Riachuelo in 2003.[42]

NGOs with similar institutional mandates also had prior work experiences that aided their shared interest in the Matanza Riachuelo. For example,

---

[41] Numerous documents from bridging actors use the language of human rights to describe problems and solutions for the Matanza Riachuelo River pollution. For example, Defensor del Pueblo de la Nación (2005, 205) in *Informe especial sobre la Cuenca Matanza Riachuelo*: "[T]he residents of these neighborhoods are permanent victims of institutional violence since access to basic human rights such as health, education, housing, among others, is severely impeded." FARN (2019) in *La justicia declara que el acceso al aire libre de contaminantes es un derecho humano*, May 15, 2019: "The Cuerpo Colegiado ... has been demanding that the statutes that substantially limit contaminating gases in the atmosphere be approved.... [T]he [Court's] declaration that clean air is a human right is a great milestone for the river basin." CELS (2015, 7), in *Derecho a la tierra y la vivienda*: "We were able to strengthen a space for debate and interchange in order to center human rights as the focus of public policy on housing."

[42] Interview with Mora Arauz, Fundación Ciudad, April 18, 2016; interview Andres Napoli, FARN, March 31, 2016; interview with Horacio Esber, Ombudsman's Office, April 11, 2016.

the Metropolitan Foundation and City Foundation had both focused on urban development issues in the city, sometimes together, prior to working on the Matanza Riachuelo issue. The same was true for the environmental NGOs FARN and Greenpeace, which frequently collaborated across a wide range of environmental issues and "shared many of the same objectives and projects."[43] Similarly, NGOs whose focus has been on securing housing rights, such as CELS and ACIJ, later collaborated with the Public Defender's Office to place dignified housing and property title protections on the agenda for the river cleanup relocations.[44]

Collaborations continued between NGOs and public sector institutions and helped strengthen bridging mobilization. For example, City Foundation and Metropolitan Foundation teamed up with FARN and the Argentine Journalism Forum to organize an innovative online accountability platform for online citizen denunciations of dumping and failure to comply with the Mendoza ruling (Fundación Ciudad 2016).[45] These NGOs also participated in the four public hearings held by the Supreme Court between 2006 and 2007.[46] State-level bridges also worked together; for example, the Court consulted the Ombudsman's Office before enacting the ruling, and the Ombudsman's Office was very involved with the congressional creation of the Matanza Riachuelo River Basin Authority (Autoridad de la Cuenca Matanza Riachuelo, ACUMAR).[47]

Prior work experiences created personal and institutional relationships that further facilitated effectiveness in bridging mobilization. The Ombudsman's Office noted that "there was a convergence not just of institutional relations but of personal relations. . . . It has to do with the biography of the people involved. . . . If it had been other people, perhaps the results would have been different."[48] This was most clearly visible between "founders" or groups with a long-standing presence in the issue. "Founders" knew each other for years and trusted one another's knowledge and commitment to the cause. These groups,

---

[43] Interview with Leonel Mingo, Greenpeace Argentina, April 8, 2016.
[44] Interview with Eduardo Reese, CELS, April 1, 2016; interview with Leandro Vera Belli, CELS, March 30, 2016; interview with Noelia Garone, ACIJ, April 14, 2016; interview with Agustin Territoriale, Public Defender's Office, April 6, 2016.
[45] Despite the millions of dollars that were spent on the physical remediation of the river basin (see World Bank 2009b), international aid agencies denied CSOs requests for funding to support citizen involvement in the process, such as for bus fare. Interview with Mora Arauz, Fundación Ciudad, April 18, 2016; interviews with Andres Napol, FARN, March 31, 2016, and April 12, 2016.
[46] Interview with Mora Arauz, Fundación Ciudad, April 18, 2016; Merlinsky (2013, 105).
[47] Interview with Horacio Esber, Ombudsman's Office, April 11, 2016.
[48] Interview with Horacio Esber, Ombudsman's Office, April 11, 2016.

such as FARN and City Foundation, held strong, long-standing ties they emphasized during interviews. From the Ombudsman's perspective, the NGOs provided additional expertise they themselves lacked. Reflecting on this initial period, an attorney from the Ombudsman's Office stressed how the national NGOs and Ombudsman's Office had built a "very strong interdependence."[49]

Strong Bridges Build Robust Monitoring Capacity after Judicialization

Strong bridging mobilization not only undergirded the passage of the 2008 Supreme Court *Mendoza* ruling to remediate the river, but it also allowed for more transparent and robust monitoring of the ruling's implementation. A 1994 constitutional clause (Article 43) allowed civil society actors to participate as third parties to judicial cases involving collective rights and damages (*amparo colectivo*). Thus, numerous civil society organizations petitioned the Supreme Court to be admitted as third parties to the *Mendoza* case. Most petitioning groups had participated in the Ombudsman's working group, while a few were drawn to the case during the public hearings held by the Court.[50] More civil society organizations applied to be accepted as third parties to the case than were ultimately selected.[51] A CELS attorney explained, "when more and more organizations asked to get involved, it allowed the Court to claim that this was not about a petition from one or even twenty families, but instead, a petit ion from the entire citizenry."[52] The NGOs that were admitted as third parties to the case (the Ombudsman's Office and the NGOs FARN, CELS, ACDH, Greenpeace, and the Boca Association) worked together to increase their institutional capacity to hold responsible parties accountable.[53]

[49] Interview with Horacio Esber, Ombudsman's Office, April 11, 2016.
[50] One impacted group, Vecinos de Lomas de Zamora, was also admitted as a third party to the case but was not otherwise connected to the other groups involved.
[51] The Supreme Court, with limited understanding of the vast network of organizations that had previously worked on the issue, based their selection on a technical criterion: whether organizations had institutional bylaws that identified environmental sustainability as a key institutional mission. This left out many important organizations that had done prior work on the river, such as Poder Ciudadano, Fundación Metropolitana, and the most active group, Fundación Ciudad. Interview with Mora Arauz, Fundación Ciudad, April 18, 2012; interview with Carolina Ciancio, ACDH, April 19, 2016; interview with Diego Morales, CELS, April 6, 2016. See CSJN (2008, 3–4, 9) and *Se presentan comon terceros* (2006).
[52] Interview with Diego Morales, CELS, April 6, 2016.
[53] As the Ombudsman's Office was also admitted as a third party to the case, FARN's president, Andres Napoli, represented the remaining NGOs to be admitted as a separate third-party group as

In order to help monitor the ruling to remediate the river, the Supreme Court created a judicial advisory committee (Cuerpo Colegiado) composed of the five NGOs that were third parties to the case and the Ombudsman's Office. Sandra Botero (2018, 170) calls these spaces examples of "collaborative oversight arenas, where the court, elected leaders, private actors, and civil society agents converge to address issues." In its 2008 ruling, the Court had deemed the river's extreme pollution to be a collective rights violation that stemmed from institutional fragmentation, overlapping government jurisdictions, inadequate participation, and low accountability mechanisms (Sigal, Rossi, and Morales 2017, 145–46). Thus, the NGOs were charged with augmenting citizen participation in cleanup efforts; later their role expanded into monitoring compliance with the ruling. Monitoring exercises have been conducted as voluntary work with no financial compensation, which members noted has been both an honor and a burden.[54] However, the five NGOs have played a large role in increasing transparency about river remediation progress. The Ombudsman has convened the committee and channeled any additional petitions from other citizens that enter the Ombudsman's Office into the judicial oversight committee's work. The NGOs and Ombudsman's Office meet on average every two weeks or monthly, providing reports and feedback to the presiding federal judges charged with overseeing the ruling.[55]

The symbiotic relationship between the Ombudsman's Office and advocacy NGOs—both born out of the human rights movement—has fostered an institutional space for civil society actors with standing to influence the policy process. Lindsay Mayka (2019, 45–48) describes these processes as participatory institutions that are "infused with value" and that, due to their

---

opposed to being represented as one legal entity, ensuring that the NGOs would be able to act independently from the will of the Ombudsman. This arrangement gave the advocacy NGOs more latitude to hold industry accountable (the Ombudsman's Office was unable to make accountability demands on the private sector) and provided autonomy from future holders of the Ombudsman Office, whose institutional priorities may lie elsewhere. Interview with Andres Napoli, FARN, March 31, 2016.

[54] Multiple interviews.
[55] The federal judge of Quilmes (Judge Armella) oversaw the case until he was removed in 2012. As of 2020 the Mendoza case is overseen by a federal judge in Court Number 2 (Judge Rodriguez) and a federal judge in Court Number 12 (Judge Torres; Judge Casanello). After 2017, the Federal Prosecutor's office also played a legal oversight role.
"A 13 años del fallo "Mendoza", el Ministerio Público Fiscal presenta sus acciones más relevantes," *fiscales.gob.ar*. July 8, 2021.

informal legitimacy, are able to serve as a point for state-society interaction in policymaking. The advocacy NGOs, in the words of their leadership, have "so much weight" and "are the ones that have representativeness."[56] The NGOs' clout and long-standing work have helped compensate for an Ombudsman's Office which since 2009 has not had an elected Ombudsman.[57] Despite this institutional problem, the Ombudsman's Office has played an important organizing role, coordinating the thousands of complaints received about the river and channeling them to the judicial advisory committee, convening the NGOs, and promoting a process of deliberation and consensus. An attorney in the Ombudsman's office noted, "The question is: Why does [the Court] listen to us? . . . It's not an obligation, but it's just that there is not another strong voice. . . . It's because we have for years conducted serious work, generating analytical capacity and expertise that does not exist in other places. . . . The Court consults with us before making important decisions."[58] The long-standing ties these actors have to one another as well as their expertise have created an institutionalized process for putting the Matanza Riachuelo's ecological crisis on the policymaking agenda. One member said, "We have outlasted three presidents, seven secretaries of the environment, changes in ACUMAR, changes in the composition of the Court. We have been the most institutionalized component of the process, in part because of the participation of these five organizations and their interaction with the Ombudsman's Office."[59]

Expansive Policy Shift in Slow-Harms Remediation

I have argued that strong bonding and bridging mobilization on the Matanza Riachuelo led to an expansive policy shift toward river remediation, processes that were undergirded by a legacy of human rights mobilization that was enabled by supportive national-level political and economic conditions. The result has been a dramatic increase in policy attention for an environmental

---

[56] Interview with Andres Napoli, FARN, March 9, 2017; interview with Cristina Fins, Asociación de Vecinos de la Boca, April 6, 2016.
[57] The National Ombudsman must be selected by Congress through a bicameral decision. The Argentine Congress, for partisan reasons, has failed to agree on a candidate since 2009, as of February 2020.
[58] Interview with Leandro Garcia Silva, Ombudsman's Office, April 11, 2016.
[59] Interview with Leandro Garcia Silva, Ombudsman's Office, April 11, 2016.

issue that had historically been ignored in Argentina. This section examines what the policy shifts entailed with respect to institutional design, financial investment, and regulatory capacity for river pollution following the 2008 Supreme Court ruling. While the Matanza Riachuelo River remediation process is far from over, substantive changes are notable and have been more expansive than those in Colombia and Peru. While the cleanup process continues, slow harms on the Matanza Riachuelo River is a policy problem that is no longer in the shadows.

Institutional Innovation. The most dramatic change in the slow-harms policy shift has been the creation of a new oversight institution. In 2006, a legislative act created the river basin institution ACUMAR and armed it with a significant budget and extensive authority.[60] The birth of ACUMAR was directly tied to bridging mobilization—the Ombudsman's working group had called for the creation of a river basin authority in their 2005 report, and Congress consulted with the working group in the process of legislating its creation. When it was created, ACUMAR was an institutional innovation in Argentina, becoming the first interjurisdictional governing body not beholden to one branch of government or political jurisdiction. Thus, ACUMAR was better positioned to reduce the coordination problems of managing a river that crosses federal, state, and local jurisdictions, an institutional problem that had frustrated prior remediation efforts. ACUMAR developed cross-jurisdictional plans for solid waste management, industrial effluent monitoring, and residential wastewater infrastructure development.[61] Other jurisdictions have also created new institutions to facilitate changes, as mandated by the 2008 Supreme Court ruling. For example, the Buenos Aires public works department developed a Riachuelo waste cleanup crew, which is one of the strongest institutions involved in the river basin. The Buenos Aires City Housing Commission created a Riachuelo subunit staffed to oversee the construction of new homes and relocations and, as one social worker told me, "to create a dignity-filled space for the voices of the [impacted communities] to be heard."[62] The Court ruling also helped

---

[60] ACUMAR was given its own very large budget for the first few years to execute public works. Pedro Lipcovich, "Todo el poder al Comité de Cuenca," *El Pais*, August 29, 2006.

[61] See Sigal, Rossi, and Morales (2017, 145–46) for a complete list of ACUMAR's responsibilities vis-à-vis the 2008 Court orders.

[62] Interview with Belen Demoy, El Instituto de Vivienda de la Ciudad de Buenos Aires, April 22, 2016.

increase the resources of existing municipal environmental subsecretariats and spurred the creation of new ones (Herrera 2022).[63]

Robust Financial Investments. Financial investments in infrastructure also increased dramatically in the late 2000s, as did construction projects to improve environmental conditions on the Matanza Riachuelo River. Argentina received the largest World Bank loan ever given for environmental cleanup, US$840 million; the loan documents directly cite the important role of the 2008 Supreme Court ruling and the judicial advisory committee in the Bank's involvement (World Bank 2009b, 16). AYSA, the Buenos Aires water and sanitation utility, is constructing infrastructure for residential wastewater coverage improvements; wastewater makes up 80% of the river basin's pollutant load. The World Bank loan and the Argentine government's US$360 million counterpart commitment are financing the megaworks Richauelo system, which will include 46 kilometers of sewage tunnels and new sanitation treatment plants to benefit 4.5 million people, as only 56% of the urban population has sewage coverage.[64] These works are a massive infrastructure challenge. One engineer reflected, "There is a high likelihood of failure because if any portion of the construction projects don't work properly, none of it will ultimately work."[65] AYSA engineers noted in interviews that they were undertaking wastewater infrastructure plans prior to the 2008 Supreme Court ruling, but that now there is "more political will."[66]

Improved Regulatory Capacity. Regulatory capacity to track and fine polluters has also increased considerably, although more work remains on this front. Industrial wastewater effluent remains a challenge, but there have been advances.[67] Interviews with ACUMAR inspectors revealed the creation of an extensive cadastral mapping of all industries, a regularized schedule of inspections, levying of fines, and shutting down of contaminating industries.

---

[63] Interview with Maximo Lanzetta, Subsecretariat of Environment Almirante Brown, April 18, 2016.

[64] The current sanitation system centers around the Berazategui plant, which has long failed to adequately serve the expanding urban population. Marina Aizen, "El Riachuelo diferente que abre una esperanza," *Clarín*, July 1, 2018; "Las empresas tras la obra más grande que financia el Banco Mundial en Argentina," *El Cronista*, March 25, 2017.

[65] Interview with consultant, World Bank 7706 Project, Buenos Aires, April 13, 2016.

[66] Interviews with AYSA Engineer 1 and AYSA Engineer 2, April 8, 2016. As of 2019, these works were halfway completed, and President Macri had declared, "[P]art of the change is that these works must be completed because they are important to people, not because they will be [highly visible]. These works will not be seen, they are 40 meters under the bed of the Plata River." Laura Rocha, "Riachuelo: La Acumar tendrá nuevo president," *Infobae*, February 26, 2019.

[67] ACUMAR is responsible for regulating effluent discharge from tanneries, slaughterhouses, meat processing plants, electroplating, food manufacturing, automobile manufacturing, chemical

Inspectors reported that many small tanneries have shuttered because of both the economic crisis and the new environmental regulations that they deemed financially infeasible; by 2017 the number of tanneries on the river basin had decreased from 200 to approximately 40.[68] The long process of industrial environmental upgrading for some sectors is underway; for example, large tanneries have built secondary treatment processes and "are much closer to producing effluents that meet the environmental norms," according to one inspector.[69] Quilmes brewery stated, "[M]any factories have been closed or relocated, and they audit industries like ours frequently, and this causes us to comply."[70] In contrast, employees I interviewed at one small tannery told me, "We try to comply with ACUMAR, but it's difficult."[71] An inspector noted, "Sometimes industries have a way of lying. Maybe they won't let you enter the premises, they have you wait until they fix a contaminating leak, or they dilute their effluent sample."[72]

Change is challenging, but it continues. In 2018 the ACUMAR president said, "[I]ndustries were used to being monitored on pre-scheduled visits. Now we have surprise inspections.... [W]e are detecting more infractions."[73] Many interviewees pinned hopes on the construction of an industrial park for tanneries in the municipality of Lanus, but the project, which began in 1983, remains stalled. Yet multiple interviews revealed a highly educated and experienced workforce of ACUMAR inspectors who had retained their positions since ACUMAR's founding despite many personnel changes in leadership. Managers overseeing inspectors were also concerned with transparency and reducing potential corruption, and thus periodically rotated which industries inspectors visited.

---

companies, and the Polo Dock Sud. In addition, ACUMAR oversees pollutants related to the Ezeiza Airport, which had a massive environmental crisis in prior decades surrounding a chemical spill that was never ameliorated, as well as other pollutant discharges. Interview with Miguel Sainz, ACUMAR, March 10, 2017.

[68] Interview with ACUMAR Inspector, April 20, 2016, and March 13, 2017.
[69] Interview with ACUMAR Inspector, April 20, 2016, and March 13, 2017. In one interview, an employee at a large tannery showed me the upgraded processes they began in 2008 that eliminated industrial toxic effluent dumping. Interview with Marcelo Piatek, Jordano Curtiembres, Lanus, Buenos Aires, March 13, 2017.
[70] Irene Caselli, "Los residentes pobres de Buenos Aires conviven con uno de los ríos más contaminados del mundo," *Univision.com*, February 24, 2017.
[71] Interview, small tannery, Lanus, Buenos Aires, March 13, 2017.
[72] Interviews, ACUMAR, April 2016 and March 2017.
[73] Marina Aizen, "El Riachuelo diferente que abre una esperanza," *Clarín*, July 1, 2018.

Physical improvements along the river basin are visible. For example, by 2016 there was public access to the waterfront that was formally occupied by either commercial properties or informal settlements. Relocation of impacted communities has created a long riverside path for recreational use that also allows cleanup crews to access the waterfront. More vegetation, birds, and wildlife have emerged.[74] Sunken ships, automobiles, and shipping containers have been removed, particularly in La Boca neighborhood, where they were once ubiquitous. The waterfront controlled by the Buenos Aires Public Works Department has removed over 1,500 tons of garbage since 2018 and 90% of the solid waste dumping on the riverine mirror within the city.[75] The 2008 ruling helped create new waste management policies in the city that expanded waste collection to areas that previously had none. During an interview on his garbage barge, the director of public works of Buenos Aires told me, "Once international journalists would flock here wanting to see the most contaminated place in the world. Now they come and they see this part of the river looks like this . . . and they're disappointed. It makes for a less interesting story. There is still a long way to go, the whole river does not yet look like this . . . but improvements have been real."[76] Compared to its historical conditions, as of the early 2020s the Matanza Riachuelo has a cleaner waterfront along some portions of the river, recreational waterfront access, and much less odor emanating from the river in the municipality of Avellaneda.[77]

Ongoing Accountability and Participation. Today there are many eyes on the Matanza Riachuelo River project: journalists, university researchers, NGOs, government institutions, and everyday observers. Thus shortcomings and delays in remediation receive extensive attention. For example, many actors have characterized the cleanup process as too slow and inefficient and lamented the institutional volatility of ACUMAR. ACUMAR has had eight presidents since its inception and has been accused of being staffed by

---

[74] Interviews with Javier Garcia Elorrio, Buenos Aires City Government, DGLM Riachuelo, April 15, 2016, and March 8, 2017; Marina Aizen, "El Riachuelo diferente que abre una esperanza," *Clarín*, July 1, 2018.

[75] Interview with Alfredo Alberti, VDB, April 1, 2016; "La UCPE y especialistas alemanes recorrieron la ribera del Riachuelo," *buenosaires.gob.ar*, October 4, 2018; Supreme Court Public Hearing, November 30, 2016, available at Centro de Información Judicial, https://www.youtube.com/watch?v=1VIoKJodAq8, "Riachuelo: Se realiza una audiencia pública ante la Corte Suprema de Justicia," timestamp 16:00.

[76] Interviews with Javier Garcia Elorrio, Buenos Aires City Government, DGLM Riachuelo, April 15, 2016, and March 8, 2017.

[77] For more on positive achievements in this case as of 2017, see Sigal et al. (2017, 155–57).

unknowledgeable leadership.[78] A public hearing by the Supreme Court in November 2016 put ACUMAR officials to shame.[79] The justices were dissatisfied with the amount of cleanup that had occurred (20%) given that US$5.2 million had been spent, and much of the ACUMAR leadership resigned soon thereafter.[80] The judicial advisory committee—composed of bridging actors—presented numerous critiques during the hearings, helping to increase transparency over the proceedings.

The judicial advisory committee outlined shortcomings to the remediation process and continued to hold public officials accountable during Supreme Court hearings. In 2016, they critiqued ACUMAR's handling of solid waste dumpsite removals as superficial: 57% of the open-air sites that had been removed near the river were replaced by new ones a few short years later. Clearly solid waste management infrastructure remains a chronic problem. The Shell petrochemical processing plant, which continues to be a threat to human health, has yet to be addressed. Wastewater infrastructure construction remains too slow, with too many communities chronically underserved, and the new housing for relocated communities is on land far from city center employment opportunities. The judicial advisory committee stressed that ACUMAR's health interventions, such as their mobile health vans that test for lead poisoning in communities or their building of a hospital, was outside of ACUMAR's area of expertise, often led nowhere, and wasted valuable resources. A judicial advisory committee member said, "ACUMAR continues to have resources, but they are being gutted by being asked to do too many things."[81] Calling for a more integral socioeconomic approach to address the river contamination, FARN leader and a key "bridging actor," Andres Napoli, told the Supreme Court during the 2016 hearing, "[T]hese actions will be totally sterile if we don't address the causes that generate them."[82]

Impacted communities have argued that they have been excluded from participating; for example, they typically remain outside in an overflow

---

[78] Laura Rocha, "Riachuelo: La Acumar tendrá nuevo presidente," *Infobae*, February 26, 2019.

[79] Supreme Court Public Hearing, November 30, 2016, available at Centro de Información Judicial, https://www.youtube.com/watch?v=1VIoKJodAq8, "Riachuelo: Se realiza una audiencia pública ante la Corte Suprema de Justicia."

[80] Irene Caselli, "Los residentes pobres de Buenos Aires conviven con uno de los ríos más contaminados del mundo," *Univision.com*, February 24, 2017; interview with Andres Napoli, Cuerpo Colegiado, March 9, 2017.

[81] Interview with Andres Napoli, FARN, Cuerpo Colegiado, March 9, 2017.

[82] Supreme Court Public Hearing, November 30, 2016, available at Centro de Información Judicial, https://www.youtube.com/watch?v=1VIoKJodAq8, "Riachuelo: Se realiza una audiencia pública ante la Corte Suprema de Justicia," timestamp 16.14.

auditorium during public hearings. In a March 2018 Supreme Court public hearing, one person held a sign that read, "As [neighbors] we don't contaminate, we are the ones being contaminated and we don't have a voice."[83] Much of the cleanup progress has been predicated on the relocation of informal settlements to newly built properties on outskirt land that the city claims are adequate but that many neighbors have criticized. Relocated residents lament that their communities are broken up, that they are far removed from centrally located employment, and that those who have spent decades building up their home received meager compensation for their investment.[84] Other residents claim that the cleanup process is a sham because they continue to lack wastewater service, remain exposed to toxins, and have received no medical attention.[85]

In 2017 the National Ombudsman's Office was removed from the judicial advisory committee, and the five rights-based NGOs were left to continue their accountability oversight alone.[86] They have since teamed up more closely with other rights-based institutions that represent the voice of impacted communities that are formally excluded from the *Mendoza* case, such as the Buenos Aires Public Defender's Office and the National Public Defender's Office. A judicial advisory committee representative noted, "We continue to meet because we have a lot of issues to address. [During the 2016 public hearings] I went and presented a position that wasn't exactly mine but at least it represented all the voices."[87] The bridging mobilization outlined in this chapter created more spaces for public sector accountability.

Despite criticisms, slow harms on the river are no longer invisible or unattended. The Matanza Riachuelo River has experienced an expansive policy shift as compared to the other cases in this book. Due to the bonding and bridging mobilization examined here, the capacity for new institutions to oversee change on the river is much stronger than it was decades earlier, and transparency and citizen participation are also higher—the judicial advisory's committee's efforts reflect this. For example, ACUMAR has launched an environmental monitoring site where citizens can identify industries and their

---

[83] Andres Napoli, FARN, Twitter feed, 2018.
[84] Interview with Noelia Garone, ACIJ, April 14, 2016; interview with Eduardo Reese, April 1, 2016, CELS.
[85] Interview with Eva Koutsovitis, Foro Hidrico, April 10, 2016.
[86] This decision was undertaken due to Congress's failing to name a National Ombudsman.
[87] Interview with Andres Napoli, Cuerpo Colegiado, March 9, 2017.

contamination type; this map builds on the crowdsourcing initiative begun by different rights-based NGOs years earlier.[88] The judicial advisory committee continues to oversee activities by the presiding judges and channel information from citizens to the judicial process (although citizens can also access the presiding judge directly). The committee's reports continue to be the most accurate and informed assessment of the cleanup process. They also have clout with ACUMAR; one interviewee told me, "ACUMAR officials said that the [judicial advisory committee's] next report will be their action plan."[89] The Matanza Riachuelo River has been put on the public policy agenda, and the state has been made to answer for its role in both the contamination and cleanup efforts, even if policy wins continue to be hard fought.

Evaluating Alternative Explanations in the Argentina Case

I have argued that citizen-led efforts for more regulation and accountability around river pollution on the Matanza Riachuelo was a key driver in policy reform, and that this mobilization can be linked back to a history of human rights mobilization and supportive political and economic environments in Argentina. This social mobilization involved people from all social classes, including impacted communities (bonding mobilization), but was highly dependent on resourced NGOs and institutional allies that acted as "bridges" connecting grassroots claims to the state (bridging mobilization). But there are competing theories that could plausibly explain this variation, which appear in studies of social and environmental mobilization in other cases.

The first is that national attention turns to long-ignored problems when there is a precipitating event that serves as a flashpoint for collective action, in this case the potential triggering impact of a natural disaster. Did floods become flashpoints for change in slow-harms policymaking? In Buenos Aires, seasonal flooding is a historical problem that impacts low-income communities in flood-prone low-value land (Merlinsky and Tobías 2016, 48; World Bank 2009b, 1). The case studies show how neighbors in Lomas de Zamora fight against continual flooding due to a high water-table in

---

[88] The ACUMAR map was housed at http://establecimientos.acumar.gob.ar/Mapa/, based on the NGO led project originally housed at quepasariachuelo.com, by FARN, Fundación Ciudad, the Argentine Journalism Forum and funded by the European Union.
[89] Interview with Leandro Garcia Silva, Ombudsman's Office, April 11, 2016.

their communities, caused in part by the AYSA water utility's change in their water extraction sources. Yet despite the city's responsibility to address a problem partially of their own making, flooding has not otherwise altered the amount of policy response on river pollution. More broadly, floods in 1985 and 2013 devastated the city, but these events were not associated with long-term infrastructure upgrades or pollution remediation in impacted areas.[90] While flooding generated collective grievances, public officials typically responded with short-term fixes as opposed to comprehensive reforms.

Another prevailing explanation is that low-income residents show little environmental concern because environmentalism is a "postmaterial" value held by left-leaning affluent communities whose material needs have been met (Inglehart 1990, 56, 380–88). Socioeconomic class does not fully explain environmental mobilization in the Matanza Riachuelo because diverse socioeconomic classes mobilized for environmental causes. In Buenos Aires, middle-class residents did mobilize over environmental pollution, particularly wetlands contamination. Yet low-income communities on the urban peripheries of Buenos Aires (e.g., González Catan, Lomas de Zamora) also mobilized around environmental degradation, such as against toxic exposure from landfills and contaminated riverways and for sewage infrastructure. These "accidental environmentalists" were working-class urbanites whose level of environmental concern increased because of their heightened exposure to environmental vulnerabilities. This finding underscores recent work on vulnerability politics in extractives conflicts in Central America (Eisenstadt and West 2019, 9–11).

On the other hand, extreme poverty, when it coincides with low social capital, does disincentivize collective action. Places where economic vulnerability was highest, and residents had also newly migrated to the area, struggled to generate a robust movement for slow harms. For example, in Villa Inflamable in Avellaneda, the organization Sowing Together (Sembrando Juntos) (see Table 3.1) was a small cooperative learning space whose organizing efforts did not reach further than two to four people. Over 75% of residents are new to Villa Inflamable from shantytown removal elsewhere or from migration from nearby countries (Peru, Bolivia, Paraguay), and many neighbors continue to experience what Auyero

---

[90] "Cuáles fueron las peores inundaciones de la historia argentina," *El Once*, April 5, 2013.

and Swiston (2009, 6, 44) documented as "toxic waiting." Newer arrivals (facing extreme vulnerability) and older residents (some of whom are lower middle class) experience cross-community tensions about work, drugs, and public security, and disagree over whether they are actually experiencing contamination (Auyero and Swistun 2009, 44–50). The cases suggest that when newly arrived populations exposed to toxic hazards live in extreme poverty, social organizing around slow harms is less likely.

Relatedly, Inglehart (1977, 173) argued that environmental concern was a postmaterial value that would most likely be expressed through ecological political parties, similar to the European experience. Yet in Argentina, most environmental movements "went out of their way to avoid partisan alliances" (Amengual 2016, 157). In Greater Buenos Aires, grassroots environmental activists in Gonzalez Catan, Lomas de Zamora, and La Boca described how their neighborhood meetings about local pollution initially attracted the attention of political brokers. Brokers serving clientelistic parties insisted that environmental organizers provide them with email and mailing lists of participants. Meeting organizers described rejecting brokers' advances and navigating their pushback.[91] The Boca Neighborhood Association left their participation in the grassroots group RRR when partisan politics overtook RRR leadership, and they recounted that when the environmental focus was lost, "it didn't work anymore."[92] Furthermore, ecological political parties were weak and limited in their ability to affect environmental policy in Argentina. These include the small and now defunct Green Initiative (Iniciativa Verde) in Buenos Aires, which was active from 2006 to 2011 and was not directly involved in the river remediation cause (Amengual 2016, 157).[93]

Another prevailing explanation is that the strength of legal institutions explains policy shifts around slow harms; after all, very little had been done to remediate the Matanza Riachuelo River prior to the historic 2008 Supreme Court *Mendoza* ruling. The 1994 and 2003 constitutional reforms created judicial institutional changes on which slow-harms activists relied. These included the *amparo* (writ of protection for individual rights), ratifying international legislation on human rights, allowing for collective

---

[91] Interview with Martin Farina, Colectivo Ecologica Unidos por la Laguna de Rocha, March 15, 2017; interview with Cristina Fins, Asociación de Vecinos de la Boca, April 6, 2016; interview with Celia Frutos, Vecinos Auto convocados Contra GEAMSE de González Catán, March 11, 2017.
[92] Interview with Cristina Fins, Asociación de Vecinos de la Boca, April 6, 2016.
[93] Multiple interviews, 2016 and 2017.

cases, creating the National Ombudsman's Office (Ombudsman's Office), making the Court more autonomous after 2003, and formalizing *amicus curiae*. In addition, "judicial assertiveness" facilitated opportunities for environmental reform in Argentina. For example, well-known environmental law expert Ricardo Lorenzetti was appointed a justice in 2004 and later chief justice of the Supreme Court (2007–18) (Merlinsky 2013, 101). Yet the strength of these same legal institutional factors in Argentina (including judicial assertiveness and autonomous legal institutions) did not matter to the same extent in other places with equally strong judicial institutions, such as Colombia.

In Argentina, strong legal institutions—both laws in service of the right to a clean environment as well as judicial independence and judicial assertiveness—grew alongside the development of public sector institutions born out of a robust human rights movement. These included the Ombudsman's Office but also judges, public defenders, prosecutors, and specially appointed commissions. The push toward human rights in Argentina also helped advance institutions and procedures for greater transparency, access to information, and collective claims-making. While Argentina had rights-based legal frameworks for environmental protection, importantly the state and societal interpreters of these legal institutions were actors with rights-based goals and mandates.

This chapter traced how the Supreme Court *Mendoza* ruling was undergirded by rights-based NGOs alongside the Ombudsman's Office—what I term bridging mobilizing—before and after the ruling. Numerous interviewees noted that the Court lacked expertise on environmental issues, water quality, and housing to be effective alone.[94] The NGOs and Ombudsman's Office worked together on the Matanza Riachuelo working group years before claimants initiated litigation, contributed to the technical and institutional design of the ruling in numerous Supreme Court public hearings, and filed a motion to become third parties to the case. After the ruling, these strongly networked bridges sat on the judicial oversight committee to hold the government accountable for advancing remediation efforts. Had the legal institutions to remediate the Matanza Riachuelo River been created without citizen-led advocacy to boost their efficacy and legitimacy, they would have been just like any other environmental law passed in Latin America: little more than "paper tigers."

---

[94] Numerous interviews with Cuerpo Colegiado, 2016 and 2017.

The Power of Strong Bonds and Strong Bridges on the Matanza Riachuelo River

Institutionalizing the Matanza Riachuelo River pollution as a policy problem has been an important first step toward broader ideational change about environmental norms in Argentina. Many environmental experts, scholars, and participants in the *Mendoza* Supreme Court ruling agree that it has changed the visibility of environmental issues in the country, becoming "part of the public agenda and public conversation"[95] and "chang[ing] the mode through which environmental problems are processed ... amplifying the importance of environmental rights" (Gutiérrez and Isuani 2014, 313–14).[96] The lead plaintiff in the case, Beatriz Mendoza, summed up the change best: "This is a point of no return. It will take more or less time, we don't know, but we don't go backwards from here because awareness has been raised. Today in all the universities that teach environmental sciences and in all the law schools that teach environmental law, they study the Riachuelo court case. This now has legs."[97]

In this chapter I have argued that the 2008 *Mendoza* ruling is only as strong as the vast advocacy network behind it—including both grassroots activism (bonds) and national-level NGOs and activist public officials (bridges)—who before, during, and after the ruling paved the way for its effectiveness. Both by working through the Court as well as complementing its weaknesses, "bridges" between grassroots activists and the state have been conduits for change. NGOs that serve on the judicial advisory committee, as well as those that have not, such as ACIJ and Fundación Ciudad, have provided critical resources, such as sector-specific expertise, and material resources, such as staff charged with research and administrative tasks. Bridges also came in the guise of state allies, such as the Ombudsman's Office, the Public Defender's Office of Buenos Aires, and the National Public Defender's Office, all of whom provided further material and organizational support, largely through working closely with advocacy NGOs, with whom they have shared professional networks and personal affinities. Local activists and impacted communities have also been an important component of the advocacy network—raising awareness about many different types of

---

[95] Interview with Gabriela Merlinsky, author and sociologist, April 5, 2016.
[96] One prominent official noted that "Causa Mendoza put environmental rights at the center of politics at the national level" (Botero 2018, 178).
[97] Interview with Beatriz Mendoza, plaintiff in *Mendoza* case, March 16, 2017.

socioenvironmental problems on the river basin, helping to keep these issues in the news cycle, and channeling grievances through state allies. Remarking on the role of NGOs in the Mendoza case, a prominent environmental law expert explained, "Environmental law is a transparent right, it is democratic. It is a participatory right, a right that is based on solidarity and cooperation. It requires an active civil society."[98]

Slow harms easily become part of the everyday landscape over time. Putting slow harms on the policymaking agenda requires increasing their level of visibility first within impacted communities and then outside them; bridges between grassroots claims and the state were critical for aggregating grievances and scaling up claims. Effective bridges not only brought new resources to address slow harms but also used a rights-based framing that drew on prior experiences working together.

In the Argentina case, this occurred when NGOs and activist public officials connected environmental problems in a polluted river basin with the human rights claims-making agenda. Supportive left-of-center political administrations helped facilitate the growth of human rights organizations. The embeddedness of the human rights movement in postdemocracy Argentine institutions and public opinion created a fertile space for the issues of environmental contamination and human rights to be linked. Issue linkage—between an idea with resonance and one that had previously been unimportant—was a key ingredient in creating visibility for the Matanza Riachuelo pollution.

As the next chapter shows, access to rights-based framing and prior collective work experiences is key to understanding the strength of bridging mobilization. Old, invisible problems must be reconceptualized and approached in a new way. When claims-making over slow harms occurs but is not deeply embedded in a preexisting human rights movement, issue linkages between human rights and the environment are weak and tenuous. In Argentina, prior collective experiences in human rights claims-making gave NGOs and activist public officials legitimacy when using the human rights language in characterizing the river basin pollution as a human rights injustice to which the state was obligated to attend. The human rights frame was the conduit through which environmental problems could most visibly be seen in Argentina. This stands in contrast to the dynamics observed in the Colombia and Peru cases.

---

[98] Interview with Nestor Cafferatta, Secretario de Justicia Ambiental, CSJN, March 16, 2017.

4
Stagnated Policy Shifts in Colombia
On Strong Bonds with Weak Bridges

Colombia's abundant natural resources have historically drawn those seeking to exploit the land as well as those willing to put their lives on the line in its defense. The country's unique megadiversity and geography influenced its early adoption of environmental institutions as much as it exacerbated internal armed conflict. Remote, high mountainous terrain both facilitated guerrilla warfare and limited the territorial reach of the state for environmental protections. The state's inability to enforce its impressive environmental laws mirrored its inability to restore order in the countryside during the decades-long armed conflict. State-sponsored violence against leftist activists further weakened participatory spaces and created hostile dynamics between civil society and public officials. These tensions impacted burgeoning environmental activism.

As slow harms concentrated along the Bogotá savannah in the second half of the 20th century, so did cries from grassroots activists for improved environmental conditions. Describing efforts to protect a contaminated wetland from illicit garbage dumping by city officials in Suba, Bogotá, one activist remembered, "We linked arms to create human chains and put our bodies in front of incoming trucks, [but ultimately] everything we did, we did through judges. . . . We implemented forty-eight different judicial processes. It was the only space where we were heard."[1]

The polluted Bogotá River is a "most likely" case for reform, boasting strong bottom-up environmental activism in a country with an ecologically oriented Constitution, homegrown environmental institutions, and an autonomous and accessible judiciary. Yet the many grassroots efforts and judicial orders have not translated into significant policy change. Compared to the Buenos Aires case, policy shifts for slow-harms remediation in Bogotá have consisted of piecemeal actions led by the very

---

[1] Interview with German Galindo, founder of Conejera Foundation, August 2016.

institutions responsible for pollution, with little regulatory will or capacity to deter industrial contamination. The upgrades that have occurred have lacked transparency, accountability, and spaces for citizen participation. This chapter examines why the Bogotá slow-harms advocacy network was relatively less effective in putting slow harms on the policy agenda than the network in Buenos Aires.

The critical missing link for the Bogotá River has been strong bridging mobilization that could scale up fragmented grassroots claims and assert strong influence on the policy process. Bogotá's advocacy network contained weaker bridges that lacked material resources, a history of collaboration, and a shared vision for reform. Enabling conditions for rights-based mobilization was missing in Colombia due to decades of internal armed conflict and conservative presidential administrations that squashed, rather than elevated, the growth of a human rights movement. Conservative administrations in Colombia were more reliant on export-oriented mineral wealth extraction and more closely allied with the military than in Argentina. Under these conditions, the human rights movement in Colombia did not become a dominant and multipronged network of influence within institutions or activist networks.

Instead, Bogotá's' slow-harms mobilization was framed around environmental concern by local and underresourced NGOs, which were ultimately less effective in creating linkages with "activist public officials" than those in Buenos Aires. Given the hostile political environment in which activists operated, local environmental NGOs in Bogotá were unable to build collaborative work experiences and state-level linkages that would allow them to have the policy influence required for bold change. Unlike the slow-harms activists in Argentina, Colombian activists did not connect pollution claims to human rights messaging and otherwise lacked a coherent and resonant frame to draw broad attention to a historically invisible policy problem. Slow-harms mobilization for the Bogotá River continues and is backed by the power of the judiciary, but its impact has been more limited and has been overseen by technocrats and a judiciary with weak accountability and transparency from a narrow segment of civil society. This chapter reviews the adoption of national-level environmental frameworks in Colombia, traces the development of strong bonds with relatively weaker bridges for environmental claims-making, examines the policymaking limitations of the strong bond–weak bridge network, and reviews alternative explanations.

Environmental Institutions in Colombia: A Brief History

Even prior to Rio 1992, Colombia had an unusually robust environmental institutional framework that stood out compared to most other countries in the region (Hernández, Flores, and Naranjo 2010, 28).[2] The country's first comprehensive environmental law was the 1974 National Code for Renewable Natural Resources and Environmental Protection,[3] on the tails of the 1972 UN Conference in Stockholm, and boasted 340 articles that even included pollution fees and environmental impact assessments.[4] Prior to this, in 1954 the Tennessee Valley Authority in the United States influenced the creation of autonomous regional corporations in Colombia (e.g., Corporación Autonoma de Cundinamarca, CAR), which were regional agencies charged with promoting economic development related to water, telecoms, infrastructure, and natural resource management (O'Brien 1995, 19–20). By 1968 the National Institute for Renewable Natural Resources administered environmental oversight in regions without a CAR. Yet contradictions arose due to CAR's dual role as both facilitator of regional economic development and regulator of environmental degradation; similarly, the National Institute for Renewable Natural Resources, an arm of the Ministry of Agriculture, was tasked with protecting the same natural resources that ministry offices sought to economically develop. Thus, despite its relatively sophisticated environmental institutional framework, Colombia's "environmental considerations were strictly subordinate to those of the economy" (O'Brien 1995, 16). Dispersed and contradictory roles across national and regional organizations, small budgets relative to responsibilities, and no power to sanction environmental violations made these environmental institutions little more than "paper tigers" (Sánchez-Triana, Ahmed, and Awe 2007, 10–17; Lamprea 2016, 285).

Environmental protections received more "teeth" with the 1991 Colombian Constitution that featured environmental protections so prominently it has been referred to as the "ecological" Constitution (e.g.,

---

[2] For example, the International Convention on Wetlands (Ramsar) and the 1992 Convention on Biological Diversity. See also Rodriguez Becerra (1994) and Carrizosa Umaña (1992).

[3] Código Nacional de Recursos Naturales y de Protección al Medio Ambiente. For more on the development impulses in the mid-1970s on sustainability that influenced Colombia, see O'Brien (1995, 8–9, 16–17).

[4] The National Code was issued through Decree 2811, based on Law 23 of 1973. See Lamprea (2016, 285, n.4) for more on the limitations of Law 23. Colombia's environmental institutions date back even further, to Bolivar, the Civil Code of 1883, and the establishment of the first National Forest Reserve in 1948 (O'Brien 1995, 16).

Hernández, Flores, and Naranjo 2010, 30; Lamprea 2016, 284).[5] Routes to citizen participation on environmental issues increased dramatically following the new Constitution, which featured over 40 articles on the environment, including Article 79, which promulgated the right to a clean environment and the right to information about the environment and participation, particularly through judicial venues (Lamprea 2016, 284–85). Several new legal mechanisms allowed citizens to intervene in the courts on behalf of the environment. *Acciones populares* (or *acciones populares de grupo*) (Article 88) are individual or group lawsuits by citizens against the state; citizens could now use an *acción de tutela* (Article 86) to request injunctive relief to prevent violation of fundamental rights or request an *acción de cumplimiento* to ensure that environmental laws are upheld; *consultas previas* became a tool to ensure prior consultation of indigenous communities for projects impacting them.[6] Subsequently, more *acciones populares* focused on the right to a clean environment than on any other issue.[7] Although not widely used until the late 1990s, these judicial tools stood out among countries in the region as an extraordinary attempt to increase access to environmental rights claims.

Environmental frameworks were amplified further in 1993, when Law 99 created the National Environmental System, which established 37 organizations for environmental management, and Colombia became one of the few countries to establish a Ministry of the Environment.[8] Importantly, Law 99 also restricted CAR governance to solely environmental regulation and consolidated a previously decentralized environmental governance framework. Finally, in 2011 a new regulatory body, the National Environmental Licensing Authority, was created under the newly reconfigured Ministry of the Environment and Sustainable Development.

Despite its impressive de jure framework, environmental protections enforcement remained weak in Colombia. Effective enforcement was hindered by the "usual suspects," such as low annual environmental expenditures,

---

[5] The Constituent Assembly was influenced by the preparations for the 1992 Rio Conference as well as the debate over cultural and indigenous participation in environmental issues in the context of the 500th anniversary of the discovery of the Americas (Lamprea 2016, 284).

[6] Other new constitutional mechanisms for public participation included the right to petition public authorities and public hearings, open meetings, and referendums. The Constitution did not specify how these would be implemented.

[7] In a study of 41 collective rights cases from 1999 to 2009, the Ombudsman's Office reports that a plurality, 32%, were for the right to a clean environment (Londoño and Carrillo 2010, 81; Lamprea 2016, 284, n.5). See also Londoño (2006).

[8] For more on the development and shortcomings of the Ministry of Environment and its institutional changes, see Guhl Nannetti (2015) and Carrizosa Umaña (2015).

which remained at 0.65% of GDP in 2010 (Sánchez-Triana, Ahmed, and Awe 2007, 28; OECD 2014, 96), and opposition from the business sector (Londoño Toro 2008, 547; Sánchez-Triana, Ahmed, and Awe 2007, 24). Colombia's decentralized environmental framework also continued to pose challenges, such as CARs having limited accountability and being subject to local capture (OECD 2014, 49). Much of Colombia's environmental protections system was designed to rely on voluntary regulation and over time became hampered by conflicting roles across institutions at all tiers of government (Guhl Nannetti 2015, 51; Sánchez-Triana, Ahmed, and Awe 2007, 44). The result has been a high rate of environmental regulatory noncompliance (OECD 2014, 62).

Finally, the long history of armed conflict has impacted the country's ability to govern its natural resources. Environmental management institutions were for decades unable to have a presence in difficult-to-reach territories overrun by armed groups and narcotrafficking (Carrizosa Umaña 2015, 20). Furthermore, violence against environmental activists is not new in Colombia; it dates back to at least the emergence of the National Institute for Renewable Natural Resources, which, after it was created in 1968, suffered murders of staff as they defended the environment (O'Brien 1995, 16). Within this context, as urban environmental issues grew throughout the country, the state's capacity and political will to mount an effective response to environmental degradation remained limited.

Strong Bonding Mobilization Sends Smoke Signals

When grassroots organizing began for the Bogotá River, it was as strong as for the Matanza Riachuelo River in Buenos Aires and encompassed a much larger territory. This section describes bottom-up claims-making around toxic exposure due to construction debris dumping in wetlands, legislative protection of the right to water, and petitions for wastewater services, all of which were grievances related to pollution on the Bogotá River, a map of the river is shown on Map 4.1. The organizational forms of the grassroots groups, listed in Table 4.1, more frequently resembled social fronts rather than formal community groups. It was common for groups to form for specific issues and then disband, or for activists to view themselves as social movement participants resistant to creating a formal organization.

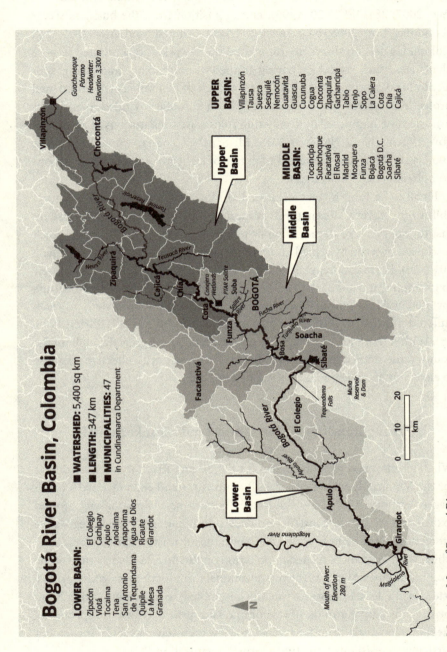

Map 4.1 Map of Bogotá River
Map by Dennis Bolt.

Table 4.1 Local Activist Groups involved in the Bogotá River (Actors in Bonding Mobilization)

Name	Dates Active	Number of Activists	Mission	Action Strategies	Judicial Advisory Committee
Conejera Wetlands Foundation (Fundación Humedal de la Conejera)	1993–	12 founding members, activist count varies (e.g., at one point 2,000–3,000 people in workshops) (3,887 Facebook likes)	Restoration and management of wetlands, rivers, and flora of Bogotá wetlands, beginning in Conejera, Suba	Litigation, direct confrontation, education (EcoBus), native seed preservation, lobbying, government alliances	Yes
Bogotá River Foundation (Fundación Rio Bogotá)	1995–2000	N/A	Environmental conservation around the Bogotá River	Local organizing, tree planting, network building	No
We are the Bogotá River (Somos Rio Bogotá)	2002–4	N/A	Support the passage of national legislation for a human right to water	Gathered signatures for referendum, network building	No
SIE Environmental Corporation (SIE Corporación Ambiental)	1999–	5 employees, numerous activists (6,085 Facebook likes)	Plan cultural and educational events with children to improve living conditions near Tunjuelo River (part of Asamblea Sur)	River awareness campaigns, marches, organizing, lobbying, youth educational programs, connection to Buen Vivir	Yes
Asdoas House (Corporación Casa Asdoas)	2003–?	3 founding members	Promotes environmental conservation surrounding Tunjuelo River through connection with Muisca culture (part of Territoro Sur)	Leads cultural and historic ecotourist walks and river navigations, connection to Buen Vivir	No

(continued)

Table 4.1 Continued

Name	Dates Active	Number of Activists	Mission	Action Strategies	Judicial Advisory Committee
Tunjuelo Southern Assembly (Asamblea Sur de la Cuenca Tunjuelo)	2000–2005	N/A	Promote recuperation of Tunjuelo watershed	Door-to-door neighborhood organizing, demands against Dona Juana landfill, social monitoring of industrial dumping	No
Fucha River Corporation (Corporación Vida del Río Fucha (CORVIF))	1996–	N/A (271 Facebook likes)	Recovery of Fucha watershed, a tributary of the Bogotá River	Environmental assessment studies, cultural events, lobbying, promote sustainable public works construction	No
Salitre Working Group (Mesa Interlocal de la Cuenca del Río Salitre)	2008–	76 in 2010 (521 Facebook likes)	Strengthen citizen participation to impact public policies over Salitre watershed, a tributary of the Bogotá River	Weekly meetings, river tours, publications, studies, forums, lobbying	No
Collective Planet Native House (Colectivo Planeta Casa Nativa)	2012–	N/A (2,648 Facebook likes)	Promotes environmental conservation among local community	Local cleanup brigades, river tours, tree planting	No
Fiscal Accountability Citizen Watchdog Groups for the Bogotá River (Veeduría Ciudadanía Nuestro Río Bogotá)	2010–	Activists in 42 hubs (300–400 members)	Citizen oversight of public spending on Bogotá River construction infrastructure spending	Monitor use of public funds, notify government authorities of misuse of resources, file legal and administrative complaints, influence strategic policy planning	Yes

Source: Author's compilation based on various sources, including interviews, groups' self-produced materials, and social media. See appendix for discussion of data collection strategies. Social media information taken from 2017.

Like the Buenos Aires case, claims about pollution in Bogotá also emerged from low-income community groups and were not just environmental concerns of upper-middle-class residents. Claims-making groups shared strong within-group solidarity due to family ties and decades of living in the same community. Communities faced many challenges: low-income communities lacked resources for organizing and were limited in their influence on public officials, while citywide political campaigning resulted in legislative failures. These efforts, along with those listed in Table 4.1, did, however, send strong smoke signals about the impact of pollution for aggrieved communities. Yet the smoke signaling that did occur, with few exceptions, like the Buenos Aires case, did not bridge territories and remained largely fragmented.

Wetlands Conservation in La Conejera, Suba. The first and the most prominent group to organize was the Conejera Wetlands Foundation (Fundación Humedal de la Conejera), dedicated to protecting the city's wetlands, which had declined from 50,000 hectares connected to the Bogotá River in 1950 to only 1,000 hectares by 2009 (World Bank 2010, 4). A founding member explained that when his family moved into a new apartment building in Suba, Bogotá, in the early 1990s, they were surprised to find a biodiverse wetland in their backyard that had become a dumping ground for a construction company's refuse. "I began to tell our neighbors, 'Let's get organized. This can't continue.' . . . Whatever I researched I would share with them. . . . And they were [amenable] because it was happening in their backyard."[9] They created a local committee made up mostly of housewives and documented skin rashes on residents and other health impacts due to wastewater effluent discharge. The Conejera Foundation used their robust evidence to generate 50 judicial processes against different entities, including the Bogotá water and sanitation utility, EAAB (Empresa de Acueducto y Alcantarillado de Bogotá).

What began as a superlocal family affair by resourced residents—with lawyers and biologists within the family turning their attention to this cause—branched into a formal organization with multiple sister groups, encompassing activists from different parts of the city and from diverse socioeconomic backgrounds. Their many efforts emphasized native Colombian species and horticultural practices, created training sessions for activists, biologists, and fauna experts—such as the creation of the Ecobus,

---

[9] Interview with Germán Galindo, Fundación La Conejera, August 3, 2016.

Figure 4.1 Fundación La Conejera before and after wetland cleanup campaigns.
Source: German Galindo.

an education hub for Bogotá residents on wetlands conservation—and included political lobbying and litigation. The Conejera Foundation became a training camp for many environmental activists connected to other organizations in the region and a model of environmental advocacy in Colombia.[10] Of the total number of civil society organizations interviewed, the Conejera Foundation had the largest amount of connections to other civil society organizations.[11] Leadership from the Conejera Foundation led to Colombia's signing of the International Ramsar Convention through Law 357 in 1997 and the 2006 adoption of a wetlands preservation public policy by the Bogotá city government (Alcaldia Mayor de Bogotá, D.C. 2005).[12] Although the Conejera Foundation began as a grassroots organization with strong ingroup solidarity due to the many family members who made up the group, it later became an influential NGO with bridging capacity, as will be discussed in the next section.[13]

Right to Water Signature Drives in Bogotá. Grassroots collectives also initiated political and legislative campaigns to safeguard water rights and address river pollution. In 2006, a citizen group called the National Defense of Water and Life (Comité Nacional en Defensa del Agua y la Vida) launched a constitutional referendum for the right to water as part of a broader effort to challenge the privatization of natural resources (Gómez Bustos 2014,

---

[10] Interview with Alejandro Torres, environmental activist, August 2, 2016.
[11] These findings are consistent with Palacio (2014, 90), who finds the Conejera group to have the most direct and indirect relations in her study of 14 civil society organizations in Bogotá.
[12] Interview with Germán Galindo, Fundación La Conejera, August 3, 2016.
[13] Figure 4.1 is a photograph of wetland clean up campaign by the Conejera Foundation.

88–89). The signature collection process was a nationwide effort, but in the capital region it brought together diverse citizens concerned about water access and the river's contamination. These groups created a collective called We Are the Bogotá River (Somos Río Bogotá) comprised of activists in different municipalities in Cundinamarca who worked for months to gather thousands of signatures.[14] In Bogotá and the other six main rivers of the country, activists built alliances through river navigations, marches, conferences, and lobbying (Gómez Bustos 2014, 90–92). Nevertheless, these efforts had little direct impact on policy, as environmental activists struggled to find allies in Congress. The referendum failed due to partisan intervention and blocking by the executive, and many of the citizen groups disbanded (Misión de Observación Electoral 2012, 79–80; Gómez Bustos 2014, 95).[15]

Youth Environmental Campaigns and Harnessing Indigenous Knowledge in Tunjuelo. Since 1997, working-class activists have organized along the Tunjuelo, a tributary of the Bogotá River, with a focus on improving living conditions and creating participatory spaces for "popular urban environmentalism" (Ramírez 2010, 1). One activist remarked that within-group solidarity stemmed from many lengthy battles with public officials over "thousands of socioenvironmental conflicts you can't even imagine."[16] Tunjuelo activists formed diverse participatory forums, including a participatory working table (Mesa Interlocal)[17] and social fronts made up of many grassroots groups, such as the Southern Territory (Territorio Sur) and Southern Assembly (Asamblea Sur).[18]

In Tunjuelo, social organizing around water pollution and the right to a clean environment increased dramatically after a devastating flood in 2002 left many unhoused and created a sanitation crisis for low-income communities in southern Bogotá.[19] Many Tunjuelo activists considered themselves social movement participants rather than members of formal social organizations. Over 800 people participated in the activities of the Southern Territory, and 500 young people joined regional forums and river

---

[14] Interview with Alejandro Torres, environmental activist, August 2, 2016; interview with Hector Buiprago, founder of Cantoalagua, July 29, 2016.
[15] Interview with Alejandro Torres, environmental activist, August 2, 2016.
[16] Interview with Tatiana Silva, Corporación SIE, August 3, 2016.
[17] The Mesa Interlocal pressed for municipal budgets to earmark environmental expenditures.
[18] "Los guardines del Tunjuelo," *El Espectador*, October 15, 2009. Interview with Tatiana Silva, SIE, August 3, 2016; Coordinación Asamblea Sur, "La participacion social en la solución de los conflictos del Sur de Bogotá: Cuenca Río Tunjuelo, una mirada integral en la planeacion del territorio," n.d.; interview with Arturo Sanchez, Corporación Madre Tierra, July 25, 2016.
[19] Interview with Tatiana Silva, Corporación SIE, August 3, 2016.

navigation activities in 2003, connecting with national-level youth environmental networks (e.g., Red Juvenil Nacional Ambiental). Two of the most visible and organized groups active within the Southern Territory are SIE Corporación and Casa Asdoas. The SIE Corporation (which translates to the Goddess of Water in Muisca) and Casa Asdoas emphasize ancestral traditions and the concept of Buen Vivir.[20] These groups have led camping river navigation tours for young people since 2000 to raise awareness about river pollution in Bosa, Bogotá.[21] One activist explained that "the navigations established a strong identity with [the river], with the idea that in order to have moral authority to speak about the river one needs to walk beside it" (Ramírez 2010, 2). While grievances and organizational forms have changed over time, the focus on youth campaigns has been a constant in mobilizing environmental action in southern Bogotá.[22]

Table 4.1 shows how bonding mobilization was made up of at least 10 local groups involved in bringing attention to the Bogotá River pollution since the 1990s. The grassroots organizations identified in this table are all members of groups that have themselves been directly impacted by toxic exposure to contamination and that live in the territory in which they have engaged in activism.

Yet the grassroots groups in Table 4.1 were often not distinguishable from NGOs that are discussed in the subsequent section in terms of their demand-making strategies, scale, or number of resources.[23] Both grassroots organizations and formal NGOs engaged in small-scale activism such as tree planting and river navigation, and less so on research or litigation for policy influence. The level of similarity between grassroots organizations (led mostly by activists and directly impacted by the issue area) and NGOs (led mostly by employees and not directly impacted by issue area) for the Bogotá River suggests that the environmental advocacy movement that formed in Colombia was characterized by small-scale, underresourced groups. The

---

[20] Buen Vivir is a concept in Latin American indigenous knowledge that refers to living in harmony with nature rather than dominating nature or removing human presence through conservation. See Kauffman and Martin (2014). A central tenant in Buen Vivir culture is "Do no harm." In Bogotá the concept was seen as rooted in Muisca culture and customs. Interview with Tatiana Silva, Corporacion SIE, August 3, 2016.

[21] See "Casa Asdoas," YouTube, June 10, 2014.

[22] Figure 4.2 is a photograph of a mobilization by the Tunjuelo assemblies, and Figure 4.3 is a photograph of a campaign to protect wildlife during infrastructure updates on the river by the Salitre Working Group (see Table 4.1).

[23] For more on environmental grassroots groups in Bogotá, see Hernández, Flores, and Naranjo (2010).

SLOW HARMS AND CITIZEN ACTION   125

Figure 4.2 Environmental protests, Tunjuelo Assemblies, Sur Tunjuelo, Tunjuelo, Colombia.
Source: *El Espectador*, 2020.

next section turns to whether NGOs and activist public officials were able to bridge grassroots claims to ignite a movement to remediate slow harms on the Bogotá River.

Weak Bridging Mobilization in State and Society

Like the Matanza Riachuelo River in Buenos Aires, grassroots activists in the large territory that bordered the Bogotá River were active and vocal but limited in their ability to aggregate and scale up claims. However, in contrast to the Buenos Aires case, the activist public officials and NGOs that mobilized for the Bogotá River counted on fewer resources and prior collaborations, and thus their *bridging mobilization* was less effective. In particular, the societal bridges within the Bogotá River advocacy network were unable to reorient the historically ignored problem of pollution toward a more universally resonant and urgent issue. The relative weakness of societal bridges on the

Figure 4.3 Resistance campaigns against PTAR Salitre, Bogotá.
Source: Photograph by Veronica Herrera, 2016.

Bogotá River was impacted by unsupportive enabling conditions rooted in Colombia's unresolved and fragmented human rights movement, and the subsequent unstable relationship between NGOs and conservative political administrations.

Weak Enabling Conditions: Human Rights Contested Under Reactionary Conservative Political Administrations

Unlike the Argentina case, the Colombian human rights movement has remained relatively more fragmented and under attack, and thus the human rights frame has not served a unifying role for activists working on the Bogotá River. Human rights movements strengthen under enabling conditions that create an end to human rights abuses, accountability for human rights violators, victim redress, and national reconciliation. These conditions have been elusive in Colombia. The ongoing nature of the Colombian armed conflict, the multiplicity of actors, and the lack of state-sponsored protection for human rights defenders has undermined human rights mobilization.[24] Conservative presidential administrations have played an important role in weakening human rights mobilization through alignments with military and paramilitary interests and commitments to protect extractives investments. This has limited the political capital of human rights groups and their influence on other policy issues, such as slow-moving environmental harms.

The contested political environment within which the human rights movement emerged diminished its potential size and level of consolidation. Human rights activists arose from within a leftist armed resistance which lost thousands of people to state-sponsored violence.[25] Attacks on unarmed civil society swelled during the 1990s, including against organized labor, which had the effect of dampening the development of NGOs (Rochlin 2007, 181). As human rights activism deepened, activists were violently persecuted, becoming themselves victims of the types of human rights violations they were decrying (Tate 2007, 154–61). Human rights activists faced such physical insecurity that one Human Rights Watch observer noted that activists would have to be "painfully naïve or suicidal" to continue to participate (Tate 2007, 156).

Human rights movement building has also been thwarted by internal divisions. Early activists aligned with the Communist Party, and many left-of-center Patriotic Union Party members became human rights activists when the party was attacked by paramilitaries (Tate 2007, 148, 156). Thus, human rights activists have differed on whether to align with the leftist

---

[24] The Colombian armed conflict began during the Cold War when armed guerrilla groups formed (some members originating from the 10-year partisan civil war called La Violencia, 1948–58). Guerrilla leftists called for improved agricultural working conditions and social revolution. These included the Armed Revolutionary Forces of Colombia (FARC), an arm of the Soviet-line Communists that was active in the south (Lee 2012, 30–31); the National Liberation Army, which was financially and ideologically aided by Cuba and active in the northeast; and the Popular Liberation Army, led by Maoist-oriented dissidents and active in areas north of the FARC (Offstein 2003, 103–4). In 1974, a final group formed, the M-19, who were educated, young militants who used armed struggle to promote a social democrat platform and constitutional reform; unlike their rural counterparts, the M-19 were active in cities before disbanding in 1990 and forming the political party Democratic Alliance M-19 (González-Jácome 2018, 98).

[25] The familiar apparatus of repression used by military governments in the Southern Cone remained intact in Colombia in the form of a "dirty war" where union activists, leftist party militants, human rights workers, and representatives of oppositional politics were systematically targeted (Avilés 2001, 32). Military strength and resources swelled with U.S.-backed financing associated with Plan Colombia, and military officials committed grave human rights abuses (e.g., Gallagher 2017, 1683). Yet the worst of the state-sponsored violence was administered by paramilitaries, who were responsible for the majority of 1,969 massacres, resulting in 10,174 deaths recorded between 1994 and 2003, and who are accused of taking over the country's most valuable land through extortion, blackmail, forced sales, and murder and displacing beneficiaries of government-sponsored land reform programs (Ballvé 2013; Arnson 2005, 2, 12).

guerrilla revolutionary project or condemn their actions. In addition, tensions arose as some activist groups formed professional NGOs to access international funds, and others remained underresourced grassroots activists. International funding allowed some NGOs to buy office buildings, hire workers, and achieve a new level of influence that was not widely available to all rights-based NGOs, further dividing the movement (Tate 2007, 152–54).

Numerous human rights agencies within government have been created in Colombia under international pressure and are often staffed by former activists. Yet these agencies have had duplicative roles and poor coordination and are chronically underfunded (Avilés 2001, 47; Tate 2007, 231). State officials have also feared reprisals from abusers seeking to avoid detection; human rights officials have been threatened and attacked (Tate 2007, 230, 215–26). Despite the vast challenges, the Defensoria and other state agencies continue to be staffed in part with public officials who began their careers with NGOs and continue to work to influence human rights policy from within the state. For some public officials, this has meant being dubbed by NGOs as traitors who have gone to work for the enemy (Tate 2007, 250–55).

As international pressure to adopt human rights frameworks increased in Colombia, so have the number of actors to utilize human rights language for their own purpose. For example, in the 1990s, the military created human rights offices to investigate human rights accusations, publishing human rights reports and hosting conferences. Military officers use human rights arguments to defend themselves against accusations of misconduct and argue their right to a fair trial, to defense counsel, and to face their accusers (Tate 2007, 256). By adopting human rights language in military doctrine and framing itself as a victim of human rights violations, the military has helped weaken the power of human rights framing in Colombia. Right-wing NGOs have also used human rights language to defend the rights of those victimized by guerrilla violence, and their media campaigns have gained attention (Tate 2007, 111–12). Human rights framing has been appropriated by all sides of the struggle in Colombia, and thus its moral authority is relatively more contested than in Argentina.

Furthermore, no presidential administration has expanded the power of the left and human rights organizing; instead a prolonged period of conservative presidential administrations has further attacked the movement.[26] The right-of-center Alvaro Uribe administration (2002–10) was notably

---

[26] In 2005, the government promoted its Justice and Peace Law as an example of transitional justice because it created an alternative to penal punishment for paramilitaries with reduced sentences and a

suspicious of human rights organizing, publicly denounced human rights activists as supporters of terrorism, and promoted policies that overrode human rights protections in the name of "democratic security" (Chambers 2013, 119). Uribe's political heir, Juan Manual Santos (2010–18), followed similar policies and supported military commanders and paramilitary interests when negotiating the 2016 peace deal. Iván Duque (2018–22) was harshly criticized for a crackdown by security forces in response to peaceful protests in the 2021 "national strike," prompting rebukes by 500 human rights organizations, including Amnesty International.[27]

Additionally, the 2000s saw growth in the political protection of oil and mining investments under Uribe and subsequent administrations. Compared to Argentina, Colombia's share of extractives in their market is higher, making up 11% of total revenue, 56% of exports, and 5% of GDP (EITI 2018b). The political economy of the country impacts human rights mobilization. Human rights actors were stymied by presidential administrations that courted extractivist industries and squashed the mobilizing power of human rights. Over 700 human rights defenders, particularly those defending land and environment against land-intensive industries, have been killed in Colombia since 2016.[28] The entanglement between conservative political administrations, unresolved armed conflict, and courting of multinational extractive giants has weakened spaces for civil society participation as compared to the Argentina case.

In this context, human rights defenders have struggled for protection and consolidation. Unlike the Matanza Riachuelo case, where environmental mobilization aligned with human rights mobilization, in Colombia rights-based NGOs were not involved in Bogotá River cleanup efforts. The societal bridges, or resourced outsiders, that emerged to participate in the Bogotá remediation case were mostly small, local environmental NGOs that were not otherwise previously connected with each other or state institutions. Thus, they were weaker and less effective in aggregating and scaling up claims for the Bogotá River beyond what the grassroots groups set in motion.

---

future truth commission to provide reparations for victims. The law was critiqued by opponents as a cover for Uribe's strategy to demobilize the paramilitary without sufficiently punishing them for their crimes (Rowen 2017, 96–97).

[27] Amnesty International, "Colombia: Open Letter to President Iván Duque," May 14, 2021.
[28] Human Rights Watch, "Amicus Brief on Killings of Human Rights Defenders in Colombia," April 20, 2021; United Nations Human Rights Office of the Commissioner, "Colombia: Extreme Risks for Rights Defenders Who Challenge Corporate Activity," August 4, 2022.

State-Level Bridges Aggregate and Scale Up Claims

Nevertheless, institutional allies played a role in aggregating grievances and scaling up grassroots claims associated with the Bogotá River's pollution. This section illustrates how activist officials within legal institutions and the Comptroller's Office began to address the problem of slow harms but lacked the support of powerful bridges in society with the necessary resources to help further elevate the visibility of slow harms. State-level institutions lacked embeddedness in a preexisting movement for social change and were not able to draw on the collective ideas, prior shared experiences, and resources that were available to the Argentine bridges. The first significant aggregation of claims about pollution on the Bogotá River occurred through the courts—positioning an activist lower court judge to become the actor most responsible for bridging and scaling up claims—albeit with limited external support.

State Level Bridges: Legal Institutions. Residents impacted by toxic exposure first sought to activate the newly minted right to a clean environment inscribed in the 1991 Constitution through litigation, watchdog groups, and protests. They first filed *tutelas* in the Colombian Constitutional Court claiming that the contamination on the Muña reservoir violated individual fundamental rights as pollutants were sprayed widely by the hydroelectric dam.[29] A judge responded by ordering the hydroelectric company to fumigate the area and build a forest wall intended to block the contamination. As the company dragged its feet, watchdog groups demanded the judge's orders be implemented by filing more legal petitions, and citizens mobilized in mass protests.[30] Legal rulings surrounding individual rights violations had limited success with the Constitutional Court, an institution charged with defending individual fundamental rights as opposed to collective rights.

The successful use of legal institutions—and thus a key element of bridging mobilization—finally took off in the early 2000s via a magistrate judge in the Cundinamarca Administrative Court, Nelly Villamizar, who helped aggregate claims about collective rights and became the most significant bridge

---

[29] "EEB debe limpiar represa del Muña, pero salvo mil millones," *El Tiempo*, July 15, 1993.
[30] "Inspección judicial al Muña," *El Tiempo*, December 5, 1998; "Arresto al gerente de energía," *El Tiempo*, March 28, 1999; "El Muña origina marcha de protesta," *El Tiempo*, August 1, 1998. In 2003, the Constitutional Court reviewed *tutelas* ratified in the Bogotá Superior Court and ordered the hydroelectric company to decontaminate in two years, specifying that "everything that causes damage must be compensated, particularly when these damages threaten collective security and health. "A descontaminar Muña," *El Tiempo*, September 4, 2003.

in slow-harms advocacy for the river.[31] The Administrative Court grouped several *acciones populares* filed by residents; these were litigations alleging the violation of collective rights over the contamination of the hydroelectric Muña Dam.[32] As Magistrate Villamizar explained, after numerous hearings with government entities in 2001–2, everyone insisted that they were not responsible.[33] Villamizar responded by initiating working group sessions on the river, including dozens of government entities, industries, and civil society organizations.

Judge Villamizar rendered a ruling in 2004 (1-479) that found 72 entities responsible for the Bogotá River's contamination, including 42 municipalities and 20 industries (Lamprea 2016, 297). An innovative component of the ruling was that it collectivized the complaints, previously unheard of in administrative law, which instead had tended to focus exclusively on single citizen petitions and their resolution. Judge Villamizar explained, "I made the case large and important, because I got everyone together in the same room, and held them accountable."[34] The ruling stated that the environmental damage was "dispersed" and was caused by both purposeful action and the omission or negligence of state actors (Lamprea 2016, 296–97). The ruling was historic, "without antecedent in the judicial history of the country."[35] In 2014, the Administrative High Court of Colombia (Consejo del Estado) upheld the lower court ruling, and thus the sentence to remediate the Bogotá River became settled law and unappealable. The Consejo del Estado ruling featured 17 working groups, 4 public hearings, and 50 informal interinstitutional meetings.[36] In the High Court Ruling, a much greater

---

[31] Colombia has four high courts: the Constitutional Court, the Supreme Court, the Superior Council of Judicature, and the Council of State (also known as the Administrative High Court of Colombia, or Consejo del Estado). The Administrative Tribunal of Cundinamarca (Tribunal Administrativo de Cundinamarca) is a lower court of the Administrative High Court of Colombia. These courts rule on legal claims brought against government officials and the administrative apparatus of the state. Here *acciones populares* are brought by citizens to petition administrative courts for claims about the violation of collective rights.

[32] In 1992, Sibaté resident Gustavo Moya Ángel initiated an *acción popular* against the Bogotá power company responsible for the hydroelectric Muña Dam. This was the first of many *acciones populares* waged on behalf of Sibaté against the various entities responsible for the decontamination of the Bogotá River and the Muña reservoir. "Cuando el río sueña," *El Espectador*, April 14, 2014; "EEB debe limpiar represa del Muña, pero salvó mil millones," *El Tiempo*, July 15, 1993; "Inspección judicial al Muña," *El Tiempo*, December 5, 1998; "Redacción Cundinamarca; temor por gases del Muña," *El Tiempo*, February 23, 2004.

[33] Interview with Nelly Villamizar, judge, Tribunal Administrativo de Cundinamarca, August 5, 2016.

[34] Interview with Nelly Villamizar, judge, Tribunal Administrativo de Cundinamarca, August 5, 2016.

[35] "Sentencia por el Río Bogotá," *El Tiempo*, August 29, 2004.

[36] Interview with Marco Antonio Velilla Moreno, magistrate, Consejo del Estado, July 28, 2016.

number of public agencies than civil society groups were represented in the work group sessions, a trend that would continue throughout the implementation of the ruling.

State Level Bridges: Comptroller's Office. Another institution that played a role in bridging mobilization was the National Comptroller's Office (Contraloría General de la República), charged with oversight of public sector fiscal expenditures. Constitutional reforms had created *veedurias*, citizen fiscal watchdog groups, which were participatory institutions intended to democratize fiscal oversight of public spending.[37] By the 2000s, this gave rise to the formation of many *veedurias* across all sectors where government funds were being spent, including one created for the Bogotá River.[38]

An activist public official organized 200 public hearings on the Bogotá River in 2007–8, in stadiums, libraries, and town halls throughout the river basin, where approximately 5,000 people participated.[39] In 2009 the Comptroller's Office held three day-long events with the participation of approximately 400 people, called "A Citizen Agenda for Participatory Fiscal Oversight." Participants voiced what local activists had decried for years: "The problem was not [only] the river, but the public sector management of the river. . . . First, a failure of transparency. The collective image is that government management is darker and more corrupt than the river itself. Second, the public apathy over the river, the indifference, the low participation. Third, lack of planning and coordination. Fourth, the weakness of institutional control. And fifth is the lack of coordination between actors."[40] The Comptroller's Office continued to bridge grievances and actors; in 2009, it gathered citizens and public officials in meetings in three locations on the river basin. These public hearings continued from 2010 to 2014, with a total citizen attendance rate of over 800 people.[41] The activist public official who organized these events explained, "We have to change the problem of

---

[37] The legal rights and obligations of *veedurias* were outlined in Constitution Articles 103 and 270 and numerous subsequent laws and decrees, particularly Law 850 in 2003 (Procuraduría General de la Nación de Colombia, n.d., 2–5).

[38] After 2006, incoming comptroller Julio Cesar Turbay Quintero (2006–10) pushed an agenda that included augmenting citizen participation for fiscal control of public spending on environmental problems. According to a document describing the responsibilities of the Comptroller's Office, "the defense of the environment constituted one of the most important issues and actions of this administration" (Contraloría General de la República 2010, 17).

[39] Interview with Marta Luque, Office of the Contraloria General de la Republica, August 2, 2016.

[40] Interview with Marta Luque, Office of the Contraloria General de la Republica, August 2, 2016.

[41] From 2008 to 2014, 178 meetings were held in six municipalities representing the entire river (Contraloría General de la República. n.d.).

indifference, of lack of information, so we do so by fomenting solidarity and a sense of citizen ownership of the problem."[42]

In the process of organizing public hearings along the river basin, the Comptroller's Office connected with the activists who had been involved in the 2002–4 Water Referendum, the We Are the Bogotá River group that had splintered into different local activist projects after the referendum failed. Many of these same grassroots activists became involved in the Comptroller's work. They helped create the Veeduria Network for the Bogotá River (Veeduria Ciudadania Nuestro Rio Bogotá) in 42 municipalities by 2016 and developed varying levels of capacity to influence public policy change on the river, as the following sections illustrate.

Limited Bridges within Society: Local NGOs Struggle to Aggregate and Scale Up Claims

In addition to the activist officials in legal institutions and the Comptroller's Office, several local NGOs also became involved with the Bogotá River, but they had limited ability to aggregate claims beyond what was already occurring inside legal institutions. Table 4.2 shows that six NGOs worked on the river pollution case, but compared with their Argentine counterparts, they possessed fewer of the conditions necessary to be effective bridges for slow harms. While many organizations were enthusiastic and committed, they lacked critical material resources to fund activities and disseminate their expertise and had few preexisting ties with each other or state-level institutions. Furthermore, local NGOs were more narrowly focused on environmental conservation and lacked a unifying set of ideas about how to frame slow harms for broader resonance.

Limited Funding, Staffing, and Expertise Dissemination

Despite their shared interest in the Bogotá River, the local NGOs that became involved had limited resources and were thus unable to disseminate their expertise broadly. None of the NGOs had access to international financing and thus had few material resources with which to fund activities and grow their

[42] Interview with Marta Luque, Office of the Contraloría General de la República, August 2, 2016.

Table 4.2 NGOs involved in the Bogotá River in Colombia (Actors in Bridging Mobilization)

Name	Dates Active	Number of Employees or Activists	Mission	Action Strategies	Judicial Advisory Committee
Green Living Foundation (Fundación al Verde Vivo)	1994–	Employees (3–4)	Reforestation of upper river basin	Tree planting, river navigations, carbon-offset corporate programs; conference organizing	Yes
A Song for Water (Cantoalagua)	2010–	Activists (10 founders, 10 floaters, 400 sister global sites)	Promote education and cultural awareness of water to foster better citizen stewardship	Gather large groups of singers, artists, and activists for ritualistic chants to create sacred space for water, promoting conservation	No
User Association for Renewable Natural Resources and the Defense of the Bogotá River Basin (Asociación de Usuarios de los Recursos Naturales Renovables y Defensa Ambiental de la Cuenca del Rio Bogotá, ASURIO)	2012–	Activists (500 in 2012, 30 in 2016)	Provide technical solutions, hold government accountable for river restoration	Provide technical solutions, advise Sibaté, sanitation treatment plant technologies	Yes

INPRESEC	2012–	1 employee, numerous consultants	Promote the construction of collective and collaborative river basin sustainability in Colombia	Organize small leather industries in Villapinzón, help them with legal defense, upgrade to clean production, award-winning participatory process was nationally recognized by President	Yes
Mother Earth Corporation (Corporación Madre Tierra)	1997–	1–5 Activists	Promote conservation through citizen activism	1997–98 100% Rio Bogotá activities, founded other cooperatives, some media and video, not particularly active now	Yes
Bogotá Wetlands Network (Red de Humedales de la Sabana de Bogotá)	1999–	14 nodes within the Network, membership over 50	Restoration and management of wetlands, rivers, and forests	Cleanups, forestation, education, litigation, lobbying for legislative changes, monthly meetings, *Entre Juncos* newsletter and social media	No

Source: Author's compilation based on various sources, including interviews, groups' self-produced materials, and social media. See appendix for discussion of data collection strategies. Social media information taken from 2017.

membership. Environmental NGOs formed in the 1990s, when Colombia had more access to international development aid and government funding for environmental NGOs; since these financial supports have dried up, local NGOs without international partners tend to lack access to any funding.[43]

For example, as Table 4.2 indicates, Fundación al Verde Vivo has the most fiscal resources of the local NGOs under study, with an office and four employees, yet has been unable to generate a mass membership base similar to Greenpeace's financing model. Verde Vivo relies on tree planting events, corporate sponsorship of carbon-offset programs, and government contracts to finance its operations.[44] Another local NGO, ASURIO, was also unable to generate a mass membership model; when founders tried and failed to make membership subscription-based, one leader lamented, "People were unwilling to sign up if they had to pay."[45] The remaining NGOs involved on the river, INPRESEC, Corporación Madre Tierra, and the Conejera Foundation, have no sources of funding and are structured more like volunteer-oriented grassroots organizations.[46] Furthermore, cash-strapped NGOs sometimes rely on government contracts, as is the case of Verde Vivo, which can create a conflict of interest when trying to hold government accountable.

Some NGOs had important sources of expertise but were limited as organizations due to small membership bases or internal divisions. For example, INPRESEC is staffed by one person, whose work on the river has been more of an advisor to the presiding judge than an effective bridge that connected with social groups widely. ASURIO's membership base has shrunk over time, from 500 in 2012 to fewer than 30 by 2016. ASURIO has always had a lot of expertise, as they are run by engineers with strong opinions about technical

---

[43] After Rio 1992, a wave of environmental NGOs formed in Colombia, the majority taking on the "Ecofondo" model. The Ecofondo was designed to be the NGO majority in internationally imposed debt-restructuring deals, so it developed as having NGO and government representatives and flourished throughout the country. After the 1990s, environmental groups vied for international financing, from programs such as the debt swap program and Plan Colombia, and the large ones became professionalized into bureaucratic NGOs. By the early 1990s it was estimated that over 500 NGOs had formed that worked on the environment (Gaviria 1992, 76). By 1994, at least 370 NGOs were affiliated with Ecofondos (O'Brien 1995, 21). Some have criticized the Ecofondo model for sometimes consisting of groups that have little environmental commitment and are interested only in accessing fiscal resources. Tobasura Acuna (2003, 113–14, 118) estimates that as many as 3,000 entities formed NGO-like structures to capture resources from Ecofondo's model (O'Brien 1995, 15–16, 20–22; Anonymous interview, 2016).

[44] Interview with Fernando Vasquez, director, Fundación al Verde Vivo, July 18, 2016.

[45] Anonymous interview, 2016.

[46] Figure 4.5 is a photograph of a brochure to promote environmental awareness created by Corporación Madre Tierra in its early years, when it had access to international funding through Ecofondo.

Figure 4.4 Cantoalgua ceremony, Bogotá.
Source: Photograph by Veronica Herrera, 2016.

solutions to pollution remediation. Yet as a small number of people control agenda setting, ASURIO has suffered from internal divisions and leadership breakdowns, and in 2016 the group split into two factions that are locked in a dispute over who legitimately represents the organization.

While rights-based NGOs in Argentina were able to work closely with the Ombudsman's Office and bring preexisting relationships with public officials into their work on river remediation, in Bogotá societal bridges were more limited. Few local NGOs had previously developed relationships with public officials that they could bring to bear on the river pollution case. ASURIO's initial leadership was "unwilling to work with politicians."[47] Cantoalagua was involved in gathering signatures for the 2007 constitutional referendum for the right to water, but they are mostly apolitical and shy away from policy matters.[48] Verde Vivo relied on government contracts from CAR and thus has political relationships but was not well positioned to hold these same officials accountable for their role in overseeing river remediation.

---

[47] Anonymous interview, 2016.
[48] Interview with Hector Buiprago, Cantoalagua, July 29, 2016. A motto that appears on their website is "We are not for the right or the left, we are for the earth!" (No somos de derecha ni de izquierda, somos de la tierra!). Figure 4.4 is a photograph of a water blessing ceremony by Cantoalgua.

Figure 4.5 "You are made from Water and so will be your Children." Arturo Sanchez, Corporación Madre Tierra campaign pamphlet.
Source: Photograph by Veronica Herrera, 2016.

The most significant societal bridge was the Conejera Foundation, a grassroots organization turned NGO, listed in Table 4.1 and discussed earlier. Once a grassroots family affair, the Conejera Foundation became a professionalized NGO with diverse expertise in law, biology, and conservation sciences, and emerged as a leader in the river pollution issue once it became judicialized. The Conejera Foundation also belongs to a broader network called the Red de Humedales de la Sabana de Bogotá, an umbrella group of 14 wetlands organizations which have engaged in numerous environmental projects in the city. The Conejera Foundation also has extensive relationships with city officials created over a long period of collaborations since the 1990s.[49]

NGOs Lack Unifying Frame and Prior Shared Experiences

Local NGOs involved in the Bogotá River pollution case were environmentalists narrowly focused on the problem at hand. They lacked a shared language, frame, and background with which to recast the problem of slow harms in a new light. The language they used to talk about the river pollution reflected diverse environmental goals, such as improving biodiversity and reforestation (e.g., Fundación Humedal Conejera, Fundación al Verde Vivo), generating technical solutions to complex infrastructure challenges (e.g., ASURIO), and raising spiritual awareness of the human connection to nature (e.g., Cantoalagua). These frames were distinct from one another and lacked an ideological anchor to unite them. While one NGO director said, "We are interested not in one claim, but rather the twenty claims, those of the collective,"[50] these NGOs had limited tools with which to reframe pollution in a collective manner, and their focus on environmental conservation frames failed to resonate broadly.

Before some of these NGOs started attending the working groups convened by Judge Villamizar, they had rarely collaborated. When asked to map their professional relationships, each of the NGOs on the judicial advisory committee revealed that its collaborative work had begun largely after the court ruling.[51] These NGOs continued to approach the different issues surrounding the river basin in an isolated and fragmented manner even when the judge convened the judicial advisory committee on which many of these NGOs sat.

These groups were disconnected not only from one another but also from a larger movement for change in Colombia. Most were not connected to national-level environmental NGOs (except for the Conejera Foundation, which had broad connections), nor did any national-level environmental NGO become involved in the Bogotá River case. The NGOs in Table 4.2 were

---

[49] Jhon Barros, "Especial: Así nació el movimiento ciudadano que salvo a los humedales de Bogotá," *Semana*, November 11, 2020.
[50] Interview with Fernando Vasquez, director, Fundacion al Verde Vivo, July 18, 2016.
[51] See the appendix for more on mapping exercises during interviews.

not involved with human rights groups in Colombia, nor did any human rights groups in Colombia become involved in the Bogotá River case. The Colombian human rights movement has grown in a weakened and stagnated manner amid the armed conflict, and thus compared to its Argentine counterpart did not develop the social capital and political influence that would have potentially aided environmental causes had these two issues been more forcefully linked for the Bogotá River.

Lacking a shared set of experiences from a history of collaborative work, these NGOs worked with a much more limited set of alliances and organizational tools. Once they were convened by the presiding Cundinamarca Administrative Court judge Villamizar when forming the judicial advisory committee, these local NGOs—relatively weak and fragmented compared to the Argentina case—took their marching orders directly from the Administrative Court.

Weak Bridges Struggle to Build Monitoring Capacity after Judicialization

Weak bridging mobilization was evident in monitoring efforts following the High Court ruling for remediation of the Bogotá River. Bridges in both state and society struggled to hold government officials responsible for complying with their cleanup and regulatory obligations. Societal bridges were relatively weak and very dependent on state intermediaries. These challenges are evident when examining three accountability-seeking routes: the judicial advisory committee, citizen watchdog groups (*veedurias*), and the work of the Public Prosecutor's Office. These three efforts have been fragmented, poorly coordinated, and lacked, among other things, a strong advocacy network that could bring sufficient resources to bear on the problem and have more influence within the media, public opinion, and public policy circles.

Judicial Advisory Committee

As in the Buenos Aires case, the historic ruling to remediate the Bogotá River in 2004 was accompanied by the creation of a judicial advisory committee (called a citizen verification committee, *comité de verificación*) to help oversee the ruling's implementation.[52] The committee was composed by Judge Villamizar of NGOs and a branch of the Public Prosecutor.[53] The selection process of the NGOs was ad hoc: the presiding judge chose NGOs she observed attend the public hearings held prior to 2004. One NGO leader said, "She chose those of us she felt she could trust."[54] The organizations included leaders from INPRESEC, ASOMUÑA, a business association in Sibaté,[55] la Fundación al Verde Vivo, Girardotemos, la Fundación Humedal de la Conejera, and the groups SIE, Movimiento por la Vida, Corporación Madre Tierra, la Fundación Amigos del Planeta, and la Fundación Ambiental Alto Magdalena (Tribunal Administrativo de Cundinamarca 2004, 459–60). Only some of these organizations are listed in Tables 4.1 and 4.2 because only a portion of the organizations identified in the judicial ruling as members of the judicial advisory committee went on to participate in it.[56]

The judicial advisory committee was weaker than its Argentine counterpart, by both institutional design and membership. Unlike the Argentina case, where the committee meets independently and sets its own agenda, in Colombia the judicial advisory committee is overseen by and reports to the administrative judge presiding over the case. The more limited autonomy of the Bogotá committee is further exacerbated by the weak preexisting ties between the NGOs. Their limited prior history of collaborative work or legal case of their own on behalf of the river (e.g., they did not independently bring their own litigation to the court or become third parties to existing litigation) makes them less likely to coordinate outside of the committee.[57] The

[52] Verification committees are outlined in Law 472 1998, Article 34.
[53] The ruling also states that environmental and agrarian prosecutors (*procuradores judiciales ambientales y agrarios*) in each municipality under the jurisdiction of the ruling were to also serve on the committee (Tribunal Administrativo de Cundinamarca 2004, 460).
[54] Anonymous interview, July 26, 2016.
[55] ASOMUÑA is not listed in Table 4.2 because it is a business association rather than an NGO. This small business association is financed by dues that are paid by small industry and businesses in Sibaté, one of the communities most impacted from the river's pollution. Their president, Walter O'Campo, has been very active on the judicial advisory committee.
[56] For example, Amigos del Planeta Fundación Ambiental Alta Magdalena and Movimiento por la Vida never participated beyond the public hearings, and despite being named on both rulings as formal members of the judicial advisory committee, never attended meetings. Sometimes one NGO created a "shell NGO" for a specific alternative purpose but was run by the same member. For example, Fundación Amigos del Planeta was formed in 1999 by the Fundación Humedal de la Conejera members in order to fight a legal battle over wetlands with Mayor Peñalosa; despite being named in the ruling as a separate NGO, its members are the same as the Conejera. Similarly, Girardotemos was the legal entity of one activist, Hernando Robles, who later formed ASURIO. Both Girardotemos and ASURIO are listed as part of the judicial advisory committee in 2004. Interview with Medardo Galindo, Fundación Conejera, July 19, 2016.
[57] The one important exception is the legal work of the Fundacón Humedal la Conejera, which acted on their own and not on behalf of the committee. They (under the name Fundación Amigos del Planeta) asked the judge to add them as third parties to the *acción popular*, which is one of the reasons

committee is overly dependent on the will of a single judge, which creates periodic conflicts over accusations of abuse of power and makes the committee fully dependent on the will and tenure of one individual.[58]

From its 2004 inception, the Colombian judicial advisory committee did not have the benefit—and resources—of a horizontal accountability agency such as the Ombudsman's Office to convene, organize, and provide autonomy from Court directives, nor did the Public Prosecutor play this role.[59] In this context of fragmented agendas and weak support from other horizontal accountability institutions, the NGO membership of the committee has changed considerably over the years, with NGOs being added or removed from the 2004 and 2014 versions of the committee.

Despite their hard work, the judicial advisory committee has faced numerous challenges in their efforts to build monitoring capacity. Some problems are the same as those in the Argentina case; for example, the Court did not give the committee funds for transportation or administrative expenses. One interviewee lamented that although the overseeing judge had the authority to decide how to fund the oversight, and that typically oversight is financed by the guilty parties in a suit, Judge Villamizar had opted to not press guilty parties to pay for these expenses.[60] Another challenge was related to the "soft power" that the committee wielded. One participant observation session of committee oversight activities found full attendance by the seven active civil society organizations (see Tables 4.1 and 4.2), but only one of the many government agencies that had been called to the oversight meeting actually attended, the Botanical Garden, which had the least amount of direct responsibility for the river's contamination.[61] Even though some groups, such as the *veedurias*, noted that due to court backing they were now in a better position to cajole government agencies to share information than

---

Amigos del Planeta were put on the judicial advisory committee as a distinct NGO. Furthermore, in 2005 the Conejera (under the name Fundación Amigos del Planeta) appealed the ruling arguing against the location and number of sanitation treatment plants being proposed in the sentence and asked the Consejo del Estado to consider other alternatives based on an environmental impact assessment. Interview with Medardo Galindo, Fundación Conejera, July 19, 2016.

[58] The committee met for two and a half years before being dismissed in 2006 due to the presiding judge fighting a corruption charge of which she was ultimately resolved. The committee was mandated to be reconvened after the 2014 Consejo del Estado ruling, only meeting again in 2016.

[59] In 2014, the Consejo del Estado ruling added other horizontal accountability institutions, such as the Ombudsman and additional delegates from the Public Prosecutor's Office to serve on the judicial advisory committee (Consejo del Estado 2014, 1246). As of interviewing in 2016, the Ombudsman's Office had yet to convene or participate on the committee.

[60] Anonymous interview.

[61] Participation observation of Judicial Advisory Committee Oversight Meeting, August 2, 2016.

prior to being on the committee, it seemed that it was more difficult to secure attendance by government agencies in judicial advisory committee meetings if the judge herself was not in attendance.[62]

Fiscal Oversight Route: Citizen Watchdog Groups

State-level bridges—in the form of the Comptroller's Office—allied with citizen watchdog groups (*veedurias*) to seek accountability over public spending on infrastructure related to river remediation. The *veedurias*' capacity for holding government accountable is limited by several common problems. First, *veedurias* are overly dependent on the material and organizational resources of the Comptroller's Office; one public official told me, "If the Comptroller's Office does not convene people, it doesn't happen."[63] Many community members lack resources necessary for travel to and from meetings; thus the initial participatory deliberation meetings organized by the Comptroller's Office were much more well attended because the Comptroller's Office did the organizational heavy lifting and facilitated transportation.

When *veedurias* act alone, they are much less effective. Actual oversight meetings, where *veedurias* are to gather independently, document infractions, and communicate with appropriate authorities, are not funded and are thus much more difficult to imbue with real monitoring capacity. The *veedurias* suffer from information asymmetries due to limited access to government data and limited power to enforce compliance with requests for sharing government information (Herrera and Mayka 2020, 7).

Veedurias are also subject to strongman boss rule. The agenda of these citizen watchdog groups centers on a small number of people, sometimes just one. In these cases, leaders use the group to push an agenda—whether partisan or otherwise—and fail to engage in deliberative consultation with members.[64] Some interviewees noted that the *veeduria* leadership on the judicial advisory committee did not represent the opinions of the wider base of *veeduria* membership.

---

[62] Interview with Jorge Achury, Red de Veedurías, 21 July 2016.
[63] Anonymous interviews, July–August, 2016.
[64] For example, in a WhatsApp chat with *veedurias* from Chia, Cundinamarca, where I belonged and received thousands of notifications in 2016–18, the group was dominated by the personal agenda of one community leader who rarely convened meetings or sought community input. Many initial invitees asked to be removed from further communications.

Finally, in the cases where *veedurias* identify public sector spending malfeasance and provide photographic documentation, their ability to generate accountability is dependent on the government agencies to which they send requests. For example, farmers and neighborhood association leaders that formed a *veeduria* in Mesitas de Colegio (in El Colegio), a rural community 223 kilometers from Bogotá, note that despite their documentation, photographs, and petitions, "there are no authorities here," and say, "We participate, and document, but . . . the authorities . . . they don't listen to us."[65] In some regions, *veedurias* have suffered threats to their lives given the high social violence against activists in Colombia.[66] Thus, the monitoring capacity of *veedurias* is frequently fragile and uneven unless boosted by partnerships with other government agencies.

The Public Prosecutor and the Challenge of Sanctioning

State-level bridges—in the form of the Public Prosecutor—have worked with the *veedurias* to boost monitoring capacity, yet this initiative has also been plagued with important challenges. Charged with prosecuting public officials for misconduct and noncompliance with the ruling, the Public Prosecutor's Office is another route for seeking accountability through removal of public officials or levying fines. One attorney in the Public Prosecutor's Office stressed that accessing information has been difficult because mayors provide inaccurate data or dozens of boxes of files to deter him from identifying relevant information. In these cases, the *veedurias* are his "eyes and ears": "I don't trust the public officials. When I investigate the claims made by some *veedores*, they are often true."[67]

Other challenges include the limited education and experience that many mayors have. An official in the Prosecutor's Office lamented, "[Mayors] often do not understand how government works . . . and what their obligations are under the law."[68] Whether due to noncompliance or outright criminal activity (such as corruption, particularly through the kickbacks or outright theft of funds for construction projects), mayors are difficult to prosecute. Describing the theft of funds for a sanitation treatment plant on the last day

---

[65] Interviews with seven community leaders in Mesitas de Colegio, Cundinamarca, July 24, 2016.
[66] "¿Quién ve por las veedurías ciudadanas?," *El Heraldo*, August 11, 2013.
[67] Interview with Jorge Castillo, Procuraduria General de la Nacion, July 29, 2016.
[68] Interview with Jorge Castillo, Procuraduria General de la Nacion, July 29, 2016.

of a mayor's administration in Chia, Cundinamarca, the Public Prosecutor's Office attorney said he lacked the resources to acquire initial information and relied on the *veedurias* to keep him abreast of developments. Officials in the Public Prosecutor's Office lament that the institution had yet to provide more staff to monitor the dozens of public officials whose municipalities are implicated in the Bogotá River ruling and to bring charges. "We need to open disciplinary investigations on all of them . . . the forty-seven mayors, the six ministers, all of them, because they have not complied. It is only through force that they will begin to comply with their obligations."[69] The Public Prosecutor's Office continued to develop plans for organizing civil society and the *veedurias* into committees that could play a bigger role in seeking accountability for compliance with the ruling. However, given limited staff and resources, efforts to organize citizen oversight beyond existing channels had yet to take off.

Stagnated Policy Shift in Slow-Harms Remediation

Although the Bogotá River had strong bonding mobilization from grassroots activists, the relatively weak bridging between local environmental NGOs and public institutions was insufficient to spark a comprehensive policy shift for the Bogotá River pollution crisis. The weakness of weak bridges in society was influenced by a fractured legacy of human rights mobilization and conservative political administrations that weakened rights-based NGOs.

Here I review how weak bridging mobilization for the Bogotá River, compared to the Buenos Aires case, has led to a "stagnated" reform process, with lower institutional innovation and financial investments and very little regulatory capacity to enforce pollution standards. Unlike reforms in the Matanza Riachuelo River case, policy shifts for the Bogotá River did not include a new river basin institution with resources and authority to police and fine polluters. Instead, existing public sector agencies responsible for the pollution crisis are the actors overseeing cleanup efforts with little accountability. While some advancements have been made since the Administrative Court rulings, the Bogotá River remediation process remains underresourced and lacks transparency. The process has not included significant spaces for citizen participation and the judicial advisory committee has been kept at arm's

---

[69] Interview with Jorge Castillo, Procuraduria General de la Nacion, July 29, 2016.

length compared to the Buenos Aires case. NGOs and activist public officials continue to struggle to influence policy change and hold polluters and responsible public sector agencies accountable.

Institutional Smoke and Mirrors. While new institutions have been created to oversee pollution redress, these have not been imbued with sufficient authority, resources, or citizen oversight mechanisms. For example, the Administrative Court ordered the creation of a river basin authority, the Strategic Committee for the Bogotá River Basin (Consejo Estratégico de la Cuenca Hidrográfica del Río Bogotá, CECH), but unlike ACUMAR's institutional design in Argentina, CECH was composed of the very institutions that were condemned in the ruling.[70] Being both judge and jury is problematic and allows the condemned institutions to limit the participation of civil society actors. NGOs on the judicial advisory committee lamented their exclusion from this important decision-making space, noting, "The decision-making will happen there—by the agencies that were found guilty in the case—and we are not there. . . . How can we monitor if we can't participate in the decision-making?"[71] Furthermore, the CECH is intended to be temporary and give way to a permanent river basin authority, but the creation of such a space has been repeatedly delayed. Cundinamarca CAR, which has been in place for decades, is the primary agency overseeing the remediation of the river, but only in the areas under its jurisdiction (which excludes Bogotá).

Access to information about the pollution remediation progress has been limited. Perhaps in an effort to create the appearance of social accountability, the CECH created an online environmental observatory, ORARBO, which is an information-sharing portal that provides pollution metrics on the Bogotá River. This observatory is intended to "democratize information" and serve as a way for civil society groups to identify environmental problems and share information. Yet the observatory is composed primarily of government agencies named as guilty parties in the Administrative Court ruling. The number of government agencies officially recognized by ORARBO, 62, far outweighs the number of civil society groups, 3. Paradoxically, polluting

---

[70] These included the Environmental Ministry (Ministerio de Ambiente y Desarrollo Sostenible), the Bogotá water utility (EAB), the Bogotá Department of the Environment (Secretaria Distrital de Ambiente), the Cundinamarca Secretariat of the Environment, CAR, and mayors from the municipalities of Cajicá and La Mesa. Other invited guests included the National Comptroller (both the environmental office and the citizen participation office), and the Public Prosecutor.

[71] Interviews with Medardo Galindo, Fundación Conejera, July 19, 2016; interview with Arturo Sanchez, Corporación Madre Tierra, July 25, 2016.

industries are also on the ORARBO,[72] and only two of the previously mentioned NGOs, ASURIO and the Conejera Foundation, are listed as part of the oversight mechanism. It is unlikely that government agencies, without external pressure, will voluntarily provide access to information about progress delays or backtracking, and NGOs are outnumbered. Thus, citizen groups have had limited space and leverage to hold public sector agencies and polluting industries accountable.

Limited Financial Investments. Rather than imbue new institutions with authority and resources, as had been the case for the Matanza Riachuelo, existing institutions relied on new responsibility reallocation and limited financial commitments to complete public works projects for the Bogotá River. The Cundinamarca CAR was charged with updating the Salitre sanitation treatment plant (northwest of the city) and recuperating the river's flood zones. These tasks were tackled with a modest World Bank loan disbursed in 2011 for US$250 million (World Bank 2010), a much smaller financial commitment than those made for the Matanza Riachuelo River.[73] EAAB, the Bogotá water utility, is charged with finishing the wastewater main connections that will take residential wastewater from neighborhoods to the sanitation treatment plants once construction is complete on the latter. These wastewater mains (*interceptores*) have been under construction for so long that their use life is expiring, and many worry that they will be unusable once they are inaugurated.[74] EAAB is also charged with finalizing the construction of a second wastewater treatment plant, the Canoas plant, that will treat Soacha's wastewater and 70% of Bogotá's. These projects have been criticized by those concerned that population growth following the initial design of the plants have made them underequipped to provide full sanitation coverage. NIMBY siting protests have also surrounded the PTAR Salitre plant development, a photograph of this campaign is seen earlier in this chapter in Figure 4.3. Critics complain that the plant design has had little public deliberation or input.[75]

Constrained Regulatory Capacity. The Bogotá River does not have a river basin authority with the financial resources that the Matanza Riachuelo River

---

[72] El Observatorio Regional Ambiental y de Desarrollo Sostenible del Río Bogotá (ORARBO), http://orarbo.gov.co/es/directorio-actores-ambientales, accessed May 28, 2020.
[73] Interview with Anibal Acosta, administrative director, CAR, August 2, 2016. CAR, the Bogotá Department of the Environment, and the EAAB water utility signed an accord to split responsibilities between themselves to attend to the ruling in 2007 called Convenio 171.
[74] Interview with Susana Muhamed, secretary of environment under Gustavo Petro, July 27, 2016.
[75] Multiple interviews.

developed, and thus regulatory capacity has been much lower. Progress to date has largely sidestepped confronting politically powerful private-sector interests. Few interviewed were willing to discuss industrial discharge and the thorny task of enforcing regulation. CAR does not have an industrial regulation team with inspectors, in contrast to ACUMAR in Argentina.

Regulating industry is not a primary task of the CAR agency, and there is no coordinated government body at the regional or federal level that has taken on this role. Instead, fragmented responses abound. For example, CAR has instated drones to monitor effluents throughout the river's long trajectory,[76] but data gathering alone—without the political will to shut down politically powerful polluters—has yielded weak results. CAR has made some progress, but it has been based on a narrow set of goals (restoring flood zones, removing 8 million tons of solid waste, constructing the Salitre plant) and has avoided addressing the pollutant discharge levels because doing so is not within its mandated tasks.[77] Judicial advisory committee members insisted that the judicial proceedings largely sidestepped industry and the energy company accused of environmental damages in the Muña Resevoir, EMGESA, despite their repeated pleas to hold these actors accountable.[78] CAR does not have the authority to interfere with the Ministry of Mines and Energy, which authorized the 24 mining sites, some of which are tied up in litigation over how they impact river pollution.[79] The political battles between the state—and perhaps also the judiciary—and powerful private-sector interests in mining, energy production, and some manufacturing have largely been avoided. Instead, CAR and the presiding judge have left these regulatory battles to municipal authorities.

Mayors vary greatly in both their interest in regulating industry and their capacity to do so. In the tannery region of Villapinzón, where the river begins, pressure from the Administrative Court ruling has helped to push for more regulatory measures against small tanneries. Small-scale polluters, which have limited political power, have been vilified, shut down, and fined. Larger polluting tanneries with more resources have upgraded to greener production processes and invested in sanitation treatment technologies. Recently upgraded tanneries complain that many smaller operations

---

[76] "Con drones y cámaras vigilan el Río Bogotá las 24 horas: La CAR Cundinamarca y Codaltec instalaron 14 torres de control para monitorear el afluente," *El Tiempo*, May 17, 2019.

[77] "Avanzan las obras de planta para sanear el 50% del río Bogotá," *Conexion capital*, October 10, 2019.

[78] Interview with Medardo Galindo, Fundacion Conejera, July 19, 2016.

[79] Zonas de Mineria en la Sabana de Bogotá, Angelicalozano.com.

continue to operate clandestinely and produce lower priced leatherware because they ignore new environmental regulations.[80] Indeed, one small-scale tannery owner told me, "They shut me down, but I work at night or on the weekends."[81] Closer to Bogotá, city officials stress that they have shut down 23 leather tanneries.[82] In explaining the closing of polluting industries in Bogotá in 2016, a mayor's aide said, "[T]hese types of actions . . . are focused on complying with the Sentence from the Consejo del Estado that ordered the recuperation of the river."[83] Clearly the ruling has created some momentum for change in some parts of the river, but it remains to be seen whether the weak and fragmented accountability structures that currently oversee the river restoration process are enough to tackle this wicked policy problem.

Limited Accountability and Participation. The Administrative Court ruling has created more news coverage and increased public debate and visibility over the Bogotá River. Media coverage following the 2014 ruling shone a spotlight on the right to a clean environment. For example, the newspapers *El Tiempo* and *El Espectador* ran blogs for the river, which reported updates to compliance with the ruling from different government agencies. Artists and musicians have created benefit concerts and annual river navigations, and the city made May 12 the annual Day of the River, signaling that the work of grassroots organizations and legal institutions has created more visibility for change (Herrera and Mayka 2020, 9).

Yet the amount of accountability and citizen input is significantly more limited than that for the Matanza Riachuelo River remediation process. Government agencies continue to limit access to information, and the judicial advisory committee has had little impact on bringing shortcomings and delays to light or championing rights of communities impacted by toxins or relocations. For example, CAR relocated an impacted riverine community in El Porvenir in the municipality of La Moscera, which included 188 families and small businesses. In this community, 45 small businesses and 25 families were waste pickers, a significantly smaller number than those on the Matanza Riachuelo riverbanks due perhaps to the topography of Bogotá and the rural nature of much of the Bogotá River (World Bank 2010, 17). Interviews with CAR social workers who oversaw the relocation stressed the

---

[80] Anonymous interview, 2016, Villapinzón.
[81] Anonymous interview, 2016, Bogotá.
[82] "Por contaminar el Río Bogotá, sellan 23 curtiembres," *El Tiempo*, November 18, 2018.
[83] "Sellan empresas que contaminan el agua en Bogotá," *El Espectador*, October 16, 2016.

care with which relocations were conducted, that residents now owned the title to the new property, that residents were living in much better conditions and further removed from toxic contamination.[84] Yet interviews inside of the new compound revealed that neighbors now lived further apart from one another in a gated community, and small mom-and-pop stores now experienced no foot traffic and were financially struggling.[85] Unlike the judicial advisory committee in Argentina (Cuerpo Colegiado), the judicial advisory committee in Colombia was not involved in facilitating citizens' voices in the relocation conditions or compensations for impacted communities.

The historic sentence to remediate the Bogotá River helped put into motion some policy actions that had previously been mired in paralysis. It helped create more urgency for some government agencies to attend to remediation changes, such as CAR, EAAB, and the Bogotá Department of the Environment. However, the sanctioning authority of the court is limited when it is just a reflection of a beleaguered activist judge and a small number of underresourced public servants—the weakness of other potential bridges in society stands in sharp contrast to the more successful case of reform in Argentina, showing how strong bonds with weak bridges can limit slow harms remediation.

Evaluating Alternative Explanations in the Colombia Case

I have argued that a stagnated policy shift in slow harms remediation occurred for the Bogotá River due to weak bridging mobilization from and between activist public officials and NGOs that lacked both material resources and histories of collaboration. These weak bridges for slow harms were influenced by prior periods of weak human rights mobilization and conservative political administrations in Colombia. Resourced bridges are critical for connecting local grievances about slow harms to the state. How well do alternative explanations about environmental mobilization hold up for explaining the level of policy shift for the Bogotá River?

Did precipitating events brought about by natural disasters shape policy changes toward river pollution remediation? In Bogotá, just as in Buenos Aires, flooding is a periodic problem, exacerbated by La Niña weather

---

[84] Interview with Laura Olier, CAR consultant, August 9, 2016.
[85] Anonymous interview, 2016.

patterns. For example, in 2011 Bogotá experienced the largest flood in 67 years, impacting 95% of Cundinamarca and 30,000 hectares of land.[86] Floods have impacted river policy in Bogotá: the river's swelling volume following impacts from climate change have caused engineers to begin eliminating manmade canals and increasing the river's natural flood plains in some portions of its 347-kilometer trajectory. These changes have been partially financed by a World Bank (2010, 54) loan dispersed in 2010. However, managing flood zones does not equate to changing the chemical composition of a river. Because flooding is an ongoing problem that most impacts a small number of low-income communities living in flood-prone zones that are often low-value land, floods do not create urgency among the entire population in Bogotá.

For those who are impacted by flooding, the cases here show how social mobilization can be spurred by catastrophic events. For example, extensive grassroots organizing occurred in Tunjuelo after the devastating flood of 2002. Many activists, especially youth groups, joined social fronts to draw attention to the ensuing sanitation crisis caused by flooding, and river navigations highlighted pollution remediation as a central concern. While environmental mobilization was aided by flooding, public officials tended to deliver haphazard disaster relief rather than long-term upgrades.[87] Thus, while natural disasters may sometimes activate grassroots collective action, all else being equal, flooding is unlikely to ignite more government policy attention.

As for the postmaterialist thesis, like low-income communities on the urban peripheries of Buenos Aires, working-class communities also became "accidental environmentalists" in Bogotá. Working-class communities mobilized for flood relief, but in the process also became concerned with contaminated riverways and sewage infrastructure in neighborhoods near the Tunjuelo River. Working-class activists included pollution remediation in their demands for water and wastewater service access. In Suba, Bogotá, while the Conejera Foundation began as a middle-class group, wetlands protection initiatives grew to many other communities, several of which were working class, through the Bogotá Wetlands Network (Red de Humedales de la Sabana de Bogotá). As in Greater Buenos Aires, in Bogotá communities made more vulnerable by toxic exposure did develop environmental

---

[86] "Emergencia por río Bogotá, una de las peores de la historia," *Semana*, May 18, 2011.
[87] "Bogotá, con el agua al techo," *El Tiempo*, June 10, 2002.

concern. These communities did not typically live in extreme poverty, and they also had local leadership that helped activate environmental concern. The grassroots communities where environmental concern developed were also not ones with high levels of migrancy but instead had long-standing ties with neighbors. Therefore, class was not the definitive factor in explaining which communities mobilized around environmental concern, as both lower- and middle-income communities moved to organize around harms that impacted them.

Environmental concern was not primarily led by political parties in Colombia, where parties have been conservative and left-of-center administrations have been rare. In Bogotá, conservative administrations were historically beholden to urban growth machines that prioritized development over conservation. The most environmentally oriented Bogotá mayor was Gustavo Petro (2012–15), former guerrilla fighter and M-19 member and the first leftist mayor who sought to challenge entrenched neoliberal policymaking in transit, housing, and environmental protections. Petro moved to regulate the real estate industry to protect the city's wetlands and became embroiled in several political conflicts with entrenched conservative elites. His plans were cut short when he was contentiously recalled from office, an effort organized by conservative political coalitions at the local and national levels (Eaton 2020, 7–9). Environmental activists involved in Bogotá River remediation efforts supported the Petro administration but have a general sense that elected officials are frequently problems to be circumvented. One activist noted, "When administrations come to power and seek to disrupt our environmental work, we just wait them out. We file lawsuits, organize, and lay low. If we can't work with them, we just wait. We will be here in the long run, and they will only be in power for a short time."[88] In Bogotá, as in Buenos Aires, environmental activists were only weakly connected to political parties, if at all.

Political mobilization around the environment has been a halfhearted and weak electoral strategy in Colombia. The Green Party (Partido Verde) was founded in 2009 with an ecological mandate, although its positions have been only thinly centered, if at all, on environmental issues. Leaders such as Antanas Mockus have had electoral success, but their policies did not further environmental initiatives, even when Mockus was mayor of Bogotá (1995–97, 2001–3). Gustavo Petro, elected president in 2020 with a platform

[88] Interview with Medardo Galindo, Fundación Conejera, August 2, 2016.

of environmental justice, is now best poised to further an environmental agenda if he can create the political collaborations at the national level that eluded him during his mayoral administration.

The strength of legal institutions is another potential explanatory factor for the policy changes that have occurred on the Bogotá River; after all, the Administrative High Court ruling sparked important changes after a long period of public sector apathy. Does the strength of legal institutions determine policy shifts for pollution remediation? If so, we would expect the Bogotá River case to have had high levels of policy expansion for slow harms comparable to the Matanza Riachuelo River. Colombia's legal institutions are unusually robust, and Colombian courts have a high level of capacity and judicial autonomy and low barriers to citizen engagement through litigative tools inscribed in the 1991 Constitution, such as the *tutela* and the *acción popular* (Wilson 2009, 61; Rodríguez-Garavito and Rodríguez-Franco 2015, 12–13). Some organizations, such as the Conejera Foundation, have used a full array of litigative tools to achieve smaller environmental victories, such as wetlands preservation, showing how Colombia's legal institutions can work in support of environmental protections. Judicial assertiveness was also present: the activist lower court judge Villamizar took on the ruling as a reform project with which she identified deeply. (She was frequently called the "mother of the river.")[89] Her commitment was a form of judicial assertiveness despite lacking training in environmental law. Yet the Bogotá River case shows how the strength of legal institutions and actors is insufficient for slow-harms policy change.

While the Colombian Administrative High Court generated an innovative legal ruling with grassroots input for the Bogotá River, the much more limited role societal bridges played in it is notable. In Argentina, societal bridges developed a collaborative workshop on river pollution whose report influenced the ruling, and then sat on the judiciary committee afterward; in Bogotá, bridges' roles were more circumscribed and civil society was repeatedly shut out. Thus, the ability of the Court to ensure compliance with the ruling has been much more limited. In Argentina and Colombia, two countries with very strong legal opportunity structures, judicial assertiveness, and two High Court rulings mandating river remediation, the key difference in compliance with the legal rulings has been the strength of bridging

---

[89] "Nelly Villamizar, la poderosa magistrada que prohibió las marchas," *Lasillavacia.com*, June 17, 2021.

mobilization. Legal rulings are only as strong as the surrounding support of other actors in society and supportive institutions that can influence the content and oversight of litigated policy instruments. In particular, resourced actors with legacies of prior collaborative work and united rights-based goals (e.g., NGOs, activist public officials, and rights-based institutions) can imbue judicial rulings with the oversight, pressure, and demands for transparency necessary to improve compliance with legal rulings.

The Challenge of Strong Bonds with Weak Bridges on the Bogotá River

The mixed success of policy outcomes on the Bogotá River reveals the limits of an advocacy network with weak bridging mobilization. Important advances abound due to the presence of an advocacy network: the work of grassroots activists and an activist judge sparked judicial mobilization and advances on infrastructure development. Media coverage following the 2014 Consejo del Estado ruling shone a spotlight on the right to a clean environment, although many fewer scholarly treatments and media coverage existed for the Bogotá River case than the Matanza Riachuelo case.

Yet bridges—both NGOS and activist public officials—continue to struggle to be heard. The judicial advisory committee has had very limited influence in nudging government allies to make change from within. They have largely been kept out of decision-making spaces, and engineers and technocrats have worked in a fragmented manner and made most decisions with little citizen input. Transparency and accountability have been limited, and there is no major database of new and updated information on pollution or polluters or a clear participatory venue where residents can make demands. The Muña Reservoir, the initial site of judicial mobilization, continues to be plagued with toxic contamination. Public health issues are, according to one observer, "rarely discussed."[90]

While the building of infrastructure for sanitation works continues at a rapid pace, many other issues endure. No new institutions have been created to govern the river basin and to shut down contaminating industries, and existing regulatory capacity and will to do so are low and decentralized. Unanswered questions surrounding accountability for public health impacts,

---

[90] Interview with Medardo Galindo, Fundacion Conejera, July 19, 2016.

unequal distribution of hazards among the poor, government corruption, and regulation of industrial pollution are likely to continue to mire technical efforts to address slow harms. As one activist said, "The way to decontaminate the river is to stop contaminating it,"[91] yet it has proven much easier to build new infrastructure than to stop polluters.

The stagnated policy response to date suggests that grassroots activism and activist judges are not enough to create broad-based policy change for historically ignored policy problems. In the Argentina case, slow-harms redress was ignited through strong bridges that linked prior human rights work and rights-based framing to environmental issues, working outside of the state to pressure for change within and across various state institutions, many of which had also begun to view rights-based claims-making as legible and legitimate. These bridges—with expertise, resources, and a shared history of human rights work—were well positioned to elevate a previously invisible policy problem with a powerful new message that resonated broadly.

In Colombia, societal bridges, largely local environmental NGOs, were much more limited due to the lack of key enabling conditions. The Colombian human rights movement was fragmented and under siege, fighting for transitional justice goals while the country had not yet ended the armed conflict, and was further diminished with conservative political administrations that attacked and diminished its growth. With the multiplicity of actors using the human rights frame in Colombia and the ongoing attacks on human rights NGOs, the human rights frame was not one that has translated in a comprehensive and advantageous manner to environmental issues. Not surprisingly then, human rights NGOs were not involved in the river case and the case was not broadly framed as one about human rights injustice.

Society-level bridges were left without an overarching movement from which to draw on, and no attendant unifying and galvanizing frame. They remained narrowly focused on smaller monitoring tasks on the judicial advisory committee, and some were focused on river restoration tasks, not unlike small-scale grassroots activists throughout the large territory. Similarly, activist state officials, like the lower court judge of Cundinamarca and some in the Public Prosecutor's and Comptroller's offices, continued to work within existing institutions resistant to change with limited resources and few connective ties to one another.

---

[91] Interview with Fernando Vasquez, director, Fundación al Verde Vivo, July 18, 2016.

When bridges are not embedded in a prior history of working together or do not share a set of preexisting norms and goals, they have a much higher hill to climb when attempting to influence public policy. They are unable to transfer prior work experiences or frames of meaning onto new problems. They may not have clout or cachet in existing policy circles; they may also not have a name in the media or public discourse. Bridges without organizing experience may struggle to bring many diverse people and viewpoints together.

The Colombia case illustrates how weak bridging mobilization struggled to dismantle the policy status quo within both state institutions and polluting coalitions. Weak bridges have fewer reputational and ideational resources with which to confront politically powerful actors resistant to change. Bridges with limited material resources and low political leverage may also be less effective in creating space for accountability and citizens' voices. Increasing access to information as well as the number of venues for citizens to hold government accountable are likely to require confronting powerful interests. Underresourced bridges are not well positioned to increase transparency and data sharing against public officials determined to shut them out. Underresourced bridges can bring expertise to the table, but they will likely need support from other politically influential actors to be successful in their oversight responsibilities and to help bring more citizen engagement to the policymaking table.

5
Uninitiated Policy Shifts in Peru
The Challenge of Weak Bonds with No Bridges

Legend has it that on January 2, 1934, a resident of Huarochirí province in the Lima region of Peru, Eduarda Córdova, kneeling down and lifting her arms to the sky, cried out, "I would rather be killed by bullets then to live poisoned!" before she and four others were brutally massacred by government troops.[1] On the upper basin of the Rímac River, peasants had fought against a mining company that released arsenic fumes into their land, soil, and air and was protected by government forces. Today the struggle to secure environmental rights in Peru continues to be filled with conflict, and conditions on the Rímac have not much changed.

Like Colombia, Peru is a megadiverse country with ample natural resources and a tumultuous history of internal armed conflict. This armed violence has cast a long shadow and continues to negatively impact the development of environmental institutions and participatory mobilizing. Slow-moving harms surrounding the contaminated Rímac River have received little policy attention and continue to be invisible to policymakers and elected officials. This chapter examines the slow-moving harms of the Rímac River basin, investigating why and how its invisibility has deepened over time.

Despite the Rímac being the only source of drinking water for the Lima-Callao metropolitan region, collective citizen action has yet to materialize around this policy issue. Grassroots mobilization—or bonding mobilization—over slow harms in the Rímac is limited and drowned out by concerns over targeted, fast-moving harms, such as natural disaster relief and resisting relocation. The limited grassroots activism from impacted communities, particularly on the peri-urban and rural banks of the Rímac,

---

[1] Fernando Leyton, "El Río Rímac en constante amenaza por 17 relaves mineros," *La Republica*, August 5, 2017; "San Mateo de Huanchor: La historia heroica de un pueblo contra la contaminación minera en el Perú," *RedRímacNoticias*, January 14, 2011.

has not been accompanied by bridging mobilization. Neither NGOs nor state activists have emerged to raise awareness of contamination and aggregate and visibly scale up claims. This chapter examines the limited amount of bonding mobilization surrounding slow harms before investigating the spaces within the NGO community and state-level institutions where bridging mobilization would have likely occurred had it emerged. These include potential state allies such as legal institutions and the Ombudsman's Office (Defensoría del Pueblo del Perú), as well as the NGO landscape.

Weak enabling conditions rooted in the legacy of fractured human rights mobilizing and conservative presidential administrations inhibited the growth of resourced bridges. Following the internal armed conflict in Peru, conservative presidential administrations came to power that have been strongly aligned with prior military officials and export-oriented mineral wealth extraction. More so than in Colombia, in Peru the extractives industry has had an open-door policy with international extractives capital, and these dynamics have seeped into varied government institutions, including the judiciary.

Furthermore, suspicions from government officials of linkages between citizens and leftist terrorist groups continue to linger and provide a convenient excuse for officials eschewing accountability. This setting has not provided fertile soil for human rights actors to strengthen or participatory mobilization to emerge, and it has simultaneously generated a real threat to incipient environmental protections. In this context, bridges have failed altogether to emerge, and there has been no accountability-seeking over slow harms for the Rímac to date.

Yet organized groups continue to make demands surrounding *fast-moving* targeted harms throughout the countryside, besieged by the aftermath of an extractives boom that has polluted the air, water, and land and threatened the livelihood of thousands. Against their demands lie accommodationist government policies, designed to curry favor with international investors by diluting environmental standards despite the growing number of socioenvironmental conflicts unregulated investment has brought. This chapter reviews the adoption of national-level environmental frameworks in Peru, traces the absence of network formation via weak bonds and missing bridges in the wake of armed conflict, examines the preservation of the policy status quo for polluters, and reviews alternative explanations.

Resignation and policy inertia for the Rímac's pollution reflects the conditions in many Global South cities. What follows traces the history of development of the Rímac, whose banks became first a space for urban migrants seeking economic opportunities and later a refuge for internal refugees fleeing state-sponsored violence in the countryside. Located in a seismic zone and besieged by toxins both immediate and dispersed, poor communities near the Rímac navigate complex risk perceptions over the scale and scope of harms. Yet they continue to wait, resigned to environmental suffering as policymakers, technocrats, and NGOs focus on what they perceive to be more pressing policy problems. The prosecutor for environmental crimes in the Ministry of the Environment explained:

> No one cares about it because it has become part of us. When you talk to people about the Rímac, they think of the Rímac as just that, a dirty river. And when you feel it is part of the landscape, it's as if when you come home to your house each day, and there is a dead lightbulb, but you don't feel like changing it. And you know the room has a dead lightbulb, but you think of it as part of the decor of the room. If you survey everyone who lives by the Rímac, they will all say, "The river has always been dirty." It's a fact, it's just a given.[2]

Environmental Institutions in Peru: A Brief History

More so than in Argentina and Colombia, Peru's environmental institutions are young and born to satisfy international requirements rather than as a response to domestic stakeholders. Like most countries in the region, Peru has historically created multiple, malleable institutions to manage the country's natural resources. Some of the most notable were the General Directorate for Environmental Health (DIGESA), established in the 1940s, the National Office of Evaluation of Natural Resources in the 1960s, and the issuance of the Code for Environment and Natural Resources in 1990 (World Bank 2006, 39).[3] Historic "paper tiger" institutions, such as DIGESA, with official responsibilities for safeguarding environmental resources but little de facto efficacy, continue to oversee pollution regulation.

---

[2] Interview with Julio Guzman, MINAM prosecutor, and special prosecutor for environmental crimes, May 3, 2017.
[3] For more on the history of Peru's environmental institutions, see World Bank (2006, 9, 20–39); Ministerio del Ambiente (2016, 33–34); OECD (2016, 33–34).

In 1993, President Alberto Fujimori's auto-coup led to a constitutional crisis that replaced the 1979 Constitution from the statist military government of that time with a new Constitution aimed at, among other things, boosting foreign investment. Like Menem's constitutional amendments in Argentina in 1994, Fujimori's 1993 Constitution was an autocratic power grab, but it also brought the nation in line with international currents on environmental issues. The 1993 Constitution was heavily influenced by international accords and the Rio 1992 conference rather than bottom-up pressure for improving environmental stewardship.[4] "Environmental issues were treated with the logic of making them clear and accessible to investors, and making rules that would not be so costly so as to create obstacles" (Pulgar Vidal 2006, 140, 150). The prioritization of the economy over the environment continued after Peru restored democratic rule in 2000.

Aided by donor funding, Peru had some success in containing deforestation and boosting biodiversity management (World Bank 2006, 217; OECD 2016, 58), yet the problems of environmental degradation continued to mount as unplanned urbanization, mining booms, and climate change exacerbated environmental health risks. Increases in emergencies caused by natural phenomena from climatic variability rose by 54.6% from 2003 to 2013 in Peru, a country particularly vulnerable to extreme weather events (OECD 2016, 21, 39). By the late 2000s the costs of environmental degradation were estimated to be nearly 4% of the country's GDP, as reflected in increased morbidity and mortality and decreased productivity (World Bank 2009a, 1). Institutional responses have been inadequate and poorly funded. Between 1999 and 2005, annual environmental expenditure averaged around 0.01% of GDP, a small fraction of the costs of environmental degradation, and low by international standards (World Bank 2009a, 8–9).

The institutional framework for environmental policy changed dramatically in the late 2000s and appeared, at least on paper, to finally be prioritizing environmental degradation. President Alan García created Peru's first Environmental Ministry (MINAM) by decree in 2008, and Peru received a US$330 million loan from the World Bank to reconfigure its environmental development framework. Official reports stressed that García was motivated by the impact of global warming on the Peruvian Amazon and public outcry over environmental crises like lead poisoning at La Oroya (World Bank 2009a, 7–12). Yet it was widely known that strengthened environmental

---

[4] See OECD (2016, 58); Pulgar Vidal (2006).

regulations were a precondition for a bilateral trade agreement with the United States, negotiated by Democrats in the U.S. Congress (Collyns 2008; Weisman 2007).[5] Thus, calls for strengthened environmental regulation were imposed from abroad, not negotiated by bottom-up pressure from Peruvian NGOs, activists, or political leaders.

Despite reorganizations of existing environmental institutions and creation of new ones, Peruvian environmental institutions continue to be deeply beholden to foreign extractives investment. The creation of the Environmental Ministry consolidated over a dozen agencies that had previously had de jure shared responsibilities, but in practice duties had often been duplicative and diluted across agencies, and continue to have limited regulatory authority.[6] The decentralization process in the 2000s transferred environmental and territorial governance functions to regional and municipal governments (OECD 2016, 29) and has shifted more environmental stewardship responsibilities to tiers of government poorly prepared to administer them. The Agency for Environmental Assessment and Enforcement (OEFA), created in 2008 to enforce environmental degradation, operates under an environmental framework that is accommodationist to industry, especially mining. The strength of the mineral extractive sector makes government officials more apathetic to citizen grievances regarding environmental problems.

Nevertheless, environmental degradation has become more visible in the Peruvian media, where legacies of mining pollution as well as high-profile environmental conflicts receive ample coverage. The mining town of La Oroya being listed as one of the 10 most polluted places in the world (Blacksmith Institute 2013), and extreme weather events such as El Niño in 1998 and 2011, increase issue visibility of environmental problems. Yet most environmental conflicts and movements, to the extent they exist, do not address slow harms.

Environmental movements related to environmental and economic impacts of mining on rural communities have emerged in Peru. Because Peru decentralized to local government decision-making over mine siting, revenue expenditures, and environmental impact assessments, local governments have been incentivized to approve projects and enjoy voluntary

---

[5] Interview with Jose Luis Vasquez Vega, MINAM, Dirección General de Investigación, April 28, 2017. See the US-Peru Trade Promotion Agreement, implemented on February 1, 2009. The World Bank (2009a) loan,was issued soon after the trade agreement negotiations.

[6] For an overview, see OECD (2016, 29–35).

contributions from companies which help finance local political campaigns (Arellano-Yanguas 2011, 620–24; Eaton 2010, 1215–19). These dynamics underlie local government support for mining over enforcing environmental regulations.

Socioenvironmental conflicts have skyrocketed in Peru, most of them related to claims of imminent harms from mining. Socioenvironmental conflicts were up by over 300% over the period 2010–15 (OECD 2016, 40).[7] Mining conflicts often involve *frentes*, broad bands of civil society organizations and sometimes subnational political actors (Jaskoski 2014a, 874). The director of the social conflicts' office in the Ombudsman's Office explained,

> When a *frente de defensa* forms, that means the conflict has already escalated. The public has then organized around a problem that has grown too much.... Organizations that have already tried different mechanisms to have their problem resolved, they get to a point where these unattended problems lead them to band together.... This is a critical point, because at this point the distance between the state and society is very wide, there is no dialogue, no response.[8]

Although these conflicts sometimes involve water scarcity, such as a contentious case in the Andean highlands of Cajamarca, there have been instances of mobilizations around what I term "rapid targeted harms," as communities mobilize against incoming transnational mining companies. Many of these conflicts arise from communities' negotiations that seek greater material compensation or more participation in the decision-making process (Jaskoski 2014a, 874; Bebbington et al. 2008, 903).

Peruvian environmental institutions are relatively young and have largely been imposed from abroad. They reflect the interests of donor agencies and countries on the initiating end of multilateral agreements over home-grown pressures. Government agencies thus play a delicate balancing game between not upsetting the status quo dominance of polluting coalitions while also playing lip service to international environmental norms. When addressing environmental issues, public officials adopt a firefighting strategy centered

---

[7] The Environmental Justice Atlas crowd-generated map of social environmental conflict marks Peru as having the seventh-highest number of conflicts in the world as of September 9, 2019 (https://ejatlas.org/).

[8] Interview with Giselle Huamani Olivo, Ombudsman's Office, May 3, 2017.

on what is most aflame: highly visible, rapid, targeted harms. In contrast, slow harms on the capital city's river have a long history of being ignored.

Weak Bonding Mobilization

Lima's Rímac River, as seen in Map 5.1, has had much weaker bonding mobilization than the Bogotá and Buenos Aires river basins, and the claims-making that has emerged has centered on imminent threats rather than slow-moving environmental hazards. This section describes the grievances shared by residents living near the river, such as contamination of agriculture in the upper basin and dangers from flooding and landslides closer to the city center. As in Buenos Aires and Bogotá, riverine communities in Lima fear being relocated with little compensation and far from employment opportunities. This section illustrates the challenges residents face, including dismissive public officials and toxic uncertainty as communities fight for the right to stay put even among toxic hazards. While risk perceptions vary, local awareness of the long-term health impacts of pollution has remained relatively low as compared to threats with a shorter time horizon, such as relocation or building collapse due to natural disasters. Thus, bonding mobilization has been relatively weak, and smoke signaling over slow harms has not emerged en masse on the Rímac River.

Mining Tailings and Contaminated Agriculture in San Mateo. Environmental concern is most detectable in the rural countryside of the upper basin of the Rímac. Rural communities in San Mateo in the province of Huarachirí, where the Rímac begins, know firsthand the costs of slow harms on the river. One farmer said, "We are the impacted ones that are irrigating with this dirty water in San Mateo. . . . These grasses feed from the soil that is contaminated. . . The livestock is contaminated, and we are eating contaminated food."[9] Here the mining tailings from the Tamboraque mine generate ongoing damages, Figure 5.1 captures a view of the tailings. A hydraulic expert noted, "These tailings impact the rural communities in the upper basin of the Rimác, communities whose problems perhaps we don't pay enough attention to [in Lima], because . . . we don't see it."[10]

---

[9] *Documentary: Historias de Agua,* produced by Red Muqui and KillaKuyay, December 13, 2017, time stamp begins 36:30.

[10] Monica Untiveros, civil engineer, hydraulic resource specialist, on *Documentary: Historias de agua*, produced by Red Muqui and KillaKuyay, December 13, 2017, time stamp begins 35:10.

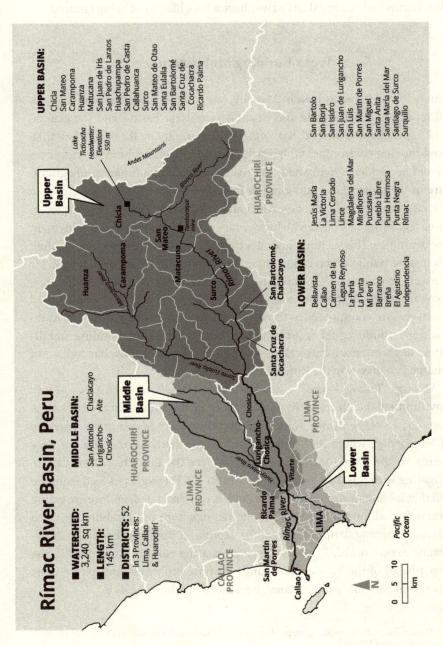

Map 5.1 Map of Rímac River
Map by Dennis Bolt.

Figure 5.1 A view of tailings of the Tamboraque mining in San Mateo de Huanchor, Peru, 2017.
Source: NurPhoto SRL/Alamy Stock Photo.

In 2016, farmers in the region organized a collective called the Platform for the Defense of the Upper Basin of the Rímac River (Plataforma por la Defensa y Promoción del Medio Ambiente en la Cuenca Alta del Río Rímac) to speak with Congress.[11] They were told to come back with data documenting the presence of heavy metals. The local pastor who has organized the collective said, "When I came to San Mateo in 2016, I found in the community a willingness to get to work. They motivated me to organize events, build capacity, and travel to see how others were organizing. We have an objective, and it's not just to get together and talk."[12] After returning with a detailed study conducted by an engineer, however, their demands stalled, and the mining tailings have yet to be relocated.

---

[11] "Lima: El drama de los pobladores del Río Rímac y los residuos minerales." Servindi.org (Comunicación intercultural para un mundo más humano y diverso), March 2, 2018.
[12] Roger Leiva, San Mateo, Huarochirí, quoted in "Ciudadanos de la cuenca del Río Rímac se unen para exigir atención por contaminación con metales," *LaMula.pe*, November 29, 2017.

Toxic Uncertainty and Resisting Relocation in La Margen Izquierda, Lima Cercado. Residents facing toxic uncertainty are often conflicted about multiple perceived risks, or if dangers pose risk at all. Officials estimate that 196,978 residents live in a 500-meter radius from the banks of the Rímac River across 10 districts.[13] Historically, many riverine residents migrated from the countryside. During Peru's internal armed conflict in the 1990s, persecuted indigenous communities such as the Shipibos, Asháninka, Awajún, and Wampis fled the Amazon and resettled in Liman shantytowns.[14] Along the riverbanks, precariously built homes lie on soft soil and visibly tilt toward the river; dangers are further compounded by Lima's seismic fault line and torrential flooding and landslides from El Niño storms.

La Margen Izquierda (MIRR) is an informal settlement along the Rímac's edge in Lima Cercado in the lower basin of the Rímac. Here residents face deep poverty and government negligence. As Wainwright (2017, 13–14) argues, knowledge of pollution cannot be separated from other challenges residents face, such as finding work. An industrial zone, residents—one study estimates a MIRR population of over 80,000—work predominantly as urban recyclers next to a historic landfill (International Development Research Centre, n.d., 2). As in Bogotá and Buenos Aires, Lima's urban recyclers provide an important environmental service, while also separating the "unrecyclable" material into mounds that fall into the river. Some residents are employed in nearby factory work and are unlikely to mobilize for pollution remediation for fear of undermining their employment security.[15] Residents exposed to toxins face uncertainty about the extent and causes of pollution and vary in how they interpret associated risks. One resident lamented, "How will we live? For too many years we have tolerated that nothing is done. I am sick from so much contamination, and my grandchildren are also sick."[16] Residents organized a small rally for protection against one factory's air pollution, lamenting, "[T]he municipality does not attend to

---

[13] The Rímac's riverine communities are concentrated across a 58-kilometer-long stretch of riverbank in the districts of Callao, Carmen de la Legua Reynoso, Lima, San Martín de Porres, Rímac, El Agustino, San Juan de Lurigancho, Ate, Lurigancho-Chosica, and Chaclacayo (Autoridad Nacional del Agua 2019, 7–9). Interview with Alejandro Diaz, Ombudsman's Office, May 3, 2017.

[14] Ruxandra Guidi, "Indigenous Residents of Lima's Cantagallo Shantytown Confront an Uncertain Future," *Americas Quarterly*, November 11, 2015; interview with Alejandro Diaz, Ombudsman's Office, May 3, 2017.

[15] "MIRR Margen Izquierda del Rio Rimac," June 10, 2008, YouTube, accessed August 18, 2022.

[16] "Contaminación en el Río Rímac: El lamento del Río Hablador," TV Perú Noticias (Panorama), January 11, 2014, timestamp 6:42.

us."[17] Conflicting notions about the degree of contamination, whether toxins are an imminent threat or a part of the everyday landscape, stymie grassroots organizing in highly vulnerable communities.

Toxins have spread across an urban periphery defined largely by self-built housing and communities with years of experience defending what they have themselves built. Lima's long history of self-help approaches was fueled by government policies that provided little assistance to migrants: "Conservative policymakers tried to cultivate an ideology of squatter 'self-help': squatters should be granted small plots if they could prove through hard work and initiative that they deserved to be homeowners" (Stokes 1995, 26; Dietz 1977). Self-built housing, disconnected from public infrastructure, grew amid government responses that eschewed any responsibility. Residents are distrustful of local officials, who are viewed as hostile, negligent in providing social services, and also guilty of polluting through mass dumping of municipal waste on the Rímac. Residents throughout the metropolitan area watch as trucks loaded with garbage from private vendors and municipal agencies dump solid waste directly into the river daily.[18]

In this context, MIRR communities have frequently resisted relocations away from the central area where self-help networks and economic opportunities are strongest. Local elected officials have proposed revitalization projects for the Rímac and been met with opposition. Plans to build a greenway and connected transit lines, the Vía Parque Rímac, were resisted by protestors in 2012–14, who decried the low amount of compensation offered for their homes and vehemently opposed forced relocation.[19] A local leader said, "[W]e do not want to be relocated, nor do we want money. What we want is the resolution of this problem. We want a working table [*mesa de dialogo*] to propose our solutions."[20] The Shipibo-Conibo indigenous

---

[17] "Vecina de la Margen Izquierda, Cercado de Lima, Asociación de Vecinos del Distrito del Cercado de Lima," Facebook Watch, timestamp 4:10.

[18] "Ate: Camiones arrojan desmonte y basura al Río Rímac," *24 Horas*, June 5, 2017; "SJL (San Juan de Lurigancho) contamina al Río Rímac," Willax TV, November 11, 2013.

[19] The Vía Parque Rímac (formerly Linea Amarilla) project was begun by Mayor Luis Castañeda Lossio (2003–10, 2015–18) and later adopted by Mayor Susana Villarán (2011–15); it would have created 25 hectares of green space and helped remediate the Rímac River. The project would have entailed forced relocations of hundreds of families, Figure 5.2 shows a photograph of a protest campaign against Mayor Villarán rejecting relocations. "Villarán: Vía Parque Rímac es una gran obra que inició Castañeda," *Radio Programas del Perú*, February 16, 2013; "Pobladores de zona del Río Rímac protestan por temor a ser desalojados," *RPP.PE (RPP Noticias)*, February 1, 2012; "Familias del margen izquierdo del Río Rímac no aceptan las tasaciones," *La República*, July 20, 2011; "Bloquean Puente Santa María en protesta contra Vía Parque Rímac," *Redacción Peru21*, October 9, 2013.

[20] "Siguen las protestas por parte de vecinos al proyecto Vía Parque Rímac," *Generación.com*, June 27, 2013.

Figure 5.2 Residents protest relocations for Proyecto Rio Verde, 2014.
Source: El Comercio.

community, which had settled near a former landfill in the MIRR, saw the community they had rebuilt once again under attack.[21] A broad swath of residents of MIRR protested en masse and the project was abandoned.

Decrying Immediate Threats from Natural Disasters in Lurigancho-Chosica. Residents have blocked roads and marched to plead for services and infrastructure support after natural disasters, an immediate threat due to increased climate variability. In 2018 residents took to the streets to decry government's response to mudslides and flash floods associated with rains from El Niño as the Rímac threatened to overflow in the district of Lurigancho-Chosica in the middle basin of the river. Figure 5.3 is a photograph that illustrates the damage from flooding on residential communities. Residents blocked the central highway and demanded the government build a containment wall on the riverbank.[22] One resident yelled, "[The government] doesn't help this population. We are in a bad way. . . . [T]he flashfloods will destroy our homes!"[23] Other neighbors cried, "[W]e need help urgently. . . . Authorities have fallen asleep," and "What we want is for the central government to

---

[21] Ruxandra Guidi, "Indigenous Residents of Lima's Cantagallo Shantytown Confront an Uncertain Future," *Americas Quarterly*, November 11, 2015.

[22] "Río Rímac: Bloquearon la Carretera Central por falta de obras," *El Comercio*, January 23, 2018.

[23] "Vecinos de Carapongo bloquearon Carretera Central para exigir obras de prevención," Latina Noticias, January 23, 3018, timestamp: 0:44.

Figure 5.3 Landslides and floods in Lurigancho district, Chosica, Peru, 2017.
Source: REUTERS/Alamy Stock Photo.

declare a state of emergency and begin to solve this problem."[24] Given the extreme physical and economic vulnerability faced by Lima's riverbank communities alongside limited government support, grievances have centered on perceived imminent threats rather than exposure to toxic hazards.

No Bridging Mobilization in State and Society

Rights-based mobilization and participatory collective organizing has been extremely limited in Peru compared to Argentina and Colombia, and no policy shifts toward river remediation have occurred. Potential bridging actors, such as state-level institutions or NGOs, have not emerged to coordinate and aggregate claims surrounding slow harms on the Rímac River. Potential bridges within the state are hamstrung by the political influence of mining interests that infiltrate government agencies and legal institutions. Potential bridges within society are undermined by public agencies' hostility

---

[24] "Chosica: Desviación del Río Rímac deja más de 50 damnificados," La noche es Mía, January 24, 2018, timestamp: 10:12.

toward citizen participation and a commodity boom cycle that perversely lowered international investment in NGO aid. These constraints are rooted in weak political and economic enabling conditions for change, to which the next section turns.

Hostile Enabling Conditions: Human Rights Attacked Under Antagonistic Conservative Political Administrations

Peru's human rights movement has been under assault since its inception, and thus the rights-based frame has not served a unifying role for Rímac River bridging mobilization. While human rights mobilization gained some traction during a brief period of national reconciliation and accountability-seeking initiatives following the end of the internal armed conflict in 2000, future right-wing administrations aligned with military officers and the extractive industries closed the small window of influence for human rights claims-making. Human rights actors continue to fight for basic democratic freedoms and the rights of indigenous groups, but their low level of policymaking influence reflects the closed spaces for participation for civil society more broadly in Peru. These hostile enabling conditions underlie anemic mobilizing for environmental harm reductions.

The Peruvian armed conflict (1980–2000) pitted the guerrilla group Shining Path (Sendero) against numerous military and paramilitary forces.[25] The conflict's origins are rooted in the 1980 national elections, which saw the end of a military government, but also incipient terrorism as the Maoist-Communist splinter group Sendero burned ballot boxes and attacked military, police, and civilians in rejection of the democratic experiment.[26] The armed forces responded with a "dirty war" that included martial law, massacres, arbitrary arrests and disappearances, summary

---

[25] Sendero was determined to undermine democratic institutions and mount a Maoist-inspired social revolution. Led by Abimael Guzmán, Sendero split from the Communist Party and integrated itself into the Andean Quechua-speaking region. Ideologically, Sendero emphasized the class struggle, anti-imperialism, the centrality of the peasantry as the "masses," and, perhaps most critically, violence. Citing Mao, Guzmán declared, "[V]iolence is a universal law . . . and without revolutionary violence one class cannot be substituted for another, an old order cannot be overthrown to create a new one" (quoted in Starn 1995, 406–9). See also Soifer and Vergara (2019, 2–6).

[26] Prior to Fernando Belaúnde Terry's (1980–85) democratic government, Peru had been governed by the right-wing military government of Morales Bermúdez (1975–80), which enacted contentious austerity measures and followed a left-wing military regime under Juan Velasco (1968–75) that pushed for nationalization and mobilization of popular sectors (Cornell and Roberts 1990, 533; McClintock 1984, 49).

executions, torture, and sexual violence. In 1984, 4,319 murders and forced disappearances were reported (Americas Watch 1992, 14). Sendero's violence increased when Alan García (1985–90) came to power and the Marxist terrorist group Túpac Amaru Revolutionary Movement began. President García's *mano duro* policies, supported by the paramilitary forces' Rodrigo Franco Command, increased human rights violations.[27] By the end of García's term, half of the population was living in an emergency zone, and the death count had risen from 1,359 in 1985 to 3,452 in 1990 (Youngers 2003, 139–40).

As the conflict worsened, so did threats on the lives of human rights activists and suspicions from government forces about activists' motives and whether they supported leftist insurgents. Human rights groups coalesced into an umbrella organization called the National Human Rights Coordinator (Coordinadora Nacional de Derechos Humanos) in 1985, uniting 67 organizations throughout the country. In addition to documenting human rights violations, the Coordinadora provided legal defense for victims and information about forced disappearances and arbitrary detentions for international campaigns (Youngers 2003, 133–89). Peruvian human rights groups took cases to the Inter-American Commission of Human Rights, frustrated with slow efforts for justice at home (González-Ocantos 2017, 145).

The armed conflict, and hostility toward organized civil society, swelled under Fujimori's administration (1990–2000).[28] Fujimori's counterinsurgency teams improved surveillance to capture Sendero's leader, Guzmán, which drastically reduced the violence and helped further cement Fujimori's public support. Clandestine military units continued to engage in targeted killings and forced disappearances and tortured civilians under special units such as the Colina Group, responsible for the Barrios Altos massacre and other crimes. It would later come to light that Fujimori's administration also ordered forced sterilizations of thousands of poor, indigenous women and men.

---

[27] These included the Cayara massacre of 1988, the execution of 200 to 300 inmates during prison riots in Lima, and, according to UN reports, the forced disappearance by military and police forces of more people than any other country (Root 2012, 22–25; Youngers 2003, 140; Americas Watch 1992, 90–95; Amnesty International 1994).
[28] Fujimori quickly moved to enact wide-ranging neoliberal forms, known as Fujishock, as well as authoritarian tactics under an obstructionist Congress. His 1992 *autogolpe* (self-coup) shut down Congress, suspended the Constitution, and purged the judiciary, enjoying initial public support in Peru but condemnation internationally (Cameron 1994, 145–63).

Fujimori's administration was concerned that human rights groups posed a threat to the regime's public image, and especially its international reputation. In this context human rights groups were sometimes also appeased, and they won major concessions such as legislation on racial discrimination, women's rights and family violence, and torture, and notably, the creation of the Human Rights Ombudsman's Office in 1996. The Ombudsman's Office was, unwittingly for the Fujimori administration, a Trojan horse that hired human rights activists as staff. After the political violence faded and Fujimori sought a third term, the Coordinadora's public image improved. The newspaper *El Comercio* included a special feature on human rights every week for one year during the 50th anniversary of the Universal Declaration of Human Rights. Human rights discourse was moving into the mainstream during this time, buoyed by Fujimori's stifling of democratic freedoms (Root 2009, 460–61). Human rights organizations would have a rather limited window of influence once Fujimori's regime came to an end. Interim President Valentín Paniagua created a Truth Commission by decree in 2000 which held televised hearings between 2001 and 2003, collecting over 17,000 testimonies and overseeing evidence collection in 2,000 mass grave sites. The human rights accounting revealed that the majority of deaths were in indigenous communities that were attacked by government forces and guerrilla warfare.[29] This accountability work was further deepened by President Alejandro Toledo (2001–6), who had a Quechua background and campaigned on promises to support transitional justice, including reparations, and ending impunity for the armed forces (Root 2012, 73–74). During these administrations, activists and their allies staffed the Ministries of Foreign Relations, Justice, and Women's Affairs, the Ombudsman's Office, and the Solicitor General's Office.

When the formerly disgraced president García returned to office (2006–11), the era of support for human rights NGOs quickly ended. As a president who himself was being investigated for past abuses, García was hostile to the human rights agenda; the Truth Commission had charged him with political responsibility for human rights violations committed during his first government (Gonzalez-Ocantos 2017, 147, 161; Burt 2009, 401). García responded by deploying intimidation tactics against the courts and appointing advisors who had been former generals. When Fujimori's followers, also hostile to

---

[29] The death toll was over 69,000 killed and disappeared, with the government responsible for half of these deaths; 75% of those killed were indigenous, mainly from Ayacucho, Huancavelica, Huánuco, and San Martín (Root 2012, 459; Paredes 2019, 176; González-Ocantos 2017, 143; Barrantes Segura 2012, 3).

human rights activists, became an emboldened congressional opposition, the window for expanding the influence of human rights activists and NGOs narrowed further. Human rights NGOs participated very little in congressional debates over human rights–related bills; business lobbyists had much more influence (Gonzalez-Ocantos 2017, 163–65). Fujimorismo, a political movement that strengthened after the defeat of Sendero, became an enemy of human rights actors who rejected the "firm hand" approach of Fujimori's government (Vergara and Encinas 2019, 240).

Future administrations were increasingly hostile to the human rights agenda, and the power of human rights as a politically influential movement waned. One human rights lawyer noted, "[O]ur enemies have become more powerful; the armed forces have regained their political influence and the government has forged an alliance with them in order to anchor its power" (Gonzalez-Ocantos 2017, 160). The election of President Ollanta Humala (2011–16), a former military officer who had committed grave human rights abuses when fighting Sendero, was a further blow to the human rights agenda.[30] Humala brought former military officers into his administration (Root 2012, 127). Most soldiers implicated in human rights violations in Peru have never been brought to justice.[31] The entanglement between presidential administrations and former military officers was especially pronounced in the Peruvian case and further explains a repressive approach toward civil society organizing.

Furthermore, the conservative orientation of Peru's presidential administrations—and its consequences for institutionalized citizen participation—cannot be separated from Peru's political economy. Assessing fractures in citizen participation in Peru, Vergara and Encinas (2019, 243) write that "a strong conservative right was consolidated that prioritized the maintenance of market freedom but placed less importance on other freedoms ... [and] was based more on influence than on public deliberation." Peru's economy is dominated by extractives, which make up 11% of its total revenue, 67% of its exports, and 12.5% of GDP—in 2018, a surge in extractive investment increased to nearly US$5 billion (EITI 2016). This growth

---

[30] In 2017, the extent of the atrocities to which Humala was connected came to light, including both the crimes and an attempted cover-up. Human Rights Watch (2017) reported that "soldiers who claim to have served under Humala's command said ... that they killed detainees, then dismembered their bodies, filled them with rocks, and threw them into the Huallaga river."

[31] According to human rights groups, prosecutors have achieved rulings in only 78 cases related to abuses committed during the internal conflict, and only 17 convictions as of May 2017 (Human Rights Watch, n.d.).

was dramatic in the 2000s: between 2002 and 2007, Peru experienced a 65% increase in foreign direct investment (FDI) in mineral extractives, becoming the world's biggest producer of silver, second in zinc and copper, third in tin, fourth in lead and molybdenum, and fifth in gold (Arellano-Yanguas 2011, 620). As FDI in mineral extractives has increased, so has the amount and severity of social conflict and repressive government responses to citizen claims-making.

Public officials are distrustful of organized civil society, partly because the armed conflict blurred the lines between who supported the armed insurgents and who was an innocent civilian. There have been "frequent tensions between NGOs and the government and crackdowns on NGO activities."[32] A high-level official in the Ombudsman's Office characterized the situation this way: "There are lots of NGOs, but they are stigmatized. There is a discourse in the government that NGOs are being financed, that they profit from conflict.... Government officials feel threatened. They do not have the knowledge, they are very biased, and don't understand the objectives or mission of the NGOs. They have never worked with them."[33]

Human rights NGOs in Peru are continuing to fight to establish basic democratic freedoms and rights of indigenous groups, but they are relatively underresourced and do not have a seat at the policymaking table. The Coordinadora remains active, with 82 Peruvian NGOs and the support of at least 12 international partners. Their national campaigns focus on reparations, promoting peaceful dialogue with government authorities, the right to social protest, and protecting the right to prior consultation for indigenous communities.[34] Much of the influence of human rights policymaking is circumscribed inside the Ombudsman's Office, an unusually strong defender of rights within a hostile political climate (Pegram 2008), as opposed to embedded in diverse government agencies.

The hostile enabling conditions of weak human rights accountability and conservative presidential administrations aligned with both military officials and an extractive sector have dampened the development of autonomous rights-based organizing by potential bridges in Peru, broadly speaking. The following sections examine how both potential societal

---

[32] International Center for Non-Profit Law, Civic Freedom Monitor, Peru, August 3, 2022.
[33] Interview with Giselle Huamani Olivo, Ombudsman's Office, May 3, 2017.
[34] Coordinadora Nacional de Derechos Humanos, website, http://derechoshumanos.pe/coordinadora-nacional-de-derechos-humanos/. See also Paredes (2019, 187–96).

bridges and state-level institutions have been weakened by these background conditions and have yet to mobilize around slow harms on the Rímac River.

Missing State-Level Bridges: Few Routes for Activating or Aggregating Claims

Activist officials have failed to champion slow harms for the Rímac River in Peru, in sharp contrast to the Argentine and Colombian cases, where a selection of reform-oriented public officials helped to both activate and aggregate claims. This section examines the role of the courts, public prosecutors in the Environment Ministry, and the Ombudsman's Office in advancing protections for slow harms. Overall, legal institutions have been closed to environmental claims-making in practice even though the de jure processes for environmental litigation are in place. In addition, the Ombudsman's Office has been active in aggregating claims-making over imminent harms but is reluctant to confront powerful state institutions via lawsuits. The fight against slow harms on the Rímac, weakly articulated by grassroots claims-making, has had no leadership from public institutions. The hostile enabling conditions of conflictual state-society tensions from decades of civil war and capture of public institutions by the mining sector is evident in the following section, which examines the lack of aggregation of anemic claims over pollution.

No Bridges within Legal Institutions

In Lima, legal institutions have not been used as a site for contesting slow harms, in contrast to the cases in Buenos Aires and Bogotá. The legal framework for environmental rights protection is intact; the Peruvian Constitution allows victims of environmental harm to present a writ of protection (*amparo*) individually or collectively.[35] Further reforms in 2006 made it possible for environmental harms to be recognized as urgent (e.g., oil spills, mining tailings on water sources) and thus waived the clause in

---

[35] The 1993 Peruvian Constitution (Article 2.22) guaranteed the "fundamental right to enjoy an environment that is balanced and suitable to one's life," a right that is echoed in the General Environmental Law (Ley General del Ambiente, Ley 28611 in 2005).

the Peruvian judicial system of exhausting prior routes before bringing a lawsuit.[36]

Despite the availability of these legal instruments to protect against environmental harms, the amount of environmental litigation remains relatively low.[37] The Peruvian Supreme Court (Tribunal Constitucional) has sided with economic interests over environmental protections in its rulings. In 2020, the Supreme Court ruled in favor of the constitutionality of Law 30230 (known as the *paquetazo ambiental*), a bundle of measures passed by President Humala's government that would reduce environmental sanctions in pursuit of attracting private investment. The lawsuit had been brought by the regional government of San Martín, a group of citizens, NGOs, and indigenous organizations. The Court upheld the reduction in environmental regulations enacted by OEFA, reduced the authority of MINAM in territorial planning and determining protected area status, and undermined the legal standing of indigenous lands and right to prior consultation. In addition, critics note that the last four Supreme Court rulings on laws with environmental content have been ruled unfounded, further disempowering environmental activists seeking support in the judicial system.[38] Previously there have been individual *amparos* about issues such as illegal mining, but no collective cases were brought for violation of environmental rights.[39]

MINAM is hamstrung both politically and in terms of information gathering. One environmental prosecutor explained this lack of autonomy: "[In MINAM] any activity we want to undertake, we need to have political support, because if we act independently, the politician sees it as an act of insubordination."[40] Furthermore, legal experts view the cost of creating sufficient

---

[36] "Entrevista a César Landa, sobre el amparo ambiental," Instituto Peruano de Protección Ambiental, timestamp 12:10.

[37] Based on a search of the Peruvian Constitutional Court database, and consultation with the head prosecutor of the Peruvian Ministry of the Environment, I estimate the number of *amparos* brought before the Peruvian Constitutional Court for the violation of environmental rights is likely between 15 and 40. A search of the Peruvian Constitutional Court online database for *acciones de amparo* using the search words *derecho de gozar de un medio ambiente* returned 40 cases; using the search words *derecho de gozar de un medio ambiente equilibrado* returned 30 cases; using the search words *un medio ambiente adecuado y equilibrado* returned 15 cases. (The broad term *medio ambiente* returned 498 cases, many of which include false positives, for example cases that are not about the violation of the right to the environment but rather reference "environment" to signify context or setting). None of the *amparos* are about rivers or the Rímac. See Tribunal Constitucional de Gobierno de Perú online portal, accessed July 22, 2020.

[38] "[Video] Expertos de la SPDA analizan sentencia de TC sobre Ley 30230 o Paquetazo Ambiental," *SPDA Actualidad Ambiental*, June 20, 2020.

[39] Interview with Isabel Calle, SPDA, May 5, 2017.

[40] Anonymous interview, MINAM, May 2017.

admissible evidence to prove contamination in bodies of water or air as prohibitive, both in terms of technical complexity as well as financial costs. One interviewee estimated that as many as 5,000 samples would need to be drawn from the Rímac River to begin a collective suit, and there was only one laboratory in Peru designed to measure this content, which has been inoperative since its inauguration because "testing supplies are unavailable."[41] The burden of proof falls on the plaintiffs in the Peruvian legal system, and experts find the necessary threshold to prove the contamination to be discouragingly high.

In 2017, MINAM had 17,000 open investigations for environmental crimes; many have been absolved and did not result in a guilty verdict.[42] When a crime is found to have been committed, the agency levies a fine. These measures seem to do little to disincentivize further environmental deterioration, although they do lend the appearance of state action and compliance with international trends toward environmental stewardship. On paper, prosecutors can, through judicial processes, impose a minimum of 3 and a maximum of 10 years in prison for environmental crimes, depending on their gravity, but it remains to be seen whether judges will implement such measures in the current political climate.[43] Prosecutors in MINAM, despite being some of the best environmental attorneys in the country, are politically unable to act independently and serve as a bridge for slow-harms claims-making.

Research on legal empowerment (Joshi 2017, 162–63) suggests that legal rights need to be activated or promoted by institutions or outsiders. An attorney in MINAM said, "[T]here is not a strong culture of civil litigation over environmental damages, it is not common. People do not know this mechanism exists, and there is no institution that consolidates it, that pushes the topic."[44] In Peru, the only NGO focused on environmental justice, Sociedad Peruana de Derecho Ambiental (SPDA), has not pursued litigation; their director explained, "The judicial system takes a long time, and it's complex. . . . Communities feel that starting a judicial or an administrative process does not serve them, so the solution has been these *mesas de dialogo*. . . . It is easier to shut down a highway and make a public official come to the region and establish accords than to begin litigation."[45] It is unclear whether the low

[41] Anonymous interview, MINAM, May 2017.
[42] Anonymous interview, MINAM, May 2017.
[43] Delitos Ambientales, MINAM, minam.gob.pe, accessed August 11, 2020.
[44] Delitos Ambientales, MINAM, minam.gob.pe, accessed August 11, 2020.
[45] Interview with Isabel Calle, SPDA, May 5, 2017.

level of grassroots claims-making is caused by the low level of activation by resourced outsiders; nevertheless, impacted communities have not pursued legal routes to claims-making over slow harms.

No Bridging within the Ombudsman's Office: Fast Harms over Slow Harms

Another potential bridge for slow harms advocacy is the Ombudsman's Office. The Peruvian Ombudsman's Office was created during Fujimori's term by a Congress seeking a democratic counterbalance to the authoritarian regime.[46] Supported by 38 field offices nationwide, the Ombudsman's Office gathers data, documents, advises, and mediates conflicts between citizens and public officials and is a source of transparency and information in a country that continues to suffer the aftermath of both terrorism and authoritarianism.

The Ombudsman's Office has been a leader in the creation of institutional responses to social conflicts. By 2019, many Peruvian state institutions had created social conflict offices, but the first one was in the Ombudsman's Office in 2004 with a case that gripped the nation. In the Antiplano region of Puno in the Llave district, a mayor was dragged from his home and publicly lynched by a group of citizens who accused him of corruption, of which he was posthumously absolved. Yet citizens, after many attempts to reach state officials, and "sensing that their petitions were ignored, that they were not being taken seriously, dragged him out and killed him."[47] At least 10,000 people stood by and did nothing, and the lynching was filmed and shown on television. In explaining the Ombudsman's Office role in conflict mediation, one attorney noted, "We needed to take this role on because . . . their problems, misunderstood, generated a situation of much violence, which led to more rights violations."[48]

The number of social conflicts tracked by the Ombudsman's Office has grown dramatically. Attorneys in the Office note that the decentralization processes have unleashed conflicts between, on the one hand, mayors who themselves feel pressured or even sometimes under physical threat from

---

[46] Juanita Darling, "Ombudsman Rewriting Peru's History," *LA Times*, November 7, 2000.
[47] Interview with Fabiola Alburqueque, Ombudsman's Office, May 3, 2017.
[48] Interview with Fabiola Alburqueque, Ombudsman's Office, May 3, 2017.

citizens and, on the other, the national government, whose responses are often weak or incomplete: "The problem with the state is that it doesn't seem to understand that social conflicts will be transformed and attended to when their structural causes are addressed."[49]

According to the Ombudsman's Office, socioenvironmental conflicts now make up the majority of reported social conflicts in Peru. In 2018, 66% (116 of 176) of all total conflicts were due to socioenvironmental issues, and 62% of these were mining related (Defensoria del Pueblo 2019, 8, 21–22). Despite the growing number of socioenvironmental conflicts, few of them are over claims related to slow harms. The attorney charged with aggregating environmental conflicts in the Ombudsman's Office explained, "The city has grown in such a disorganized fashion, all the wastewater effluents have been thrown in the river, and later we treat the water to consume it. It is a grave problem. Yet as a social conflict we have very few categorized as such in Lima over the issue of water."[50]

In contrast, water conflicts involving "targeted rapid harms," as described in Chapter 2, have grown in the Sierra zone related to mining activities and pollution of drinking water, agriculture, and livestock. Ombudsman's Office data show that between 2011 and 2014 there were 153 social conflicts over water issues in Peru, only 52 of which began a *mesa de dialogo* process and half of which were begun only after an instance of violence (Defensoría del Pueblo 2015, 89). The Ombudsman's Office continues to struggle with the challenge of creating an institutional culture of respect for human rights in the aftermath of the internal conflict.

Social violence can erupt from issues related to fast-moving harms, such as harms related to mining pollution, but slow-moving harms outside of mining have been much less legible. When asked whether the Ombudsman's Office has considered bringing lawsuits or other mechanisms by which to pressure the state over slow harms (as had the Argentine Ombudsman's Office), one official said, "We cannot interfere in the judicial process. What we can do is speak, give [an] opinion, if there are excessive wait times [for government responses], if there is a lack of attention to demands, we can speak up."[51] Thus, supportive institutions based on the complex legacy of human rights work in Peru, such as the Ombudsman's Office, have also not

---

[49] Interview with Alejandro Diaz, Ombudsman's Office, May 3, 2017.
[50] Interview with Fabiola Alburqueque, Ombudsman's Office, May 3, 2017.
[51] Interview with Giselle Huamani Olivo, Ombudsman's Office, May 3, 2017.

prioritized slow-moving harms and are otherwise bombarded with issues surrounding social conflicts and mining interests, or "fast, targeted harms."[52]

Missing Bridges within Society: NGOs Lack Material Resources and Autonomy

Neither have bridges in society emerged to increase awareness of slow harms within local communities or to advocate with policymakers for those impacted by toxic exposure on the Rímac. A history of NGO suppression by government forces has further closed the political space of activism around environmental justice issues in Peru that we have seen thrive in other countries. National-level NGOs lack autonomy because they are dependent on the state for government contracts. Because Peru is a mining economy with an accommodationist alliance between government officials and mining companies, the survival of the national NGO community has in part been dependent on their acquiescence and neutrality. In this context, international NGOs focus on apolitical issues such as biodiversity and tread lightly on more contentious environmental conflicts that emerge from the extractive economy. The factors associated with strong societal bridges—material resources and a shared history of collective work—have been missing in Peru, as this section examines.

NGOs Lack Material Resources and Autonomy

As of 2020, there were a total of 1,449 NGOs registered with the Peruvian Agency for International Cooperation. Environmental NGOs make up one-third of all NGOs in the country, totaling 455 environmental NGOs in 2020, 142 of them working in the Lima-Callao metropolitan region.[53]

---

[52] Other potential sources for bridging, such as the Comptroller's Office, which in other countries has been a source of support for slow-moving harms, has in Peru helped maintain the status quo. One official noted, "Here the Comptroller's Office only supervises once the money has been spent, not before, and that is one of the principal complaints because at that point there is no point, there is no way to recuperate the money if it has already been misspent. You may find those responsible, but the money doesn't return, the project does not get built, and we continue with the same problem" (interview with Fabiola Alburqueque, Ombudsman's Office, May 3, 2017).

[53] Official registration in the registry allows NGOs to legally participate in consultancy projects using international or national funds, public hearings, and multiparty agreements (*convenios*). Figures derived from Agencia Peruana de Cooperación Internacional (2020) on August 11, 2020.

Of these, only a few are sufficiently resourced to have professional staff, offices, and international financing.[54] These include SPDA (established 1986), Derechos Ambientales Recursos Naturales (established 2004), and ProNaturaleza (Fundación Peruana para la Conservación de la Naturaleza) (established 1984). A small number of human rights NGOs have also worked on environmental issues, such as El Instituto de Defensa Legal (established 1965) and Centro de Estudios y Promoción del Desarrollo) (established 1967).[55] International NGOs with offices in Peru are careful to avoid becoming entangled in potentially contentious local conflicts and thus play no role in slow-harms policy issues.[56]

Influential Peruvian NGOs have had to limit their critiques of the state and polluting industries because many work closely with government agencies. As an SPDA director admitted, "We want [mining] activity and investment projects, but that they be sustainable."[57] NGOs rely on access to consultancy projects from government and thus have reasoned that it is important to stay neutral. Another SPDA employee told me, "We do not seek to confront, or halt investments, or create obstacles. Our vision is sustainable development, because we recognize that politics, the current president, is tied to acceleration of the economy, of private sector investment, and for us this does not fundamentally represent an obstacle for the environment."[58] NGOs such as SPDA use their resources to conduct research, advise Congress, and push for legislation and environmental standards within existing government institutions. They see their role as neutral conciliators.[59] For NGOs that

[54] Of the 142 environmental NGOs registered in the Lima-Callao metropolitan region, 67% had functioning websites. It is likely that registered NGOs may not frequently have resources for permanent staffing, rent, and other operating expenses, but 2/3 prioritized external visibility, which may be related to accessing government or international resources. Figures derived from Agencia Peruana de Cooperación Internacional (2020) on August 11, 2020. We used internet searches for each listed environmental NGO in Lima and Callao to determine whether the NGO had a working website (search conducted the week of August 11, 2020).

[55] Other NGOs that work on environmental issues in Peru, with varying institutional formats and agendas, include CooperAcción (established 1997), which has been working on extractives and the right to prior consultation, and Asociación Servicios Educativos Rurales (established 1980), which works on rural issues surrounding water and sanitation and democratization.

[56] International NGOs with offices in Lima include the Nature Conservancy, Wildlife Conservation Society, CI, Conservation Strategy Fund, World Wildlife Fund, and Oceana. These are largely conservation societies focused on protected areas, biodiversity, and ecosystem preservation. Their long in-country presence and financial support in Peru's megadiverse ecosystems has helped make Peru a regional leader in creating protected areas. International conservation NGOs keep a distance from partisan politics and try to maintain a neutral position with government, making them poorly positioned to take on industrial polluters.

[57] Interview with Isabel Calle, SPDA, May 5, 2017.
[58] Interview with Carol Mora, SPDA, May 4, 2017.
[59] Interview with Isabel Calle, SPDA, May 5, 2017.

survived the Fujimori years, striking a delicate balance between neutrality and targeted strikes on key issues has been key to their longevity.

However, most Peruvian NGOs working on the environment are smaller groups, foundations, or networks that rely on a hodgepodge of funding and have limited operating budgets, if any. These may consist of expert volunteers who come together to pitch projects for consulting jobs with government entities or international donors. For example, NGOs such as Instituto de Promoción para la Gestión del Agua (established 1994) is a loose association of experts, and Agua-C (Asociación para la Gestión del Agua en Cuencas) (established 2003) is an agglomeration of civil society groups that have financing only for specific projects.[60] Some members' sole source of income is small, periodic consultancy contracts. These NGOs are directly tied to professional associations, such as the national engineering association, and some also have or have had positions in government, for example at the National Water Authority (ANA) or MINAM. It is unclear how many experts belong to these types of association-style NGOs and simultaneously work for government agencies, but these arrangements make it difficult for NGOs to be autonomous or pursue agendas contrary to the status quo. Oftentimes consultants are contracted by the government or international financing for projects that do not come to fruition, creating a robust market for consultancy projects that go nowhere.[61]

NGOs, accustomed to accessing international aid, have been shrinking as they have had to self-finance after the commodities boom made Peru a middle-income country on paper and international aid shifted to countries with lower GDPs. One observer noted, "It's not that [NGOs] are disappearing, it's that [their activities] are getting smaller,"[62] while others report that NGOs are dissolving at a rate of one per year.[63] A member of the NGO Agua-C described what happened after several years of working with foreign aid on an Integrated Water Resource Management initiative: "The program was approved, we signed accords [*convenio*], it was administered for two and a half years . . . and then in 2006 the Dutch aid left the country, like almost all of the international aid, and they left us hanging, halfway through the process."[64]

---

[60] Interview with Fanel Guevara, Agua-C, May 11, 2017.
[61] Conversation with Peruvian consultant and academic, Latin American Studies Association Conference, Environmental Studies Section meeting, May 2016.
[62] Interview with Isabel Calle, SPDA, May 5, 2017.
[63] According to Julia Cuadros, president of la Asociación Nacional de Centros. "Cada año desaparece una ONG de Perú por reducción de fondos," *Gestión*, May 8, 2015.
[64] Interview with Fanel Guevara, Agua-C, May 5, 2017.

Finally, AquaFondo (Fondo de Agua para Lima y Callao) is a water fund organized by the Nature Conservancy and financed by the private sector, multilateral aid, and the Peruvian government. Few Peruvian stakeholders outside of government officials and private-sector interests are involved in AquaFondo, and it is upheld by foreign interests. The fund sometimes finds it difficult to work with Peruvian officials, particularly SEDAPAL, the water and sanitation utility, which is not accustomed to doing green projects and has invested little money in supporting green infrastructure. As of 2017, AquaFondo had not invested directly in projects that would remediate the Rímac. Speaking on the lack of action on recuperating the river, a director of the AquaFondo said, "There have not been [government] interventions on water. The Rímac has been a major concern, there has been extensive investments in studies, and research, and document generation, but they are repetitive, they don't end up being diffused, and there are many institutions doing the same exact thing. And every year they update the plans, and they spend the money on consultant project after consultant project."[65]

Few Resourced NGOs Work on Fast Harms and Tread Lightly

The few NGOs that work on environmental justice in Peru have limited tools with which to press their claims. SPDA is the main environmental justice organization in Peru, and approximately 30 of its 50 employees have law degrees. A spokesperson for SPDA noted that although they used litigation early on, for example to petition the release of the right to information (*habeas data*) on acts surrounding a spill of mining tailings in 1997, litigation was no longer a course of action they pursue. Nevertheless, SPDA organizes free legal clinics in Loreto, Madre de Dios, and Lima, and they are working on legal empowerment strategies to make citizens aware of their rights to prior consultation surrounding mining and extraction, among other rights.[66]

In this context, NGOs have not served as a strong counterweight to polluting industries, although some groups that are registered as NGOs and function more like grassroots activists have made important advances. The most important ally has been the organization Red Muqui (established

---

[65] Interview with Mariella Sanchez Guerra, AquaFondo, May 4, 2017.
[66] Interview with Isabel Calle, SPDA, May 5, 2017.

2003), a network of 20 civil society organizations that have engaged environmental issues through their work resisting mining activity. Red Muqui has assisted grassroots collectives in furthering the mining tailings issue on the Rímac, such as the Platform for the Defense of the Upper Basin of the Rímac River that was active in San Mateo. Red Muqui helped organize congressional meetings in 2019 and disseminated information about water contamination in Peru through a documentary they helped produce.[67] Their strategies are more confrontational than those of NGOs such as SPDA, and they have fewer linkages to the state, yet they are the only formal organization that is working to bring attention to this issue.

Thus, the environmental NGO landscape in Peru has not invested in slow-harms remediation in this policy arena. One expert noted, "There is not one NGO working on the recuperation of rivers."[68] The possibility of government consultancy projects has disincentivized resourced NGOs from critiquing government agencies. Public officials are also suspicious of NGOs; some officials still associate NGOs with what they consider to be leftist terrorist groups from the armed conflict.[69] Other NGOs with more vocal stances against mining interests tend to have limited resources and influence. The fragile legacy of human rights network building after democratization has not translated into a robust environmental justice network for either societal groups such as NGOs or government institutions.

No Policy Shift in Slow Harms Remediation

The lack of weak bonds and absent bridges is set against a mining economy that has captured the state, and state-level hostility toward activists is an unresolved legacy of the armed conflict. This combination of factors results in pollution continuing to be an everyday, accepted issue by the state, despite lip service to the contrary. Thus, slow harms continue unabated, and remediation of the Rímac—despite its role in Lima's drinking water supply—is

---

[67] "Foro: Peligros en la cuenca del Río Rímac y alternativas de solución," *Servindi.org* (Comunicación intercultural para un mundo más humano y diverso), February 26, 2019; "Peligros en la Cuenca del Río Rímac y alternativas: por riesgos inminentes, Ley de Remediación de Pasivos Ambientales debe ser discutido y aprobado," *Diario Uno*, March 1, 2019.

[68] Interview with Julio Guzman, MINAM prosecutor, and special prosecutor for environmental crimes, May 3, 2017.

[69] A central legacy of the armed conflict is that the political left became associated with terrorism and thus became stigmatized (Muñoz 2019, 218–21); this stigmatization is evident in public opinion (Vergara and Encinas 2019, 12) and also in the types of institutions examined in this book.

not a policy priority. This section examines how, on the three dimensions of policy shift—institutional development, financial investments, and regulatory capacity—there has been very few changes to the status quo.

Institutional Morass and Limited Financial Investment in Reform. Numerous actors and institutions contribute to the appearance of policy action, but no concrete improvements have emerged to date, and no single institution is primarily responsible for addressing the river's remediation. Moreover, despite the vast resources SEDAPAL spends in treating the Rímac's polluted water for potability, the government has not invested in pollution remediation, nor has it partnered with international agencies to begin to finance reforms.

The jurisdictional complexity of the institutions that oversee the Rímac does little to address the policy problem and helps government officials evade accountability. At least five government agencies, 43 districts of the Metropolitan Municipality of Lima, and governments of Huarochirí located in the Lima department are involved in governing activities impacting the river. These include MINAM, ANA under the Ministry of Agriculture and Irrigation, OEFA, DIGESA, and SEDAPAL. Interviews at MINAM, ANA, DIGESA, and OEFA revealed numerous instances of overlapping responsibilities, as well as obfuscations of roles of other agencies. For example, water quality testing and human health impact fall under the auspices of MINAM, ANA, DIGESA, and SEDAPAL, all of which had different narratives about what standards were acceptable and what actors were most responsible for pollution. These overlapping roles not only serve patronage appointments but obfuscate responsibility. Lamenting the situation, a MINAM official explained:

> The model of segmented management by sector creates traps for addressing problems. When MINAM has declared environmental emergencies in Peru . . . they create a dialogue table [*mesa de dialogo*]. What happens? Everyone shows up. ANA arrives and does what they always do, take their samples, and find that the water meets quality standards. DIGESA also comes and takes their samples, finds that the water is fine. MINAM also. But they don't attack the overall problem. When we proposed toxicology studies, everyone balked. Each agency fulfills their limited responsibility, and nothing happens. . . . It doesn't work when it works in parts.[70]

---

[70] Anonymous interview, 2017.

Citizens impacted by environmental disasters make demands and continue to wait, unsure of which government entity is responsible for addressing their problems. A Chosica resident sums up their experience in getting the state's attention after devastating flash floods in 2017: "Not the federal government, nor the state, have helped. We spoke with the municipality, and they tell us it's [the responsibility of] the Ministry of Agriculture. We speak to the Ministry of Agriculture, and they say it's the municipality. Unfortunately, we live marginalized by the state."[71] It is difficult for citizens to attribute blame to specific entities and seek accountability. These dynamics have all worked together to create muted government responses that by accident or by design maintain the status quo.

To oversee the Rímac, rather than create a comprehensive plan that includes horizontal institutions and societal stakeholders, officials created a multisectoral commission that includes only government agencies. The commission is composed of 15 different government agencies (among them, ANA, DIGESA, OEFA, SEDAPAL) and charges them with seeking international resources and further designing studies for river remediation.[72] As of 2017, a project funded by South Korea was under development but had yet to be executed. The lack of political will to address structural problems—including housing, waste collection, and public services—as well as an accommodationist approach to polluting firms, limits what technicians can accomplish. The World Bank (2014) has undertaken background studies for a project to extend sanitation services and improve the water and sanitation system in northern Lima; however, it would entail involuntary resettlement, and it is unclear whether the project will be politically feasible. For the time being, projects to dramatically reduce wastewater pollution and remediate the river are mired in policy stasis.

Handcuffing Regulatory Authorities. Regulatory authorities have for long been beleaguered and underresourced and were practically dismantled in the mid-2010s. When Humala's government passed Law 30230 in 2014 and the Supreme Court upheld it in 2020, regulatory authorities lost the little sanctioning power they held to mitigate environmental harms. SPDA's director suggested, "Ollanta Humala began as a president that was close to the left, but along the way, pressure from the business sector pushed him to the

---

[71] "Chosica: Desviación del Río Rímac deja más de 50 damnificados," La noche es Mía, January 24, 2018, timestamp 10:00.

[72] This is called the Comisión Multisectorial para la Recuperación de la Calidad de los Recursos Hídricos de la Cuenca del Rio Rímac.

right.... [This Law] was due to pressure from the business sector on the Peruvian government... and the result is a regulatory authority that is not allowed to enforce sanctions and fines."[73] Law 30230 allowed the environmental regulatory agency, OEFA, to forgive environmental infractions by industry for a period of three years with only a few exceptions. Law 30230 officially allowed firms that already had some form of an environmental regulatory oversight on paper, however inadequate, to essentially ignore environmental standards. Firms argued that before fines could be levied, they should be given a grace period (*adecuación*) that would allow them to make necessary changes, but environmental advocates responded that laws requiring firms to have environmental impact studies dated back to the 1990s and was nothing new. Furthermore, Law 30230 redirected the funds from the fines that OEFA did levy directly back to the public treasury and national budget as opposed to remaining within OEFA to continue boosting environmental regulatory capacity.[74]

One investigative report found that the Peruvian government lost at least US$11 million to mining companies in the first year, which benefited 49 mining companies during what critics called an "environmental amnesty."[75] NGOs such as SPDA and various civil society organizations tied to the Coordinadora Nacional de Derechos Humanos brought legal demands against the unconstitutionality of Law 30230 and petitioned Congress to make changes.

Despite the law's objective to stimulate more extractive investments and increase the public treasury's coffers, economic growth slowed during this time due to falling international commodity prices.[76] Proponents of the law had argued that it would help improve environmental performance, as firms would be motivated to comply if there was less threat of sanction. Instead, during this period the number of environmental infractions recorded by OEFA increased, for example from 10% to 37% in the extractives sector, 24% to 76% in hydrocarbons, and 2% to 76% in the fishing industry. A director

---

[73] Interview with Isabel Calle, SPDA, May 5, 2017.

[74] Interview with Carol Mora, SPDA, reported in Milton López Tarabochia, "Perú: El 'paquetazo ambiental' cumplió con sus objetivos?," *Mongabay.com*, February 1, 2017. See also Richard O'Diana Rocca, "La inconstitucionalidad de la Ley 30230 y el Proyecto de Ley 3941," *CAAP.org.pe*, n.d.

[75] Esteban Valle Riestra, "Los 30 millones que no cobró el gobierno en multas mineras," *Convoca.pe*, August 2, 2015.

[76] Between 2002 and 2013, Peru was one of the fastest growing countries in Latin America, with an average annual GDP growth rate of 6.1%. Between 2014 and 2018, annual GDP growth slowed to an average rate of 3.2% due to lower international commodity rates, particularly copper. See https://www.worldbank.org/en/country/peru/overview.

of OEFA admitted that Law 30230 "could not be considered a preventative mechanism, as it does not dissuade environmental infractions. . . . [T]here were more incentives to commit environmental infractions and less costs to doing so."[77]

Furthermore, interviews with OEFA officials revealed that regulatory practices in Peru are underfunded and shrouded in secrecy. The Ombudsman's Office published a report surveying OEFA's progress on monitoring the closure of mining tailings, which in 2015 had amounted to a visit of 33 of the 36 documented sites, but only six administrative proceedings. The Ombudsman's Office declared this to be "insufficient, which is why it is urgent to intensify regulatory and sanctioning measures" (Defensoría del Pueblo 2015, 7–8). Similarly, OEFA had registered 156 hydrocarbon environmental damages but pointed out that "[documentation] serves no purpose if no one is held responsible" (Defensoría del Pueblo 2015, 7–8). As of 2015, no responsible parties had been identified, nor had remediation plans commenced, despite 72 hydrocarbon environmental damages being classified as high risk by OEFA. Even when indigenous communities and their allies use smartphone technology to document environmental degradation to defend their rights, their reports only go as far as OEFA's front door.[78]

When OEFA officials were asked in interviews to identify the industries that were being monitored by the agency, they gave vague answers. Inspections have been levied on a small number of firms on OEFA's roster, and officials were loath to reveal information about inspection schedules, selection criteria, or inspection protocols. When pressed, officials explained that given a limited budget, they chose the industries to monitor with annual visits based on multiple criteria that prioritized firms involved in "social conflicts." Furthermore, if a firm received a visit one year, it would not be visited the following year, and assessments of what zone is involved in a social conflict varies considerably over time.[79]

OEFA officials monitored firms based on the highly variable agreements and standards that businesses had previously established. A OEFA director explained, "We monitor for compliance with the commitments that were made when the firm was approved. So, if it's a firm that is twenty years old,

[77] Milton López Tarabochia, "Perú: El 'paquetazo ambiental' cumplió con sus objetivos?," *Mongabay.com*, February 1, 2017; "OEFA reconoce impacto nocivo de la Ley del 'Paquetazo Ambiental,'" *Convoca.pe*, November 9, 2016.
[78] Dan Collyns, "After Years of Toxic Spills, Indigenous Peruvians Use Tech to Fight Back," *The Guardian*, December 14, 2017.
[79] Interview with Francisco Garcia, director of Dirección de Evaluación, OEFA, May 4, 2017.

it has an environmental standard that is twenty years old. We monitor what is written on the paper. If the firm has been granted a transition period and it expires in five years, we monitor that. We cannot [seek compliance] with what is not within their commitments."[80]

Hiring practices in OEFA, ANA, and other government agencies reflect how Peru has deprioritized building regulatory capacity for environmental standards. The majority of OEFA employees are contract workers, including all inspectors. When an inspection is scheduled to occur, inspectors are hired, and all equipment is rented, including cars inspectors use to get to sites. Inspectors who work by contract can work for other agencies; it was unclear whether they could also work for private industry.[81] Because of this, an OEFA director said, "Public-sector professionals rotate all the time. You are never going to find someone who only works on [one issue] for ten years. You ask me the exact number of people who work in OEFA, but it's hard to say."[82]

Researchers who have studied the hiring practices of firms and public officials in Peru characterize the relationship between the two as a "revolving door":

> In each government, people who have tons of money finance the electoral campaigns. Once the administrations are formed, they start to decide which government positions are handed out . . . and here certain actors from the private sector . . . come through the door and they go back and forth. There is a marriage between the big firms, especially the extractives industry, and the highest government officials.[83]

Law 30230 only made official the Peruvian government's long-standing accommodationist practices with polluting industries. Even before the law was passed, 80% of the environmental infractions and levied fines detected by OEFA between 2010 and 2011 were suspended, despite the infractions being deemed "grave or very grave."[84] Political pressure has resulted in regulatory

---

[80] Interview with Francisco Garcia, director of Dirección de Evaluación, OEFA, May 4, 2017.
[81] Interview with Sonia Aranibar Tapia, subdirector of Evaluación de la Calidad Ambiental, OEFA, May 4, 2017.
[82] Interview with Francisco Garcia, director of Dirección de Evaluación, OEFA, May 4, 2017.
[83] Francisco Durand, professor, on *Documentary: Historias de Agua*, produced by Red Muqui and KillaKuyay, December 13, 2017, timestamp 17:00. See also Vergara and Encinas (2019, 242–43).
[84] Esteban Valle Riestra, "Los (s) 30 millones que no cobró el gobierno en multas mineras," *Convoca.pe*, August 2, 2015.

practices that have such little authority or agency that they are practically nonexistent.

Keeping Citizen Participation at Arm's Length. While the process of attending to slow-moving harms in Buenos Aires and Bogotá has involved complex struggles for augmenting citizens' voices and participation, in Lima citizen participation has been much more elusive. Broadly speaking, the left's prior association with terrorist groups provides a convenient excuse for public officials to ignore citizen demands when they surface. When pressed in interviews, officials revealed that citizen demands in the sector were vexing and suspicious. One Water Ministry official remarked, "We have to be careful with citizens, because they ask for *mesas de dialogo* but many of them are either terrorists or just want to be paid off."[85] When asked how many *mesas de dialogo* DIGESA officials had participated in over water quality issues, the official said, "I don't know how much of it I can share."[86] One attorney in the Ombudsman's Office reported that MINAM had stopped authorizing *mesas de dialogos* "because it opens up too many fronts."[87] The executive director of SPDA noted that under the Pedro Pablo Kuczynski administration (2016–18), "MINAM has closed considerably, it is not a ministry with open doors."[88] A former OEFA director of environmental regulations who has also been a former mining executive summed up the position of many public officials: "The discourse against mining from these sectors [who are radicals], is based on a history of arguing that mining produces extensive contamination. In reality, the environmental frame is only a tool that legitimizes the movement, but what is really behind it all is a fight for a redistribution of mining rents."[89]

Government officials' distrust of organized citizen demands has shaped the type of citizen participation they have invited into forums related to the Rímac's governance. For example, multiple studies have been conducted to create river basin councils, but their implementation has been uneven. In 2017, an attorney in the Ombudsman's Office described the situation: "[Some initiatives have begun], but they have not had the necessary implementation.

---

[85] Anonymous interviews April 2017 and May 2017.
[86] Anonymous interview, May 2017.
[87] Interview with Giselle Huamani Olivo, Ombudsman's Office, May 3, 2017.
[88] Interview with Isabel Calle, SPDA, May 5, 2017.
[89] William Póstigo, ex-president of Activos Mineros S.A.C. (2014–15) and ex-president of the Tribunal de Fiscalización Ambiental OEFA (2010–14), on *Documentary: Historias de Agua*, produced by Red Muqui and KillaKuyay, December 13, 2017, timestamp 28:53.

Those pilots, and other [propositions] . . . after ten years of passing the national hydraulic law on river basin councils, they were going to create one for each department, or interregionally. But this hasn't happened."[90] ANA has planned to roll out 29 councils and has created 12 as of 2020, yet it is unclear to what extent they are operational. A council was created for the Rímac (Consejo de Recursos Hídricos de Cuenca Chillón-Rima-Lurín). The committee's website states, "[The participants] were selected through a democratic process, in which all institutions related to water management could choose their representative," yet the committee's composition is heavily skewed toward public officials and their allies. Of the 19 positions on the council, few represented civil society interests. Most were members of either regional or local governments, rural or urban service providers, the electricity company, or the cement association. Yet the government agency members of the multisector commission are not the same as the agencies on the river basin council, further obfuscating roles and responsibilities. Financed in part by foreign aid and multilateral assistance and housed within the institutional purview of the ANA, the river basin councils appear to keep out citizen groups that question or demand accountability.[91]

In 2019, civil society groups joined a meeting with congressional members on the issue of mining tailings on the Rímac. The Platform for the Defense of the Upper Basin of the Rímac River (Plataforma de la Cuenca Alta del Rio Rímac), and the Coodinator for the Defense of the Rímac River Basin (Coordinadora de Defensa de la Cuenca del Rio Rímac), were accompanied by the NGO Red Muqui. The forum was sponsored by the Congressional Commission for Indigenous and Afro-Peruvian Environmental Issues (La Comisión de Pueblos Andinos, Amazonicos, Afroperuanos, Ambiente y Ecologia).[92] These grassroots organizations continue to pressure for the removal of the mining tailings on the Rímac in the upper basin. Congressional debates also continue over strengthening the laws governing mining tailings

---

[90] Interview with Fabiola Alburqueque, Ombudsman's Office, May 3, 2017.
[91] Consejos de Recursos Hídricos de Cuenca Chillón, Rímac, and Lurín, Autoridad Nacional de Agua, ana.gob.pe, accessed December 12, 2020.
[92] Other groups included Frente de Defensa de los Intereses de Chicla. "Foro: Peligros en la Cuenca del Río Rímac y alternativas de solución," *Servindi.org* (Comunicación intercultural para un mundo más humano y diverso), February 26, 2019; "Peligros en la Cuenca del Río Rímac y alternativas: Por riesgos inminentes, Ley de Remediación de Pasivos Ambientales debe ser discutido y aprobado," *Diario Uno*, March 1, 2019; "Foro sobre los peligros en la Cuenca del Río Rímac y alternativas de solución," *Congreso.gob.pe*, n.d.

and environmental damages from extractives. Notably, none of the civil society groups represented in these congressional forums is involved in the state-sponsored river basin council. To date, the few grassroots groups pushing for comprehensive change do not have a seat at the policymaking table.

Evaluating Alternative Explanations in the Peru Case

The Rímac River is a case of uninitiated reform, and thus the methodological objective of this chapter has been to show that the factors that explained high reform in Buenos Aires and moderate reform in Bogotá were indeed missing for Lima. I have documented how weak bonds were accompanied by missing bridges for the Rímac River, resulting in no policy shifts toward reforms. This lack of environmental advocacy mobilization was rooted in weak political and economic enabling conditions, involving historic repression of human rights actors by conservative political administrations aligned with extractivist industries. How do alternative explanations about environmental mobilization hold up for understanding the lack of environmental mobilization in Lima for the Rímac River?

First, what has been the role of natural disasters in igniting attention toward slow harms on the Rímac? The Rímac has a long history of flooding: 120 major overflow events have been documented, with heavy rains in 1578, 1650, 1728, 1750, 1790, 1828, 1876, 1891, 1925, 1982, 1997, and most recently 2017, when at least 67 people were killed in mudslides.[93] Natural disasters are imminent threats in Lima for riverbank communities whose homes are precariously built on soft soils. Much more so than in Buenos Aires and Bogotá, large portions of Lima were "self-built" by migrants, and riverbank self-built dwellings represent much of the city's low-income housing; these areas are especially vulnerable to climate change–induced physical insecurity. Here residents do make a greater number of collective claims when flooding and flash floods loom. For example, Chosica and La Margen Izquierda face extreme vulnerability when El Niño weather patterns overflow the Rímac, and residents can easily become stranded in floodwaters or witness their homes toppling. Yet residents continue to wait for services and resources that are

---

[93] "Peru Suffers Worst Flooding in Decades," *The Atlantic*, March 20, 2017; "El Río Rímac inundó Lima muchas veces," *Diario Uno*, March 26, 2017; "Lima's Time Bomb: How Mudslides Threaten the World's Great 'Self-Built' City," *The Guardian*, June 20, 2017. Destructive El Niño events have occurred in 1972–73, 1976, 1982–83, 1997–98, 2002–3 (Subgerencia de Defensa Civil 2013, 3).

slow to materialize. Flooding events have done little to help overhaul how the river is managed. Although extreme events make headlines and may generate temporary relief from government, many are habituated to the rivers' flood risks. Flooding events have not, all else being equal, induced policy changes for pollution remediation.

Overall, the three river basin case studies show that flooding events do generate more claims-making from impacted residents—whether as regular, periodic occurrences (as in the cases of some communities in Lomas de Zamora, Buenos Aires) or as ad hoc extreme crises (as in the cases of communities on the Lima river banks). Grassroots organizing around flooding occurred in low-income communities in all three cities, but only in Tunjuelo, Bogotá, did a singular high-impact flooding event generate environmental claims-making. In that case, those responses reached the state—however imperfectly—only when they were amplified by bridges such as an activist judge and working groups within the Comptroller's Office.

How do socioeconomic factors contribute to bonding mobilization in Lima? Lima's riverbank communities provide evidence that extreme poverty can stifle collective action, particularly when combined with high rates of migrancy. Riverbank communities' level of poverty in Lima is comparable to the Inflamable neighborhood of Buenos Aires in Dock Sud, Avellaneda, where residents are consumed by exposure to toxins and yet social organizing has been muted. High poverty levels and relatively weaker social ties in neighborhoods where residents have more recently migrated from other regions, such as the riverbank communities, can make social organizing less likely. Therefore, socioeconomic factors can influence organizing around environmental degradation, but it is not the only determinant, and low-income communities show environmental concern in several communities surveyed in this book, especially as concerns relate to health risks. The Lima case further shows how communities living in deep poverty tend to have few available tools for collective action. In the case of Lima's riverbank communities, resignation over slow harms is driven by histories of state repression, conservative self-help housing policies that fueled distrust and acquiescence, and high rates of resident turnover due to legacies of armed conflict.

The postmaterial thesis suggested that environmental concern would manifest in political parties, which did not occur in Latin American countries, where political parties and environmental activists are rarely allies. Lima has been governed predominantly by conservative political parties aligned with business interests, and environmental concern has not been central to the city's electoral landscape. A notable exception was the unexpected election of Mayor Susana Villarán (2011–14), whose ascent put a leftist in City Hall for the first time in 25 years. Villarán came close to being a bridge for slow-harms advocacy; she had been a vocal human rights activist in the 1990s and participated in anti-Fujimori protests and the transition government of Paniagua (Dosh and Coyoli 2019, 268–69). Villarán took up the Vía Parque Rímac, a previously stalled plan to create 25 hectares of green space and help remediate portions of the Rímac River. The project failed after riverbank communities organized around their right to stay or be adequately compensated.[94] As an environmental cause, the project had few allies, limited resources, no public participation, and was attacked by both Villarán's conservative enemies and grassroots bases. Broadly speaking, Villarán's electoral promises were not as centered around environmental justice as the Bogotá mayor who also faced a recall, Gustavo Petro. Nevertheless, Villarán came closest to pushing for river remediation in Lima but lacked the governing capacity and political support to be effective. Surviving a recall, she did not win reelection and was thwarted by attacks from the right, limited grassroots support, and inadequate party machinery (Dosh and Coyoli 2019, 275). Not all leftist mayors are environmentalists, but the few environmentally oriented mayors who have come to power in the region have faced strong right-wing opposition. Nationally, environmental issues have very little representation, if any, among Peru's political parties; for example, the Green Alternative Party has almost no electoral presence.

Finally, to what extent do weaknesses in legal institutions in Peru contribute to the lack of policy reforms for slow harms? Peru's Supreme Court did not have the autonomy and independence of Argentine and Colombian judiciaries; their rulings on environmental issues mirrored executive and legislative priorities of accommodating mining interests. Peru's Supreme Court defended Law 30230 (the *paquetazo ambiental*) as constitutional and gave regulatory agencies the green light to not enforce environmental infractions.

In Argentina and Colombia, grassroots activists accessed the courts and used legal institutions as one of many tools to press their claims. While Peru has the right to a clean environment inscribed in its 1993 Constitution and the legal recourse of *amparo* individually or collectively, these laws have no authority in practice due to a hostile judicial climate and have been little

---

[94] "¿Qué pasó con Rio Verde, la obra que tenía como objetivo recuperar la ribera del Río Rímac?," *La República*. October 18, 2022.

used. In Peru, the Court's alignment with extractivist interests closed off legal routes to the few actors working on environmental justice. Other potential bridges, such as the Ombudsman's Office and high-level NGOs such as SPDA, signaled that they were not interested in initiating litigation given the nature of the closed legal system. While the Bogotá River case showed that legal institutions were alone insufficient to provoke a comprehensive change in slow-harms policymaking, the Rímac River case suggests that supportive legal institutions comprise a key element to the facilitating structures for environmental mobilization that are sorely felt when they are missing.

Taken together, the three cases show how supportive legal institutions, where they exist, are products of citizen advocacy and mobilization. The activation of laws reflects the movements and societal pressures that helped either create them (as was the case in the 1991 Colombian Constitution and the 2003 Argentine judicial reforms) or activate them (as was the case for Argentina's slow-harms mobilization). Under extreme hostile enabling conditions such as Peru's armed conflict, and conservative administrations that repress citizen participation, citizen movements for transparency and rights claiming are unlikely to form. Because Peru lacked social movements for change, either broadly for judicial autonomy and democracy strengthening or more narrowly for environmental protections, the existing legal frameworks for Peruvian environmental issues have little practical authority.

Weak Bonds with No Bridges: Resignation to Contamination

Like many cities in the Global South, Lima's Rímac River pollution continues as an embedded part of the everyday landscape rather than an urgent policy problem. Several characteristics are similar across the three metropolitan regions: riverine land with high pollutant loads houses low-income communities with tenuous housing protections and economic ties to centrally located jobs; residents lack wastewater and waste collection services; and a changing climate exacerbates existing vulnerability. Unlike in Buenos Aires and Bogotá, Lima's Rímac is the principal source of the city's drinking water, requiring massive investments to ensure potability—and yet, in contrast to Argentina and Colombia, neither public officials nor NGOs have made an attempt to put river recuperation on the policy agenda. The state remains silent and, in many senses, complicit. As an attorney in the MINAM noted, "There are battles that can be won, and others on which we continue to wait to fight."[95] Everyone, and no one, is responsible. Contamination of the Rímac represents slow harms whose visibility has remained unchanged, or worse, become even more invisible as apathy has settled and other socioenvironmental conflicts have drowned them out.

In Peru, the enabling conditions for reform were weakest of the three cases. Like Colombia, Peru experienced intense political violence for many decades that further diminished the growth of organized civil society and autonomous NGO development. Both Colombia's and Peru's transitions to democracy brought conservative administrations to power that were determined to undermine or repress human rights groups and NGOs. While conservative administrations in all three countries courted international investments, in Peru the accommodationist alliance with the international extractive industry was most dominant and damaging for slow-harms attenuation. This chapter showed how in Peru, conservative political administrations created accommodationist policies for mining across legal institutions, environmental institutions, and government agencies that interact with organized civil society. Fast, targeted harms from mining conflicts occupy all spaces for environmental concerns, made more contentious because of the persistent belief by public officials that civil society activism is linked to terrorism.

In this context, bridging mobilization was entirely absent for slow harms. The few NGOs working on environmental issues do not work on slow harms or water pollution; most NGOs lack material resources and are dependent on government contracts. Enabling conditions were most hostile to organized civil society and human rights mobilization in Peru due to the relationship between political violence and mineral wealth extraction. Peru shows how environmental rights are most insecure in contexts where civil society is fighting for basic protections against physical insecurity.

Rather than broad-based policy change on the Rímac, NGOs working on environmental issues in Peru focus on conservation issues or on helping local groups seek limited compensation for mining-related damages. Human rights groups and institutions, such as the Ombudsman's Office and the National Human Rights Coordinator, have participated in congressional hearings over the constitutionality of assaults on environmental protections, but their reach is limited. Rights-based claims-making has little effect in

---

[95] Interview with Julio Guzman, MINAM prosecutor, and special prosecutor for environmental crimes, May 3, 2017.

Peru; neither NGOs nor state activists have been able to translate initial claims for democratization and accountability for military crimes onto the construction of more robust accountability institutions. No NGO or single institution emerged as a key leader for slow harms; the few actors that work on related topics do so in a fragmented manner; it is difficult to determine which nodes would form part of a network were one to emerge.

Not surprisingly, bonding mobilization, or grassroots activism by impacted communities, has also been limited on the Rímac, although not as limited as bridging activity. Residents exposed to toxins have focused mostly on imminent threats, such as dangers from flooding and landslides, rather than slow-moving environmental hazards. Given the history of an absent state and political violence, riverbank communities in Lima do not want to be relocated far from the city center and lose what they themselves have built. Residents have a deep mistrust of public officials whose promises have little follow-through and who historically have insisted that communities solve their own problems. Perhaps when bridging mobilization is limited, bonding mobilization is also likely to be weak if the former helps to activate and aggregate the latter, as we saw to different degrees in Argentina and Colombia.

Gripping news coverage occasionally details how flash floods from the Rímac devastate urban communities, or how municipal authorities themselves order dumping of solid waste into the river. Limeños are not blind to environmental problems in the city; surveys show that air pollution, a lack of green spaces, and limited waste management services are key concerns. Nearly 70% of urban residents surveyed were unsatisfied with the state of the city's rivers.[96] More broadly in Peru, contamination is widespread. A study by the General Directorate of Health concluded that 30% of the population is at risk of exposure to heavy metals, 20% to metalloids such as arsenic, and 6% to hydrocarbons.[97] Nevertheless, very limited organized mobilization has emerged around this slow-moving harm among the urban residents surveyed, and those suffering the most direct impacts of toxic contamination continue to wait.

---

[96] Surveys show that in 2019, Lima residents named the most pressing environmental problems as air pollution (72%), lack of green spaces (40.9%), waste and recycling (33%, 20.7%); 68.8% of those surveyed were dissatisfied with the environmental conditions of the city's rivers (Lima Cómo Vamos 2019, 27–28).

[97] Raquel Neyra, "Peru: Castillo's Triumph and Popular Environmentalism," *Undisciplined Environments*, July 8, 2021.

6
Cities, Pollution, and Democracy

We are living through an onslaught of environmental disasters. Wildfires in California. Tsunamis in Indonesia. Flash floods in India. Deforestation for palm oil cultivation in Malaysia. Environmental accidents from fracking in Australia and oil drilling in Ecuador. Many environmental crises are the consequence of climate change, but some, such as water pollution and toxic siting, have different causes. While some environmental problems make headlines, others fly under the radar for decades. All environmental problems have the potential to inflict bodily harm, yet they do so at different rates and tempos and distribute harms unevenly across different communities. Distinct temporalities shape whether harms are visible to us and others. To understand environmental politics, we must contend with how harms move in time.

This book examined *slow harms,* environmental dangers that accumulate slowly over time and target specific communities. These harms present gradual (as opposed to imminent) threats and dispersed (as opposed to concentrated) geographic proximity to bodily harm. Slow harms accumulate so gradually and in such a layered manner that they often escape scrutiny for years. Dangerous toxins spread throughout communities and become part of the everyday landscape. Generations are born into these settings, and the associated risks are often largely invisible. The activities that give rise to the harms, whether from industrial effluent discharge or residential waste dumping, also become familiar, a given. Residents may not remember a time when things were different.

Temporalities influence the possibility for collective action. Citizen collective action is always difficult to generate, regardless of the policy problem. Many environmental problems involve common pool resources, whereby it's difficult to exclude those who use or degrade the resource, and anyone who can access the resource can diminish it. Yet the label "common pool resources" involves many different types of environmental harms with differing time horizons and levels of visibility—not all common pool resource problems are equally challenging around which to mobilize. Slow-moving targeted harms—the topic of this book—are especially difficult to incentivize action around; their opaqueness and multigenerational characteristics make slow harms a low-level priority to activists and policymakers alike. In many cases, problem identification for impacted communities may take years, if it happens at all. For communities with grassroots leadership aware of the problem, they often make demands on government that go unheeded. Difficult to detect and document, slow harms often accumulate in obscurity with little accountability.

The Argument and Cases Revisited

Why and how do cities address slow-moving environmental harms in the Global South? This book unpacks the strategies of citizen collective action and the linkages that networks of actors make to each other and to the state in their pursuit of harms reduction. While organized local grassroots pressure from impacted communities—what I term *bonding mobilization*—was a critical component of policy change, it was insufficient. Bridging activists were resourced outsiders that helped break through the impasse of stalled policymaking; these were found in both state (e.g., Ombudsman's Office, legal institutions) and society (NGOs, universities, etc.). The book argued that strong *bridging mobilization* drew broad attention to slow harms and connected grievances about pollution to powerholders within the state. The strongest bridges possessed material resources such as money or expertise and prior histories of collaborative work.

The book's cases illustrated how in South America, the most effective bridges for slow harms were not rooted in environmental organizing but instead in human rights networks. The strongest bridges emerged in countries with strong human rights actors and national-level supportive presidential administrations from the center left. In Argentina, multiple leftist presidential administrations oversaw a period when human rights groups were physically protected and gained social legitimacy and when human rights principles and practices penetrated government institutions. Bridging activists for slow harms were able to credibly reframe river pollution as a human rights violation and convert a NIMBY issue into a national policy problem. Bridges working on river pollution relied on preexisting networks or shared experiences from prior human rights work to assess risk, elevate its visibility, and connect others to the problem at hand. In Buenos Aires, bridges included human rights NGOs, the Ombudsman's Office, and legal institutions; these actors were able to effectively link environmental issues to human rights and push forward substantial policy changes for the Matanza Riachuelo River.

Examining these dynamics in the Colombia and Peru cases uncovers further evidence for the argument. In Bogotá, slow-harms remediation on the Bogotá River has progressed, but much more slowly and unevenly than in the Buenos Aires case. While impacted communities mobilized across the Bogotá River and were effective in drawing initial attention to their problems, the process of aggregating and scaling up grievances, or bridging mobilization has been weaker compared to the Buenos Aires case. Here state-level bridges—activist judges and bureaucrats within the Comptroller's Office—were active but worked with smaller NGOs with limited resources. NGOs had varying levels of technical expertise but drew on few material resources and lacked a common history of collaborative work. Neither the state nor societal bridges engaged the slow-harms crisis as one of equity or social rights, but rather focused on environmental conservation claims that failed to attract broader societal support outside of environmental advocacy circles.

The book argued that Colombia's bridges were weaker because they lacked a common framework of rights-based mobilization and support and protection from the state. In Colombia, conservative presidential administrations weakened the power of human rights mobilization; presidential administrations were drawn from former business leaders who viewed civil society organizing as a manifestation of support for leftist guerrilla movements amid a decades-long armed conflict. As in Peru, Colombia's conservative administrations were more closely aligned with extractivist industries, and human rights defenders were not protected. The book unpacks the policy shifts that ensued and which have entailed a limited amount of improved regulatory capacity to shut down polluting industries. Progress toward institutionalizing environmental regulation in Colombia is thus more fragile.

Finally, in Lima, mobilization around slow harms on the Rímac River have failed to materialize, and there have been no policy shifts toward remediation. Few impacted communities have mobilized around slow harms, despite intense health risks generated by toxic exposure, and thus bonding mobilization has been weak. Most noticeably, bridging activists have been absent. Public officials within the judiciary, Public Prosecutor's Office, and Ombudsman's Office have failed to address the cause of decontaminating the Rímac River against a backdrop of extremely weak environmental institutions and a precarious human rights agenda. The Peru chapter traced the rise of a limited human rights movement that was quashed by consecutive conservative administrations that were aligned with extractivist industries and were highly distrustful of civil society organizing. Presidential administrations have repeatedly sided with allies in the military, and human rights mobilization has sputtered to a halt. Civil society organizing is much weaker in the Peruvian case, and potential bridges for river pollution have failed to materialize. With both bonding and bridging mobilization being weak, Lima's Rímac River continues to be consumed by toxic slow harms, and policy shifts have yet to be initiated.

The entanglement between legacies of political violence and the nation's political economy had important implications for how environmental protections developed and the extent to which environmental activists were politically protected. Extractives make up significant shares of Colombia's and Peru's economy, but a small amount of Argentina's, giving Argentina's presidential administrations more autonomy in supporting different forms of civil society mobilization. The level of mining dependence created challenges for slow-harms reform, particularly in Peru. Partisan orientations of presidential administrations are influenced by the makeup and strength of national economic actors and vice versa. When economic actors are powerful and lack a countervailing force to check their influence, their interests can seep into institutions such as the strength of the Courts or horizontal accountability institutions such as the Ombudsman's Office. The bonding and bridging mobilization of the three cases occurred under a backdrop of powerful economic forces. Even though both Bogotá and Lima had similar amounts of mining concessions on the Bogotá River and the Rímac River, respectively, Bogotá's public sector institutions were better able to introduce some slow harms policy changes, likely due to Colombia's being less mining-captured at the political and institutional level than Peru.

Around the world, mobilization around slow harms does occur, but it is rare. This book used process tracing to reveal the power of citizen networks in shaping policy change over environmental problems in urban Latin America. This theory-building project illustrated how domestic-level political and social cleavages interact with environmental institutions that are largely imported from abroad to influence if and whether environmental problems are addressed. This approach provides a model for better understanding the possibility, and limitations, of environmental policymaking in Global South cities. As most scholarly attention—and international aid—shifts toward climate change mitigation and adaptation strategies in the Global South, careful attention to the local historical legacies of mobilization and partisan cleavages can better contextualize the challenges cities face when attending to environmental crises. In what follows I examine how the urban form provides distinct opportunities that facilitate disruption and bridging activities for environmental activism. I then turn to a discussion of the relationship between democracy and environmental institution building, probing whether the right to dissent is fundamental to the exercise of environmental protections. The book concludes by emphasizing that environmental regulation is co-produced by citizen collective action, often as a regulatory regime of last resort.

Cities as Sites of Disruption and Bridging

Social science literature focusing on environmental harms in the Global South has frequently centered rural environmentalism. Challenges for rural activism are not so dissimilar to what urban communities face. For example, rural communities struggle to access information about environmental impact assessments and their underlying data (Lora-Wainwright 2017, 22; Hochstetler 2018, 108–9), possess few spaces for consultation regarding mitigation or regulation of polluting activities (Eisenstadt and West 2019, 76–85; Jaskoski 2014b, 874), and can experience resignation and apathy due to, for example, being beholden to the polluting industry for employment (Lora-Wainwright 2017, 29–30). Rural communities opposed to extractives and siting of megadevelopment projects have used strategies that also emerge in urban communities, such as roadblocks, occupation of construction sites, coordinated participation in consultation processes, collaborations with scholars, and collective lawsuits (e.g., Hochstetler and Tranjan 2016, 506; Jaskoski 2020, 546–50). However, this book, centered on urban environmental conflicts, illustrates how urban communities grapple with environmental harms with resources and capacities distinct from their rural counterparts. These resources—such as economic and social diversity, concentrated spatial forms, and proximity to seats of power—can facilitate more opportunities for both disruption and bridging, central tasks for slow-harms activism.

Urban social life involves densely populated, diverse social relations among individuals with different occupations, racial backgrounds, ethnicities, religions, and more. Thus cities are "relational incubators," more readily facilitating the transportation of ideas and resources across diverse communities than their rural counterparts (Post 2018, 117–18; Nicholls 2008, 842, 844). Nicholls (2008, 848) argued that the economic and social complexity of cities makes them more likely to concentrate groups representing diverse issues (such as labor unions, religious groups, student organizers), who, when brought together, can be channeled to form urban insurgent networks. Physical proximity allows actors to exchange ideas and resources more easily, but it is not a panacea, as close quarters between distinct groups can also lead to more tension and segregation. In the three cases in this book, cities became sites of relational network building between diverse actors that leveraged unique resources in the urban setting to mount resistance to slow harms. For example, in Colombia, one wetland group in Suba turned into many more across the city, eventually forming a city-wide network of like-minded activists fighting for similar causes in different locations, developing tools like the Ecobus, a workshop space that brought in thousands of participants from many different backgrounds to learn about wetlands protections.[1] In Argentina, environmental grassroots organizations, such as the Rocha Collective in Laguna de Rocha, Neighbors in Defense of Santa Catalina Wetlands, and the RRR, attended each other's events for several years to "boost their numbers" and cause more disruption at their rallies.[2] Population density and diverse forms of economic and social activity can facilitate cross-linkages between groups with similar goals.

Cities also have concentrated spatial forms that protestors can exploit to increase disruption and reach more potential allies, making them "absolutely critical sites of protest" (Pasotti 2020, 14). Mass mobilizations can take over urban downtown areas with noise and spectacle to increase their impact. Urban activists are especially skilled in "occup[ying] space and thereby claim[ing] it, physically and politically, with their bodies, their noise, their banners" (Jansen 2001, 40).[3] Protest strategies can leverage close proximity

---

[1] Interview with Medardo Galindo, Fundación Conejera, July 19, 2016.
[2] Interview with Martin Farina, Colectivo Ecologica Unidos por la Laguna de Rocha, March 15, 2017.
[3] Cities have varied spatial forms, and not all urban neighborhoods have the spatial conditions conducive to facilitating diverse and layered interactions between residents and urban movement participants, such as parks and green spaces, sidewalks, and accessible center plazas. Nevertheless these spatial conditions, where they exist, tend to be more common in capital cities than in remote,

to the seat of political power (Wallace 2014, 21–22). Many cities and especially capitals house landmark public institutions such as mayors' offices or legislatures which serve as targets for protestors, whether functionally or symbolically. It is no coincidence that rural protestors often march in capital cities to increase the visibility of their demands. For example, influenced by the civil rights movement, the March on Washington became a key repertoire for U.S. social movements (Tilly and Tarrow 2015, 51–52); the downtown march is a common repertoire for movements around the world.

While slow-harms activists did not frequently generate mass mobilizations, they used downtown centers innovatively to elevate the visibility of the issues they championed. For example, the Laguna de Rocha protestors in Esteban Echeverria, Gran Buenos Aires, used their downtown city center of Monte Grande to great effect when exposing city councilors who had voted against the Rocha Wetlands reserve after being unduly influenced by industry. In the high-traffic downtown square, activists mounted oversized posters displaying the scratched-out faces of the city council members who had voted against the reserve, shaming them into reversing their votes after local media reports advertised the scandal.[4] In Greater Buenos Aires, several groups, such as the Boca Association and Neighbors Autonomously Organized against the CEAMSE in González Catan, distributed pamphlets in their city centers about their demands for river remediation and landfill closures, respectively, coordinating their outreach during certain times and days when the largest group of people would be most likely to pass by.

This book has highlighted the role of bridging actors in society, such as NGOs and academic experts. These elite actors are more likely to live and work in urban centers (Wallace 2014, 21), often in capital or secondary cities; all the NGOs involved in the Buenos Aires and Bogotá cases had offices in the capital city. Long distances and remote locations make access to bridging allies much more difficult. NGO employees, particularly in the context of limited material resources, are unlikely to travel long distances, and rural areas can present physical insecurity for outsiders. In the Colombia case, the 347 kilometers of the river made communities living further away in rural areas, such as the *veedurías* in El Colegio and farmers mobilizing

---

agrarian areas. See Pasotti (2020, 56–57) for the types of neighborhoods that facilitate protest according to the urbanist Jane Jacobs's criteria.

[4] Interview with Martin Farina, Colectivo Ecologica Unidos por la Laguna de Rocha, March 15, 2017.

against the pollution of the Muña Dam in Sibaté, more difficult to access. There, communities complained of being ignored and forgotten and that the authorities "don't listen" (Herrera and Mayka 2020, 7). Farmers in San Mateo, located over 100 kilometers from Lima, whose agriculture was impacted by mining tailings also suffered from being "out of sight, out of mind." One urban observer noted that their problems were ignored in part because "in Lima ... we don't see it."[5]

The proximity of educational institutions to city centers may increase the likelihood of accessing expert knowledge for urban groups combating pollution. Experts play important roles in environmental policymaking, from serving as quiet advisors to becoming themselves key protagonists in policy change (Figueroa and Gutiérrez 2022, 103–5). Academic experts provide communities with both knowledge and procedures for accessing difficult-to-obtain environmental information, as multiple case studies illustrate (e.g., Tang, Tang, and Chiu 2011, 338–47; Urkidi and Walter 2011, 692). Indeed, several grassroots organizations examined in this book partnered with academic experts who became members of the impacted groups' organizations. For example, a prominent member of Foro Hídrico was an engineering professor from downtown Buenos Aires, the Conejera Foundation in Bogotá had several members who became experts in the law and environmental issues, and the Rocha Collective in Esteban Echeverria was led by professors turned environmentalists.

This book also focused on the role of bridging institutions in scaling up environmental claims. Institutions such as the Ombudsman's Office, the Comptroller's Office, the Public Defender's Office, the Public Prosecutor, and the Courts become key spaces for communities impacted by pollution to champion environmental justice. However, distance from city centers and in particular capital cities may hinder access to allied institutions. This is especially pronounced for communities who lack the resources to bring claims independently. In such cases, communities need interlocutors—such as NGOs and Ombudsman's Offices—to file litigation or official claims on their behalf. Environmental litigation is an increasingly important tool for claims making, but lawyers are typically concentrated in cities and unlikely to take "multiple trips to far off pollution sites" (Stern 2013, 177). The geographic distance residents must travel can present major obstacles for seeking redress

---

[5] Monica Untiveros, civil engineer, hydraulic resource specialist, on *Documentary: Historias de Agua*, produced by Red Muqui and KillaKuyay, December 13, 2017, timestamp begins 35:10.

(Van Rooij 2010, 65). Some institutions—such as a National Ombudsman's Office—may have field offices located throughout the country, but most judicial institutions are centered in cities. Field research in Colombia and Argentina revealed that the likelihood of a municipal government or township having an environmental office with staff increases with the size of the municipality.

Mobilized groups endeavor to gain media attention to help amplify their claims, and the national media—located in capital cities—have resources that local media lack. Local media, if it exists at all, may be a single entity captured by polluting industry or otherwise constrained in their autonomous reporting due to personal ties, limited resources, or security concerns (Stern 2011, 306; Arce 2014, 22). National media reaches a larger audience, has more financial resources, and typically entails multiple potential outlets rather than a single venue. Sympathetic journalists can even themselves become bridges, passing information to multiple informants who can boost the efficacy of advocacy networks.[6] Media coverage does not determine environmental outcomes but can be an important resource for groups most able to access journalists. While slow-moving harms are difficult to mobilize around, they may be more difficult in rural areas where media coverage of complaints is less visible than for their urban counterparts.

Democracy, Authoritarianism, and Dissent as a Regulatory Tool

This book has highlighted the role citizen groups play in slow-harms mitigation, a task that was more efficacious in settings with stronger democratic institutions. How important, then, is democracy—with accompanying rights such as freedom of the press, assembly, and dissent—for environmental regulation? Could the types of bonding and bridging mobilization that shape environmental outcomes here emerge in authoritarian contexts? Does environmentalism need democracy, as the cases of river remediation advocacy suggest, or can authoritarian contexts generate sufficient environmental protections?

---

[6] In Buenos Aires, *Clarín* journalist Marina Aizen and *La Nación* journalist Laura Rocha repeatedly covered the Matanza Riachuelo and became experts in the same ecosystem of information exchange between bridging NGOs, institutions, and academic experts. Aizen (2014) also wrote a book on the Matanza Riachuelo River pollution which further increased its visibility.

The three cases show multiple instances where the strength of democratic institutions underlie the pursuit of environmental justice. For example, the grassroots activism featured in Argentina and Colombia was an example of participatory democracy practices and institutions; these included citizen councils, citizen observatories, working tables, judicial advisory committees, and citizen watchdog groups. Another instance of political openness was toleration for mass protest, rallies, and marches in Argentina, Colombia, and Peru. Public sector institutions such as judiciaries and Ombudsman's Offices were key to pollution-remediation policymaking; these were stronger in countries with greater democratic protections and less state-sponsored violence. Peru had the weakest democratic institutions, due to unresolved legacies of state-sponsored violence and mining capture of the state, which impacted the anemic mobilization over river pollution in Lima. These findings suggest that the political openness of the regime matters critically for ensuring that environmental protections are put on the policy agenda.

How do these ideas travel to countries with authoritarian regimes? Eleven Latin American countries were governed by military regimes at some point between the beginning of the Cuban Revolution in 1959 and the end of the Cold War in 1990: Ecuador, El Salvador, Guatemala, Brazil, Bolivia, Argentina, Peru, Panama, Honduras, Chile, and Uruguay. Only 3 of 17 Latin American authoritarian regimes created national environmental agencies of any kind. The few countries that had environmental institutions during military rule saw a dramatic expansion after their transition to democracy. For example, environmental agency personnel increased from 3 to over 6,000 from 1973 to 1989 in Brazil, and from 6 in 1990 to 4,758 by 2000 in Chile. Environmental spending saw a fivefold increase in Chile between the last military government and first civilian one (Hochstetler 2012b, 216). Democratization in Latin America increased regional openness to accepting international environmental norms and assistance, concentrated mostly after the 1992 UN Conference on Environment and Development in Brazil. In both Colombia and Argentina, environmental NGOS grew considerably and received international financial support after the 1990s. Thus, the end of military regimes in Latin America suggests that "democratization has been necessary but not sufficient" for establishing environmental protections in the region (Hochstetler 2012b, 217).

Democratic transitions also brought about improved environmental institutions and legislation in Central and Eastern Europe, although this has varied across countries and issue area (Hochstetler 2012b, 208–13). The post-Soviet cases show how environmentalism and political dissident are closely linked. Environmental activists were influential critics of the Soviet regime, and in Ukraine, the Baltic republics, and Georgia they embraced "eco-nationalism" movements that demanded autonomy from the Soviet state (Newell and Henry 2016, 791). Post-Communist regimes that are EU members (e.g., Czech Republic, Hungary, Slovenia, Estonia) have stronger environmental protections than those that are not, due in part to EU entry requirements but also to the strength of civil society and rule of law, among other factors (Hochstetler 2012b, 212).

In Russia, the environmental movement bloomed during Mikhail Gorbachev's reforms in the late 1980s, but it has since struggled and been marginalized by Vladimir Putin's aggressive attacks. As Russia has again become more authoritarian, NGO offices have been raided, journalists targeted, and severe legislative initiatives have been enacted to quash dissent (Newell and Henry 2016, 793). The few environmental protections that have been advanced—expansion of protected area systems and forest certifications—are tied to entry into global markets, as is Russia's participation in international environmental agreements. Environmental conflicts continue to rise (there were at least 58 major environmental conflicts in 2020) but often receive little publicity due to low levels of transparency and media access, along with collusion between business and local authorities (Demchuk et al. 2021, 11–14). Nevertheless, civil society has played an important watchdog role in some cases. In particular, environmental NGOs and the media have had some limited successes in upholding environmental impact assessments and, for example, protecting the Khimki Forest (Newell and Henry 2016, 797). The Russia case shows how political openness is directly tied to environmental protections as activists (e.g., NGOs, the media, and independents) play a crucial regulatory role in some regions. This citizen-led environmental regulation can morph into broader political dissent as the state closes spaces for assembly and contestation.

China's environmental policy arena provides a useful contrast. Like Russia, China's political regime is known for its lack of transparency, controlling of mass media, and propaganda (Demchuk et al. 2021, 2). Yet China's environmental policies have stood out in recent years as an example of climate change leadership in authoritarian contexts and contributed to the Chinese Communist Party's (CCP) popularity. The China case also counters the notion that environmental activism necessarily opens the political system, as

China's environmental policymaking and limited societal space for activism have existed alongside firm CCP control.

Civil society organizations have played an important role in environmental policymaking in China, even while lobbying is illegal and civil society organization's activities are viewed with suspicion. Despite this more closed political setting, environmental NGOs have been an important aspect of the environmental policy arena and have brought the environmental movement to China (Lora-Wainwright 2017, 23; Ho 2001, 897). The Chinese party-state "needs and fears" environmental NGOs for their expertise and for contributing to controlling risk and solving conflicts resulting from pollution (Van Rooij, Stern, and Fürst 2016, 3). Indeed, Teets (2018, 128) argues that Chinese officials are influenced by changing ideas regarding pollution through policy networks where civil society organizations play a key role, as they provide important expertise and credible information about citizen needs. In the case of waste management, Chinese activists (such as the Friends of Nature and the Natural Academy) have scaled up activities from street protests to building cross-organizational networks, linking pollution victims, local NGOs, and international resources. The bridging work of antipollution activists is aided by the CCP's larger policy initiative Ecological Civilization, which provides discursive legitimacy for antipollution policy work (Wu and Martus 2021, 500). To be effective in authoritarian contexts, NGOs must work closely with government networks and avoid controversy; these strategies protect NGOs but also narrow the types of problems they address (Haddad 2021, 91–95).

While NGOs do find some limited room to maneuver in China, other institutions associated with environmental rights protections are even more restricted. Environmental courts, for example, are spaces for contestation and small dispute resolution; they are not autonomous bodies that crack down on politically connected polluters and thus fail to tackle the country's most critical environmental issues (Stern 2014, 53–54). Citizens, prosecutors, and judges do increasingly play a role in China's environmental regulatory landscape, even if it is one that can mirror the CCP's task of social control and reflect state priorities (Van Rooij, Stern, and Fürst 2016). "Disgruntled officials" have been known to help local activists, for example, in anti-dam campaigns (Mertha 2008, 8–12), and local officials do sometimes side with activists, depending on factors such as strength and frequency of protest (Demchuk et al. 2021, 7). In both Russia and China there have been documented cases of local administrations allying with environmentalists to put pressure on local economic interests (Demchuk et al. 2021, 5–9, 11).

Ultimately, the CCP's environmental policy agenda far surpasses those of other authoritarian states such as Russia and the prior military regimes of Latin America by allowing some room for occasional responsiveness to citizens as a pressure release for managing social conflict. China is unique in its practice of "responsive authoritarianism" whereby new channels for public feedback, direct local elections, and protest is sometimes available. Although the CCP has permitted the rise of regulatory pluralism, its level of support and restriction has limited the development of a "regulatory society" that could threaten the CCP's political control. Thus "space for activism remains limited" (Van Rooij, Stern, and Fürst 2016, 6). It remains to be seen which environmental goals can be accomplished with an authoritarian arm and which ones may prove elusive without greater transparency and the right to dissent.

Citizen-Led Environmental Regulation

This book has highlighted the critical links between democratic institutions and environmental policy in the Global South. The cases suggest that any environmental law, standard, or institution with real authority is such because of sustained pressure from collective citizen action. The environmental advocacy movements examined in Argentina and Colombia prominently feature the role of activists and their allies exercising a wide range of strategies to hold governments accountable for fulfilling their legally mandated responsibility for enforcing environmental protections.

While social mobilization has played a big role in environmental policymaking worldwide, the role of organized citizen pressure in environmental institution building has been particularly pronounced in Latin America. Characterized by weak institutions with histories of political violence and attacks on labor-based organizing, social mobilization is tightly linked to the democracy-building project in the region. Democratic institution building has involved boosting horizontal accountability institutions such as the Ombudsman's Office and the judiciary, creating participatory institutions and more citizen oversight of how information is accessed and how public funds are spent. When these democratic institutions are stronger, environmental governance regimes have more transparency and accountability. At the root of these institutions is the work of citizen collective action that continues to imbue regulatory practices with real authority via continued pressure from below.

Regulation is a rule-based process that involves an institutional authority with power to impose fines or punitive measures to promote compliance with rules. The idea that more effective regulation would come via processes that are open to social pressure rather than driven by Weberian bureaucratic insulation is counterintuitive. The European model of bureaucratic capacity is essentially about insulation from political influence. Yet full-grown Weberian regulatory agencies have rarely developed in the Global South to match imported global models; institutions with weak enforcement and/or stability of rule are more common (Levitsky and Murillo 2009, 117; Hochstetler 2012a, 363). Civil society has thus had a major role in shaping the contours of Global South regulatory regimes (Hochstetler 2012a, 363). For example, in Vietnam, "community action was the key dynamic underlying state actions and corporate initiatives to reduce pollution" (O'Rourke 2002, 98), and in Argentina, societal groups achieved effective regulatory enforcement by providing regulatory institutions with resources they lacked, such as information, material resources (e.g., cars for transport), political support, technical capacity, and operational support (Amengual 2016, 29–33). It is not difficult to create an institution on paper, but regulatory enforcement is often elusive, particularly for environmental protections. This book has illustrated the large role that civil society plays in environmental governance. Citizen collective action was responsible not only for identifying problems but also for co-producing solutions. Amid recalcitrant public officials and strong economic actors, citizen-led environmental regulation was often the regulatory regime of last resort in weak institutional settings.

This book illustrates the many diverse methods communities use to press their claims and craft citizen-led environmental regulation: council meetings, rallies, petitions, marches, public hearings, media campaigns, litigation, and much more. Throughout the writing of the book, I puzzled over what to call the forms of citizen collective action I observed in response to river pollution. Advocacy movement? Social network? Social movement? Sometimes only a small handful of activists kept an issue afloat. Few forms of citizen pressure made major headlines. Yet field research revealed the far-ranging efforts communities, and their allies, make to document harms and get the state's attention. Rather than a coherent enduring social movement or obvious social network, these citizens either alone or in small groups experimented with diverse, small-scale demand-making strategies. By doing so they co-produced environmental regulation in hostile environments and in unlikely places. "Accidental environmentalists" helped to give institutions that were built to be weak and neglectable much stronger "teeth." Communities impacted by toxic contamination, and their allies, remind us that the struggle for accountability is the foundation of a more inclusive democracy.

APPENDIX
Methodological Narrative

In this narrative I plan to share with the reader not only the methodological strategies that guided the research process, but also how the project first found its legs. I first became interested in wastewater as a central problem of development during field research for my first book, *Water and Politics*. In Mexico, engineers would often insist on a field trip to the city's wastewater treatment plant and that I write about what I saw: neighbors laying down picnic blankets next to lake-like catchment areas. I came to learn the lakes were composed entirely of untreated sewage from the adjacent wastewater treatment plant, designed only for primary treatment, with no biological process of purification. Families grilled lunch and played nearby, undeterred. This was one of my first experiences with the concept of "slow harms," experienced by millions, often unknowingly. Later I would pick up Javier Auyero and Débora Swistun's (2009) book, *Flammable: Environmental Suffering in an Argentine Shantytown,* and assign it in my undergraduate courses. *Flammable*—much more so than other assigned texts—never failed to animate the classroom. Students were eager to discuss how we navigate environmental risk and how the impacts of toxin exposure are unevenly distributed. These initial seeds led me to begin researching whether and how citizen action gains traction in polluted places.

Access in the Field, Positionality, and Ethics

In this book I draw on interviews from people from diverse backgrounds: wetlands activists, Supreme Court justices, small tannery owners, shantytown dwellers, and more. My own nationality (born in Argentina but raised primarily in the United States), gender (female), sexual orientation (heterosexual), and ethnicity (Latina) worked together to enhance my ability to gain access to the groups and types of information presented and analyzed in the book. In Argentina, many interviewees welcomed me as a compatriot; a few were further intrigued when I shared that I was born in Avellaneda, the municipality home to Dock Sud and where contamination was particularly intense. Some would ask me which soccer club I favored, and I would hesitantly blurt out "Racing," recalling my grandfather as a megafan. This type of personal connection to the Argentina case inevitably opened many doors, but I also benefited from the neutrality of my U.S. background, which marked me as sufficiently outside of the conflictual partisan divide of the Kirchner years, particularly after the contentious 2015 election.

In Colombia, I was a foreigner but also originally South American, and Bogotanos were open in sharing information. Many activists and public officials who worked on river pollution in Bogotá were eager to hear about experiences of the Matanza Riachuelo River, which I shared if asked after our interview was completed. I was also able to use social media to arrange interviews; sometimes even the very highest government official would be responsive to a Facebook request from a foreign account. Being a foreign researcher opens doors that are sometimes regrettably closed to in-country colleagues, a power imbalance with which we as researchers must grapple. WhatsApp groups presented a new world of participant observation possibilities; I relied on these messages to better understand the internal deliberations between impacted communities about their grievances and demands.

In Peru, public officials were much more closed off than in the first two countries, and I struggled to get interviewees to provide information. However, being a foreigner helped me access interviews in Peru, where officials were more distrustful of environmental activists and defensive about the lack of gains on the issues being discussed. Remaining neutral in these situations was instructive; public officials repeatedly and openly discussed civil society activism as aligned with leftist armed terrorists and were uncomfortable shining a spotlight on procedures concerning environmental regulations. The variation in openness of public officials to discuss slow-moving harms and citizen activism in interviews across the three countries reflects some of the dynamics discussed in this book regarding enabling conditions for political openness. The legacies of the armed conflict were especially pronounced in Peru.

While my project was not an ethnographic one requiring extended periods immersed in specific communities, I learned a lot and am indebted to the interviewees who gave of their time to talk with me about their experiences living in areas where they were exposed to toxic pollution. These interviews took place on day trips to Villa Inflamable, Avellaneda, and González Catán in La Matanza in Argentina, and Mesitas de Colegio and La Moscera in Cundinamarca, Colombia. To access these communities, I relied on different interlocutors, such as the NGO ACIJ in Buenos Aires, which ran a legal clinic in Villa Inflamable/Dock Sud; the skilled photojournalist Pepe Mateos, who escorted me to González Catán while in Argentina; and in Colombia activists from the NGO ASURIO, who spearheaded a long bus trip to Mesitas de Colegio, and CAR engineers who provided access to La Moscera. Inevitably the presence of others impacted how interviewees responded in these settings, in ways that made them both less and more forthcoming, depending on the topic we were discussing and whether the interlocutor was viewed as trustworthy (such as the ACIJ sociologist who had strong ties to the community). The number and location of visits I participated in were shaped by convenience; I relied on the availability of willing interlocutors and their ability to access communities.

While I repeatedly made clear that the only benefit from participating in the research would be academic in nature, there were times when participants expected that I connect them with officials within the state who could address their problems. Even NGOs sometimes expressed hope that the research would bring in more resources to address the pollution problems about which they deeply cared. This may have led interviewees to exaggerate their experience with or perception of the impacts of pollution when they knew I was interested in hearing more about this topic. To mitigate this, I triangulated with diverse text-based sources as well as the perspectives of experts not themselves impacted by pollution but with knowledge of its pervasiveness and about its impacts in the communities I studied.

While most of the interviewees I spoke with did not request anonymity, I endeavored to keep my interview list confidential while I was conducting field research. Yet occasionally, given the content of our conversations, an interviewee would deduce the identity of someone who had given me access and show frustration that I had spoken with an informant they considered opposed to their cause. I navigated multiple sides of a complex policy conflict when interviewing those impacted by pollution, those negligent in addressing their responsibility in mitigating or regulating pollution, and those principally responsible for polluting. Staying neutral was not always desirable or possible. As a

Table A.1 Summary of Interviews Conducted by Author

	Number of People Interviewed	Number of Organizations or Institutions	Average Interview Length (Minutes)
Civil society organizations and impacted communities	63	31	87
Industry	14	13	70
Judicial	9	8	114
Government officials	68	28	65
Journalists and academics	8	8	104
Multiple interviews of same interviewees	15	11	68
Total number of interviews	177	88	73

researcher I was sometimes torn between showing the solidarity I felt to activists and impacted communities while also speaking to a wide range of public officials and industries that activists saw as responsible for their suffering. My own navigation of these complex issues helped me better understand the cleavages and battle lines that can be so difficult to surpass when responding to environmental harms.

Data-Gathering Strategies

Interviews and Participant Observations

The primary data analyzed for this book are drawn from interviews, participant observations, and a wide range of documentary sources. Taken together, these include information from "reactive" sources that as a researcher I helped create (such as interviews) and "nonreactive" sources which preexisted me as a researcher (such as documents and videos). I endeavored to triangulate between these two types of sources to have a fuller understanding of the dynamics at play in slow-harms policymaking (Kapiszewski, MacLean, and Read 2015, 151–60; Webb et al. 1966). I conducted field research in Argentina, Colombia, and Peru in 2016 and 2017, which included 177 interviews; most were semi-structured with a questionnaire (over 90%), and a small handful were unstructured. All interviews were recorded, and I produced typed interview notes for each interview. I had 66 interviews transcribed, including all the interviews with civil society organizations. Table A.1 provides a summary inventory of interviews.

I was also involved in 13 participant observations in Argentina and Colombia, as seen in Table A.2. I did not conduct participant observations in Peru; the low amount of policy attention to the Rímac made it difficult to find these opportunities, and thus the research trip to Lima was also shorter than those to Bogotá and Buenos Aires. The types of participant observation conducted in Argentina and Colombia varied greatly, from sitting in on judiciary advisory oversight committee meetings to ride-along with environmental inspectors and attending local grassroots group meetings that had elements of a focus group.

Table A.2 List of Participant Observations Conducted by Author

Name	Location	City	Date
Public forum on Riachuelo River cleanup	Universidad de Torcuato de Tilla	Buenos Aires	March 2016
Public forum on Petrochemical Plant in Dock Sud	Centro Franco Argentino de Altos Estudios de la UBA	Buenos Aires	April 2016
Site tour of river restoration activities	La Boca & Matanza	Buenos Aires	April 2016; March 2017
Ride-along with ACUMAR inspectors	Lanus	Buenos Aires	March 2017
Site tour of impacted communities in Villa Inflamable	Avellaneda	Buenos Aires	March 2017
Site tour of community slated for relocation	Villa 21-24	Buenos Aires	April 2016
Site tour of CEAMSE landfill	Gonzalez Catan	Buenos Aires	March 2017
Community leaders of Mesitas de Colegio meeting	Mesitas de Colegio	Cundinamarca	July 2016
Judicial Advisory Committee meeting	Gobernación de Cundinamarca	Bogotá	August 2016
Cantoalagua Water Ceremony	Jardin Botanico	Bogotá	July 2016
Tour of recuperation of waterfalls & Youth Rehabilitation Program	Delicias La Quebrada	Bogotá	July 2016
Site tour of relocated communities	La Moscera	Bogotá	August 2016
Red de Veedurias WhatsApp messaging in Chia	WhatsApp messaging	Cundinamarca	August 2016–July 2018

Text-Based Sources: Access and Selection

I relied on numerous text-based sources, which are inanimate sources that preexist researchers. These can include any form of inanimate object a researcher analyzes in pursuit of a research question, including songs, videos, government documents, newspaper articles, diaries, and media transcripts. Because text-based sources preexist researchers, they involve less respondent or researcher bias, but selecting and interpreting sources does involve choices about which sources to give more weight to and how to adjudicate between conflicting sources (Gaikwad and Herrera 2022, 2). I relied on civil society organizations' self-produced materials (e.g., social media communications, YouTube videos, radio interviews, pollution assessment reports, posters, pamphlets), as well as government documents, legal rulings, newspaper articles, and scholarly sources. Multimedia sources included TV and radio coverage, documentaries, and even music. For example,

Grammy-winning Colombian rock band Aterciopelado's song "Rio," about the Bogotá River pollution, was instructive. Lyrics by Aterciopelado's frontman Héctor Buitrago, an environmentalist and the founder of the water-chanting collective Cantoalgua, remind us to make "waves of prayers for the river." His song reflects the cultural production of environmentalism in Bogotá and helped me better understand the types of grassroots activism I observed there.

I re-created the significance of events and their relationship to slow-harms advocacy with newspaper articles. I reviewed the physical historical archives of the newspaper *Clarín* in Buenos Aires from the 1950s to the 2000s, which included clippings from most major Argentine newspapers, including *La Nación*, *Pagina 12*, and *La Voz* (in 2016), and research assistants conducted an online search of *Clarín* from 2007 to 2015 (in 2015). Research assistants also undertook a review of *El Tiempo* and *El Espectador* from 1990 to 2015 (in spring 2016) for the Bogotá case.

The variation in the amount and type of text-based sources produced from these three cases reflects their scores on the outcome of slow-harms remediation and the argument about the role of bridging activism. In Buenos Aires, hundreds if not thousands of sources were produced by legal institutions, government agencies, public utilities, and the many NGOS, foundations, and grassroots activists involved in promoting accountability. The case also received an extremely large amount of media attention. In Bogotá, fewer documents were produced overall; these included very few from academics, where the case had not been much studied, and much less media attention was also generated overall. The main producers of knowledge were legal institutions, government agencies, and the formidable grassroots organization turned NGO Conejera Foundation. In Peru most documentary information was sensationalist media coverage of environmental suffering as well as dozens of commissioned policy reports on how to approach river remediation and best practices, a disproportionate amount when considering how few of the reports' recommended policy changes had been put into practice.

As I assessed the evidentiary value of the copious amount of documents produced about river pollution in these three countries, I iteratively weighed more heavily sources that I understood through interviews were drafted by knowledgeable experts, those with firsthand accounts, those with long-standing work in the policy arena, and those who had less reason to exaggerate their position. I iteratively discarded certain documents in favor of others by consulting diverse interlocutors. In all three cases, sources disagreed with one another, and I came to learn that this at times reflected opposing positions on a complex topic. I had initially hoped to get comparative data on the three river basins in terms of the number of polluters, the types of pollution, and the resulting health impacts on different communities. Reliable metrics for these indicators were very difficult to find, especially in Colombia and Peru. The very government officials I was interviewing who offered certain data warned me that these were inaccurate, outdated, or otherwise incomplete. I thus chose to cite only the figures that came from the sources I deemed most credible and chose to present them throughout the text qualitatively rather than in a formal table that suggested parity across indicators.

Identifying Key Actors in Bonding and Bridging Mobilization

In both Argentina and Colombia, the presence of two high court rulings helped guide data collection efforts. I began by seeking contacts (or "seeds") within the judicial advisory committees for Argentina and Colombia, as both rulings listed these actors and news media covered their activity, especially for Argentina. After more interviewing I began to see that there was a larger network of formal organizations and experts who were not part of the judicial advisory committee. Through snowball sampling within the initial civil society organizations, journalists, academics, and activist public officials, I was able to identify the most active and interconnected members of the networks for slow-harms advocacy that developed in Bogotá and Buenos Aires outside of the formal institutions that had initially been my focus. These actors were typically part of formal organizations or worked with government, and thus were findable through snowball sampling or online profiles.

Grassroots activists were much more difficult to locate. Grassroots groups typically have no sources of funding for their activities; their labor is voluntary (as opposed to being an employee of an NGO); and they live or work in the impacted community. They may have less education, less media access, and fewer resources than NGOs. For impacted communities that form collectives or grassroots groups, their organizational form changes over time, as do the amount and visibility of their events or campaigns. I used online materials and secondary sources to understand organizational activity for local groups, some of whom I was able to later interview. My research team was able to gather information from local groups' online presence, such as their websites, Facebook pages, radio and blog interviews, and local media coverage that featured their activism. For each local grassroots group, I developed an evidentiary online folder of audiovisual presentations, newspaper reports, and social media activity that I triangulated with interview material. I drew on these folders to characterize each group's activity. Because of the vast territories involved and the three-decade period under study, there may be grassroots groups in adjacent municipalities that during the research period between 2015 and 2020 were not active on social media and were not connected to organizations within the capital city, and thus are left out of the network inventory. Therefore, the inventories in Chapters 3 and 4 of grassroots groups may underestimate the quantity of grassroots activism, although it does capture what I believe to be the entire universe of "bridging actors" involved in Argentina and Colombia.

In Lima's Rímac River basin, both bonding and bridging mobilization were very limited, so I adopted a different approach. I interviewed several NGOs, none of which worked directly on the Rímac issue, and officials within government to identify what activity, if any, had occurred to propel change on this issue. Strategies such as combing newspaper coverage, social media posts, and blogs did little to identify grassroots groups. Several activities that occurred after my initial field research, including a congressional hearing propelled by activists and a documentary, produced sources that helped provide more clues to flush out the contours of the very limited collective claims-making occurring on the Rímac.

Finding a limited amount of information due to the nature of the case being one of limited change, my research assistants and I then conducted an extensive search of Peruvian television news coverage that was catalogued on YouTube. Using the search terms "Río Rímac" and "Contaminación" generated hundreds of relevant videos. Here we found several illuminating instances of grassroots grievances, if only a small handful of collective organizing. We catalogued 40 news coverage clips as highly relevant; these used field reporting, talk show formats, and a small handful of government videos on the topic. These strategies proved to be useful for characterizing a "negative" case. Here I was able to establish a base of evidence to show that there had been indeed limited activities associated with policy shifting, and that the indicators associated with reforms were absent.

For the Rímac, however, I did find numerous consultant policy reports on what types of changes should be made on the river; these were commissioned by government entities and international financial institutions. The overabundance of commissioned reports relative to the low amount of policy change for Peru is striking and lends further credence to what some interviewees stressed was a "consultant for hire" market. Here, government institutions frequently use consultants to pay lip service to foreign and domestic requirements for assessment reports, but the reports are purposefully designed to be ignored.

Mapping Exercises: Understanding Network Activity and Relational Dynamics between Civil Society Organizations

When I began this project, I sought to undertake some form of network analysis and devised relational mapping exercises to accompany the interview questionnaires. The maps were designed to measure the activity level of each group or organization interviewed. I wanted to know who was in the "slow-harms network," which groups were most active, what their activities entailed, the strength of their ties to one another, and their level of state access, if any.

I asked respondents of civil society organizations to identify the civil society actors and public entities to which they were connected. I did not ask them to name a specific number of groups or actors but let them choose the number. I asked them to distinguish between strong ties (using two lines), moderate ties (one line), and weak ties (dotted line), and draw the relationship on a piece of paper. I explained that the connection could be based on prior or current shared work initiatives, sharing of information or ideas, or knowledge of personnel/people. I coded transcripts of these interviews using Atlas Ti qualitative data software, with codes developed to measure "alliances" (strong or weak), the number of shared work products between groups, and type of frame most associated with an organization's key mandate or goal (e.g., environment, urban, democracy building). I also invited interviewees to optionally identify "value language" frames to describe their group's mandate (e.g., rights, citizenship, public good, the collective).

What I quickly found, though, was that quantifying relational dynamics among organizations was too restrictive; it became nearly impossible to accurately assign distinct numbers to each group. Ties between groups shifted over time, especially for groups that had been active for decades; these shifts could not be fully captured in a questionnaire or easily displayed in a diagram, which was only a snapshot in time. Furthermore, the institutional memory of the organization was not held by one or two people drawing a diagram or answering a questionnaire. Indeed, work activities and perceptions of those activities changed based on the biographies and preferences of those involved at any given moment; groups did not always keep records, and groups both grew and dissolved, sometimes without warning. These were moving, fluid entities whose activities and even identities waxed and waned in response to the threats they confronted. I found that even self-perceptions of relational ties were not always accurate; a respondent may not have ideational affinity or preexisting ties before, for example, working with a judicial advisory committee. Yet these state-directed initiatives forged ties between unusual bedfellows, which were not revealed consistently in the self-identified ties component of the mapping exercises.

Thus, to paint a fuller picture I also used information from online and physical materials produced by civil society organizations and information revealed from other interviews about relational ties between groups (such as preexisting ties or work products) to construct the relational patterns between the groups as they appear in Chapters 3–5. The mapping exercises and interview transcripts, analyzed qualitatively through process tracing and the comparative case method, made up the bulk of the evidence I relied on to understand the formation and efficacy of bridges for slow-harms advocacy and, to a lesser extent, to understand bonding mobilization in the three cases.

References

Abbott, Andrew Delano. 2001. *Time Matters: On Theory and Method*. Chicago: University of Chicago Press.
Abers, Rebecca Neaera, and Margaret E. Keck. 2009. "Mobilizing the State: The Erratic Partner in Brazil's Participatory Water Policy." *Politics & Society* 37 (2): 289–314.
ACUMAR. 2014. "Agentes contaminantes avances." Originally accessed: http://www.acumar.gob.ar/pagina/842/agentes-contaminantes.
ACUMAR. 2022. Agentes Contaminantes: Establecimientos Declarados Agentes Contaminantes. Buenos Aires: ACUMAR. https://www.acumar.gob.ar/fiscalizacion-adecuacion-ambiental/control-ambiental-datos/.
ACUMAR. n.d. "ACUMAR caracteristicsas de la Cuenca Matanza Riachuelo." Accessed December 5, 2022. acumar.gob.ar.
Acuña, Guillermo. 1999. *Marcos regulatorios e institucionales ambientales de América Latina y el Caribe en el contexto del proceso de reformas macroeconómicas: 1980-1990*. División de Medio Ambiente y Asentamientos Humanos. Santiago, Chile: United Nations ECLAC.
ADC, CELS, FPC, FARN, and INECIP. 2002. *Una corte para la democracia*. La Asociación por los Derechos Civiles, el Centro de Estudios Legales y Sociales (CELS), la Fundación Poder Ciudadano, la Fundación Ambiente y Recursos Naturales (FARN), el Instituto de Estudios Comparados en Ciencias Penales y Sociales (INECIP) y la Unión de Usuarios y Consumidores. Buenos Aires.
Adger, W. Neil. 2006. "Vulnerability." *Global Environmental Change* 16 (3): 268–81.
Agencia Peruana de Cooperación Internacional. 2020. *Organizaciones No Gubernamentales de Desarrollo (ONGD)*. Vol. *Registradas en la Agencia Peruana de Cooperación Internacional (APCI)*. Lima.
Ahlers, Anna L., and Yongdong Shen. 2018. "Breathe Easy? Local Nuances of Authoritarian Environmentalism in China's Battle against Air Pollution." *China Quarterly* 234: 299–319.
Aizcorbe, Matías, Fernandez Bouzo, María Soledad, Alejandra Gil, and Regina Ricco. 2007. "Las organizaciones territoriales en el sur del Área Metropolitana de Buenos Aires: Construcción social y política del conflicto ambiental." *IV jornadas de jóvenes investigadores: Instituto Gino Germani, Facultad de Ciencias Sociales* Universidad de Buenos Aires.
Aizen, Marina. 2014. *Contaminados: Una inmersión en la mugre del Riachuelo*. Buenos Aires: Random House Mondadori S.A.
Alcaldia Mayor de Bogota, D.C. 2005. *Política de humedales del Distrito Capital*. Bogotá: Departamento Técnico Administrativo Medio Ambiente.
Alcañiz, Isabelle, and Ricardo A. Gutiérrez. 2009. "From Local Protest to the International Court of Justice: Forging Environmental Foreign Policy in Argentina." In *Environmental Change and Foreign Policy: Theory and Practice*, edited by Paul G. Harris. London: Routledge, 109–120.

Alcañiz, Isabella, and Ricardo Gutiérrez. 2020. "Between the Global Commodity Boom and Subnational State Capacities: Payment for Environmental Services to Fight Deforestation in Argentina." *Global Environmental Politics* 20 (1): 38–59.

Alcañiz, Isabella, and Ricardo A. Gutiérrez. 2022. *The Distributive Politics of Environmental Protection in Latin America and the Caribbean*. Cambridge: Cambridge University Press.

Allen, Adriana. 2003. "Environmental Planning and Management of the Peri-Urban Interface: Perspectives on an Emerging Field." *Environment and Urbanization* 15 (1): 135–148.

Amengual, Matthew. 2016. *Politicized Enforcement in Argentina: Labor and Environmental Regulation*. New York: Cambridge University Press.

Amengual, Matthew. 2018. "Buying Stability: The Distributive Outcomes of Private Politics in the Bolivian Mining Industry." *World Development* 104: 31–45.

Americas Watch. 1992. *Peru under Fire: Human Rights since the Return to Democracy*. New Haven, CT: Yale University Press.

Amnesty International. 1994. *Peru: The Cayara Massacre: The Cover-Up*. Vol. AMR 46/015/1994.

Arce, Moisés. 2014. *Resource Extraction and Protest in Peru*. Pittsburgh, PA: University of Pittsburgh Press.

Arellano-Yanguas, Javier. 2011. "Aggravating the Resource Curse: Decentralisation, Mining and Conflict in Peru." *Journal of Development Studies* 47 (4): 617–38.

Arnson, Cynthia J., ed. 2005. *The Peace Process in Colombia with the Autodefensas Unidas de Colombia-AUC*. Report on the Americas 13. Washington, D.C.: Woodrow Wilson Center.

Auerbach, Adam. 2019. *Demanding Development: The Politics of Public Goods Provision in India's Urban Slums*. New York: Cambridge University Press.

Auerbach, Adam, Adrienne LeBas, Alison E. Post, and Rebecca Weitz-Shapiro. 2018. "State, Society, and Informality in Cities of the Global South." *Studies in Comparative International Development* 53 (3): 261–80.

Autoridad Nacional del Agua. 2015. *Autoridad Nacional del Agua informe técnico de resultados del primer monitoreo participativo de la calidad de agua superficial de la Cuenca del Río Riamc*. Lima: Autoridad Nacional del Agua.

Autoridad Nacional del Agua. 2019. "Delimitación de La Faja Marginal Del Río Rímac." Resumen Ejecutivo. Lima: Autoridad Nacional del Agua.

Autoridad Nacional del Agua. n.d. "Observatorio Del Agua Chillon, Rímac, Lurín: Vertimientos y Contaminación." https://observatoriochirilu.ana.gob.pe/. Accessed December 6, 2022. Lima: Autoridad Nacional del Agua.

Auyero, Javier. 2014. "Toxic Waiting: Flammable Shantytown Revisited." In *Cities from Scratch: Poverty and Informality in Urban Latin America*, edited by Brodwyn Fischer, Bryan McCann, and Javier Auyero. Durham, NC: Duke University Press, 238–62.

Auyero, Javier, and Debora Alejandra Swistun. 2009. *Flammable: Environmental Suffering in an Argentine Shantytown*. New York: Oxford University Press.

Avilés, William. 2001. "Institutions, Military Policy, and Human Rights in Colombia." *Latin American Perspectives* 28 (1): 31–55.

Ballvé, Teo. 2013. "Grassroots Masquerades: Development, Paramilitaries, and Land Laundering in Colombia." *Geoforum* 50: 62–75.

Bardhan, Pranab. 2002. "Decentralization of Governance and Development." *Journal of Economic Perspectives* 16 (4): 185–205.

Barrantes Segura, Rafael. 2012. "Reparations and Displacement in Peru." International Center for Transitional Justice and The Brookings Institute, July. https://www.ictj.org/publication/reparations-and-displacement-peru.

Bates, Robert H. 1999. *Open-Economy Politics: The Political Economy of the World Coffee Trade*. Princeton, NJ: Princeton University Press.

Beamish, Thomas D. 2001. "Environmental Hazard and Institutional Betrayal: Lay-Public Perceptions of Risk in the San Luis Obispo County Oil Spill." *Organization & Environment* 14 (1): 5–33.

Bebbington, Anthony, Leonith Hinojosa, Denise Humphreys Bebbington, Maria Luisa Burneo, and Ximena Warnaars. 2008. "Contention and Ambiguity: Mining and the Possibilities of Development." *Development and Change* 39 (6): 887–914.

Beer, Christopher Todd, Tim Bartley, and Wade T. Roberts. 2012. "NGOs: Between Advocacy, Service Provision, and Regulation." In *The Oxford Handbook of Governance*, edited by David Levi-Faur. Oxford: Oxford University Press, 323–38.

Benford, Robert D., and David A. Snow. 2000. "Framing Processes and Social Movements: An Overview and Assessment." *Annual Review of Sociology* 26: 611–39.

Bennett, Andrew, and Jeffrey T. Checkel. 2015. "Process Tracing: From Philosophical Roots to Best Practices." In *Process Tracing: From Metaphor to Analytical Tool*, edited by Andrew Bennett and Jeffrey T. Checkel. New York: Cambridge University Press, 3–38.

Berman, Sheri. 2020. "Crises Only Sometimes Lead to Change. Here's Why." *Foreign Policy*, July 4.

Bertonatti, Claudio, and Jorge Corcuera. 2000. *Situación ambiental de la Argentina 2000*. Buenos Aires: Fundación Vida Silvestre Argentina.

Blacksmith Institute. 2013. *The World's Worst 2013: The Top Ten Toxic Threats: Cleanup, Progress, and Ongoing Challenges*. New York: Blacksmith Institute and Green Cross Switzerland.

Bodea, Cristina, and Adrienne LeBas. 2016. "The Origins of Voluntary Compliance: Attitudes toward Taxation in Urban Nigeria." *British Journal of Political Science* 46 (1): 215–38.

Botero, Sandra. 2018. "Judges, Litigants, and the Politics of Rights Enforcement in Argentina." *Comparative Politics*. 5 (2): 169–87.

Bourdieu, Pierre. 1985. "The Forms of Capital." In *Handbook of Theory and Research for the Sociology of Education*, edited by J. Richardson. Westport, CT: Greenwood, 241–58.

Brass, Jennifer N., Wesley Longhofer, Rachel S. Robinson, and Allison Schnable. 2018. "NGOs and International Development: A Review of Thirty-Five Years of Scholarship." *World Development* 112: 136–49.

Brown, Phil, and Edwin J. Mikkelsen. 1997. *No Safe Place: Toxic Waste, Leukemia, and Community Action*. Berkeley: University of California Press.

Brysk, Alison. 1994. *The Politics of Human Rights in Argentina: Protest, Change, and Democratization*. Stanford, CA: Stanford University Press.

Bueno, Maria del Pilar. 2012. "Los vaivenes de la diplomacia climática Argentina (1989–2011)." In *Argentina y Brasil: Proyecciones internacionales, cooperación sur-sur e integración*, edited by Carla Morasso and Gisela Pereyra Doval. Rosario, Argentina: Editorial de la Universidad Nacional de Rosario, 134–54.

Bullard, Robert D. 1993. "Anatomy of Environmental Racism and the Environmental Justice Movement." In *Confronting Environmental Racism: Voices from the Grassroots*, edited by Robert D. Bullard. Boston: South End Press, 15–39.

Burt, Jo-Marie. 2009. "Guilty as Charged: The Trial of Former Peruvian President Alberto Fujimori for Human Rights Violations." *International Journal of Transitional Justice* 3 (3).

Buthe, Tim. 2002. "Taking Temporality Seriously: Modeling History and the Use of Narratives as Evidence." *American Political Science Review* 96 (3): 481–93.

Caballero Calderón, Eduardo. 1985. "El Río Funza." In *Río Bogotá*. Bogotá: Benjamin Villegas e Asociados, 15–38.

Camargo, Guibor, Andrés Miguel Sampayo, Andrés Peña Galindo, Francisco J. Escobedo, Fernando Carriazo, and Alejandro Feged-Rivadeneira. 2020. "Exploring the Dynamics of Migration, Armed Conflict, Urbanization, and Anthropogenic Change in Colombia." *Plos One* 15 (11): 1–18.

Cameron, Maxwell A. 1994. *Democracy and Authoritarianism in Peru*. New York: St. Martin's Press.

Cao, Xun, and Aseem Prakash. 2012. "Trade Competition and Environmental Regulations: Domestic Political Constraints and Issue Visibility." *Journal of Politics* 74 (1): 66–82.

CAR. 2006. *Plan de ordenación y manejo de la Cuenca Hidrográfica del Río Bogotá resumen ejecutivo*. Bogotá: Corporación Ambiental Regional de Cundinamarca.

CAR. 2022. Información general Río Bogotá. car.gov.co/rio_bogota.

Carrizosa Umaña, Julio. 1992. *La política ambiental en Colombia: Desarrollo sostenible y democratización*. Bogotá: CEREC.

Carrizosa Umaña, Julio. 2015. "Veinte años difíciles, 1994–2014." In *La gestión ambiental en Colombia, 1994–2014: ¿Un esfuerzo insostenible?* edited by Ernesto Guhl Nannetti and Pablo Leyva. Bogotá: Foro Nacional Ambiental, 17–21.

Carruthers, David V. 2008. "Popular Environmentalism and Social Justice in Latin America." In *Environmental Justice in Latin America Problems, Promise, and Practice*, edited by David V. Carruthers. Cambridge, MA: MIT Press.

CELS. 2015. *Derecho a la tierra y la vivienda*. Buenos Aires: Centro de Estudios Legales y Sociales.

Chambers, Paul A. 2013. "The Ambiguities of Human Rights in Colombia: Reflections on a Moral Crisis." *Latin American Perspectives* 40 (5): 118–37.

Cheng, Patricia W., and Laura R. Novick. 1991. "Causes versus Enabling Conditions." *Cognition* 40 (1–2): 83–120.

Christel, Lucas G., and Ricardo A. Gutiérrez. 2017. "Making Rights Come Alive: Environmental Rights and Modes of Participation in Argentina." *Journal of Environment & Development* 26 (3): 322–47.

Clapp, Richard W. 2002. "Popular Epidemiology in Three Contaminated Communities." *Annals of the American Academy of Political and Social Science* 584 (1): 35–46.

Colchado Lucio, Oscar. 1975. "La leyenda del Río Hablador." In *Leyendas Peruanas*, Lima: Editorial Bruño. ana.gob.pe.

Coleman, James S. 1988. "Social Capital in the Creation of Human Capital." *American Journal of Sociology* 94: 95–120.

Collier, David. 1976. *Squatters and Oligarchs: Authoritarian Rule and Policy Change in Peru*. Baltimore, MD: Johns Hopkins University Press.

Collier, David. 2011. "Understanding Process Tracing." *PS: Political Science & Politics* 44 (4): 823–30.

Collyns, Dan. 2008. "Peru Sets up Environment Ministry." *BBC News*, May 14.

Commission for Racial Justice. 1987. *Toxic Wastes and Race in the United States: A National Report on the Racial and Socio-Economic Characteristics of Communities with Hazardous Waste Sites*. Executive Director: Dr. Benjamin F. Chavis, Jr. New York: United Church of Christ, 1–79.

Consejo del Estado. 2014. *Sala de lo contencioso administrativo, sección primera, acción popular*. Consejero ponente: Marco Antonio Velilla Moreno. Radicación número: 25000-23-27-000-2001-90479-01(AP). Bogotá, March 28.

Contraloría de Bogotá. 2014. *Evaluación del programa de saneamiento del Río Bogotá 2008–2013*. Bogotá: Contraloría de Bogotá.

Contraloría General de la República. 2010. *Una gestión fiscal ética y eficiente: Así cumplimos*. Informe de los cuatro años de gestión al Congreso y al Presidente de la República. Bogotá: Contraloría General de la República.

Contraloría General de la República. n.d. *Estrategias de seguimiento institucional y ciudadano a la gestión para la recuperación del Río Bogotá*. Bogotá: Contraloría General de la República.

Convenio. 2010. Convenio marco para el cumplimiento del plan de urbanización de villas y asentamiento precarios en riesgo ambietnal de la Cuenca Matanza Riachuelo. Buenos Aires: Convenio.

Corcoran, Emily, Christian Nellemann, Elaine Baker, Robert Bos, David Osborn, and Heidi. Savelli. 2010. *Sick Water? The Central Role of Wastewater Management in Sustainable Development*. Norway: United Nations Environment Programme.

Cornell, Angela, and Kenneth Roberts. 1990. "Democracy, Counterinsurgency, and Human Rights: The Case of Peru." *Human Rights Quarterly* 12 (4): 529–53.

Crenzel, Emilio. 2008. "Argentina's National Commission on the Disappearance of Persons: Contributions to Transitional Justice." *International Journal of Transitional Justice* 2 (2): 173–91.

CSJN. 2008. *Mendoza, Beatriz Silvia y otros c/ Estado Nacional y otros s/ daños y perjuicios (daños derivados de la contaminación ambiental del Río Matanza Riachuelo)*. Buenos Aires: Corte Suprema de Justica de la Nación.

Dahl, Robert A. 1961. *Who Governs? Democracy and Power in an American City*. New Haven, CT: Yale University Press.

Defensa Pública. 2014. *Revista institucional de la Defensa Pública de la Ciudad Autónoma de Buenos Aires*. CABA: Defensa Pública de la Ciudad Autónoma de Buenos Aires.

Defensor del Pueblo de la Nación. 2003. *Informe especial sobre la Cuenca Matanza Riachuelo*. Buenos Aires: Defensor del Pueblo de la Nación Argentina.

Defensor del Pueblo de la Nación. 2005. *Informe especial de seguimiento Cuenca Matanza Riachuelo*. Buenos Aires: Defensor del Pueblo de la Nación Argentina.

Defensoría del Pueblo. 2007. *Pongamos la basuar en su lugar: Propuestas para la gestión de los residuos sólidos municipales*. Informe Defensorial No. 125. Lima: Defensoría del Pueblo, República de Perú.

Defensoría del Pueblo. 2015. *Conflictos sociales y recursos hídricos*. Lima: Defensoría del Pueblo, República de Perú.

Defensoria del Pueblo. 2019. *Defensoría del Pueblo: Adjuntía para la prevención de conflictos sociales y la gobernabilidad*. Lima: Defensoría del Pueblo, República de Perú.

Demchuk, Arthur L., Mile Mišić, Anastassia Obydenkova, and Jale Tosun. 2021. "Environmental Conflict Management: A Comparative Cross-Cultural Perspective of China and Russia." *Post-Communist Economies* (34) 7: 1–23.

Diamint, Rut. 2008. "La historia sin fin: El control civil de los militares en Argentina." *Nueva Sociedad* 213 (95): 95–111.
Díaz, Myriam del Valle. 2009. *La política ambiental Argentina: Un acercamineto a su genesis y devenir en las tres últimas décadas*. San Juan, Argentina: Editorial Fundación Universidad Nacional de San Juan.
DIEGESA. 2011. *Evaluación de muestras de agua del Río Rímac y principales afluentes con datos de DIGESA y SEDAPAL*. Lima: Ministerio de Salud.
Dietz, Henry A. 1977. "Land Invasion and Consolidation: A Study of Working Poor/Governmental Relations in Lima, Peru." *Urban Anthropology* 6 (4): 371–85.
Díez, Jordi. 2015. *The Politics of Gay Marriage in Latin America: Argentina, Chile, and Mexico*. Cambridge: Cambridge University Press.
Donaghy, Maureen. 2015. "Resisting Removal: The Impact of Community Mobilization in Rio de Janeiro." *Latin American Politics and Society* 57 (4): 74–96.
Dosh, Paul, and Julia Smith Coyoli. 2019. "Lessons from the Left in Lima: Susana Villarán and the Fleeting Return of Progressive Politics to City Hall." *Latin American Perspectives* 46 (1): 263–81.
Douglas, Mary, and Aaron Wildavsky. 1983. *Risk and Culture: An Essay on the Selection of Technological and Environmental Dangers*. Berkeley: University of California Press.
Eaton, Kent. 2010. "Subnational Economic Nationalism? The Contradictory Effects of Decentralization in Peru." *Third World Quarterly* 31 (7): 1205–22.
Eaton, Kent. 2020. "Bogotá's Left Turn: Counter-Neoliberalization in Colombia." *International Journal of Urban and Regional Research* 44 (1): 1–17.
Eisenstadt, Todd A., and Karleen Jones West. 2017. "Public Opinion, Vulnerability, and Living with Extraction on Ecuador's Oil Frontier: Where the Debate between Development and Environmentalism Gets Personal." *Comparative Politics* 49 (2): 231–51.
Eisenstadt, Todd A., and Karleen Jones West. 2019. *Who Speaks for Nature? Indigenous Movements, Public Opinion, and the Petro-State in Ecuador*. New York: Oxford University Press.
EITI. 2016. "Extractive Industries Transparency Initiative: Peru." 2016. https://eiti.org/countries/peru.
EITI. 2018a. "Extractive Industries Transparency Initiative: Argentina." 2018. https://eiti.org/countries/argentina.
EITI. 2018b. "Extractive Industries Transparency Initiative: Colombia." 2018. https://eiti.org/countries/colombia.
Engel, Katalina, Dorothee Jokiel, Andrea Kraljevic, Martin Geiger, and Kevin Smith. 2011. "Big Cities. Big Water. Big Challenges: Water in an Urbanizing World." Berlin: World Wildlife Federation Germany, 1–81.
Falleti, Tulia G., and James Mahoney. 2015. "The Comparative Sequential Method." In *Advances in Comparative Historical Analysis: Resilience, Diversity, and Change*, edited by James Mahoney and Kathleen Thelen. New York: Cambridge University Press, 211–39.
Falleti, Tulia G., and Thea N. Riofrancos. 2018. "Endogenous Participation: Strengthening Prior Consultation in Extractive Economies." *World Politics* 70 (1): 86–121.
FARN. 2019. "La justicia declara que el acceso al aire libre de contaminantes es un derecho humano." Comunicado. Buenos Aires: Fundación Ambiente y Recursos Naturales. May 15.

Fearnside, Phillip M. 2006. "Dams in the Amazon: Belo Monte and Brazil's Hydroelectric Development of the Xingu River Basin." *Environmental Management* 38 (1): 16.
Feierstein, Daniel. 2006. "Political Violence in Argentina and Its Genocidal Characteristics." *Journal of Genocide Research* 8 (2): 149–68.
Feitlowitz, Marguerite. 2011. *A Lexicon of Terror: Argentina and the Legacies of Torture.* New York: Oxford University Press.
Figueroa, Lucas M., and Ricardo A. Gutiérrez. 2022. "La acción de los expertos en contexto: La aplicación de la política de protección de bosques nativos en cuatro provincias Argentinas." *Gestión y Política Pública* 31 (1): 99–126.
Finkel, Eugene, Adria Lawrence, and Andrew Mertha. 2019. "From the Editors: Cities and Urban Politics." *APSA Comparative Politics Newsletter.* 30 (1): 2–4.
Freudenburg, William R. 1993. "Risk and Recreancy: Weber, the Division of Labor, and the Rationality of Risk Perceptions." *Social Forces* 71 (4): 909–32.
Fundación Ciudad. 2002. *Foro desarrollo sostenible de la Cuenca Matanza Riachuelo: Guia de trabajo.* Capital Federal, Argentina: Fundación Ciudad.
Fundación Ciudad. 2016. "Fundación Ciudad Actividades Realizadas." Capital Federal, Argentina: Fundación Ciudad. In possession of author.
Gallagher, Janice. 2017. "The Last Mile Problem: Activists, Advocates, and the Struggle for Justice in Domestic Courts." *Comparative Political Studies* 50 (12): 1666–98.
Gaventa, John. 1982. *Power and Powerlessness: Quiescence and Rebellion in an Appalachian Valley.* Champaign: University of Illinois Press.
Gaviria, Luz Beatriz. 1992. "The Colombian Environmental Movement: Social Actor or Space for Participation?" In "Environmental Social Movements in Latin America and Europe: Challenging Development and Democracy," edited by María Pilar García-Guadilla and Jutta Blauert. Special issue of *International Journal of Sociology and Social Policy* 12: 65–77.
Giugni, Marco. 2011. "Political Opportunity: Still a Useful Concept?" In *Contention and Trust in Cities and States*, edited by Michael Hanagan and Chris Tilly. Dordrecht, Netherlands: Springer, 271–83.
Gómez Bustos, Ivette Johanna. 2014. "La acción colectiva del agua en Colombia y el referendo como acercamiento de democracia directa." *Análisis Politico* 80 (January–April): 79–103.
González-Jácome, Jorge. 2018. "The Emergence of Revolutionary and Democratic Human Rights Activism in Colombia between 1974 and 1980." *Human Rights Quarterly* 40 (1): 91–118.
Gonzalez-Ocantos, Ezequiel A. 2017. *Shifting Legal Visions: Judicial Change and Human Rights Trials in Latin America.* New York: Cambridge University Press.
Granovetter, Mark S. 1973. "The Strength of Weak Ties." *American Journal of Sociology* 78 (6): 1360–80.
Greenpeace. 2009. *Plan de rescate para el Riachuelo: Campaña tóxicos.* Buenos Aires: Greenpeace Argentina.
Greenpeace. 2012. *Cueros tóxicos: Nuevas evidencias de contaminación de curtiembres en la Cuenca Matanza Riachuelo.* Buenos Aires: Greenpeace Argentina.
Greenpeace. 2015. *Polo Petroquímico Dock Sud: La contaminación que no se ve: Aguas subterráneas en riesgo.* Buenos Aires: Greenpeace Argentina.
Grimm, Nancy B., Stanley H. Faeth, Nancy E. Golubiewski, Charles L. Redman, Jianguo Wu, Xuemei Bai, and John M. Briggs. 2008. "Global Change and the Ecology of Cities." *Science* 319 (5864): 756–60.

Grossman, Shelby. 2020. "The Politics of Order in Informal Markets: Evidence from Lagos." *World Politics* 72 (1): 47–79.
Grzymala-Busse, Anna. 2011. "Time Will Tell? Temporality and the Analysis of Causal Mechanisms and Processes." *Comparative Political Studies* 44 (9): 1267–97.
Guha, Ramachandra. 2014. *Environmentalism: A Global History*. London: Penguin.
Guha, Ramachandra, and Joan Martínez Alier. 1997. *Varieties of Environmentalism: Essays North and South*. London: Earthscan.
Guhl Nannetti, Ernesto. 2015. "Evolución del Ministerio de Ambiente de Colombia en sus primeros veinte años: 1994–2014." In *La gestión ambiental en Colombia, 1994–2014: ¿Un esfuerzo insostenible?* edited by Ernesto Guhl Nannetti and Pablo Leyva. Bogotá: Foro Nacional Ambiental, 25–113.
Guillén, Oscar, Víctor Cóndor, Mario Gonzales, and Silvia Iglesias. 1998. "Contaminación de las aguas del Río Rímac: Trazas de metales." *Revista del Instituto de Investigación de la Facultad de Ingeniería Geológica, Minera, Metalurgica y Geográfica* 1 (2): 127–45.
Guthmann, Yanina. 2017. "Análisis de la política de derechos humanos en Argentina, 2005–2015." *Estado y Derecho* 10 (19): 11–33.
Gutiérrez, Ricardo, and Fernado Isuani. 2014. "La emergencia del ambientalismo estatal y social en Argentina." *Revista de Administração Pública* 48 (2): 295–322.
Haddad, Mary Alice. 2021. *Effective Advocacy: Lessons from East Asia's Environmentalists*. Cambridge, MA: MIT Press.
Hager, Carol. 2015. "Introduction: A New Look at NIMBY." In *NIMBY Is Beautiful: Cases of Local Activism and Environmental Innovation around the World*, edited by Carol Hager and Mary Alice Haddad. New York: Berghahn Books, 1–14.
Haggard, Stephan, and Robert R Kaufman. 1995. *The Political Economy of Democratic Transitions*. Princeton, NJ: Princeton University Press.
Hall, Peter A. 1993. "Policy Paradigms, Social Learning, and the State: The Case of Economic Policymaking in Britain." *Comparative Politics* (25) 3: 275–96.
Head, Brian W., and John Alford. 2015. "Wicked Problems: Implications for Public Policy and Management." *Administration & Society* 47 (6): 711–39.
Helmke, Gretchen, and Frances Rosenbluth. 2009. "Regimes and the Rule of Law: Judicial Independence in Comparative Perspective." *Annual Review of Political Science* 12: 345–66.
Hernández, Andrés, Jorge Flores, and María Alejandra Naranjo. 2010. *Gobernanza ambiental, trayectoria institucional y organizaciones sociales en Bogotá*: 1991–2010. Bogotá: Universidad de los Andes.
Herrera, Veronica. 2014. "Does Commercialization Undermine the Benefits of Decentralization for Local Services Provision? Evidence from Mexico's Urban Water and Sanitation Sector." *World Development* 56 (April): 16–31.
Herrera, Veronica. 2017. *Water and Politics: Clientelism and Reform in Urban Mexico*. Ann Arbor: University of Michigan Press.
Herrera, Veronica. 2022. "Citizen-Led Environmental Governance: Regulating Urban Wetlands in South America." Paper presented at the American Political Science Association Annual Congress, Toronto: September.
Herrera, Veronica, and Lindsay Mayka. 2020. "How Do Legal Strategies Advance Social Accountability? Evaluating Mechanisms in Colombia." *Journal of Development Studies* 56 (8): 1437–54.

Herrera, Veronica, and Alison E. Post. 2014. "Can Developing Countries Both Decentralize and Depoliticize Urban Water Services? Evaluating the Legacy of the 1990s Reform Wave." *World Development* 64 (December): 621–41.
Hilbink, Lisa. 2012. "The Origins of Positive Judicial Independence." *World Politics*. 64 (4): 587–621.
Ho, Peter. 2001. "Greening without Conflict? Environmentalism, NGOs and Civil Society in China." *Development and Change* 32 (5): 893–921.
Hochstetler, Kathryn. 2003. "Fading Green? Environmental Politics in the Mercosur Free Trade Agreement." *Latin American Politics and Society* 45 (4): 1–32.
Hochstetler, Kathryn. 2012a. "Civil Society and the Regulatory State of the South: A Commentary." *Regulation & Governance* 6 (3): 362–70.
Hochstetler, Kathryn. 2012b. "Democracy and the Environment in Latin America and Eastern Europe." In *Comparative Environmental Pratice: Theory, Practice, and Prospects*, edited by Paul F. Steinberg and Stacy D. VanDeveer, 199–229. Cambridge, MA: MIT Press.
Hochstetler, Kathryn. 2018. "Environmental Impact Assessment: Evidence-Based Policymaking in Brazil." *Contemporary Social Science* 13 (1): 100–111.
Hochstetler, Kathryn. 2020. *Political Economies of Energy Transition: Wind and Solar Power in Brazil and South Africa*. Cambridge: Cambridge University Press.
Hochstetler, Kathryn, and Margaret E Keck. 2007. *Greening Brazil: Environmental Activism in State and Society*. Durham, NC: Duke University Press.
Hochstetler, Kathryn, and J. Ricardo Tranjan. 2016. "Environment and Consultation in the Brazilian Democratic Developmental State." *Comparative Politics* 48 (4): 497–516.
Holland, Alisha C. 2017. *Forbearance as Redistribution: The Politics of Informal Welfare in Latin America*. New York: Cambridge University Press.
Hugo, Victor. 1862. *Les Misérables*. Paris: A. Lacroix, Verboeckhoven.
Human Rights Watch. 2014. *Cleaning Human Waste: "Manual Scavenging," Caste, and Discrimination in India*. Amsterdam: Human Rights Watch.
Human Rights Watch. 2017. "Implicating Humala | Evidence of Atrocities and Cover-Up of Abuses Committed during Peru's Armed Conflict." Human Rights Watch News Release. September 7.
Human Rights Watch. 2019. World Report 2019: *Peru: Events of 2018*. Human Rights Watch.
Hummel, Calla. 2021. *Why Informal Workers Organize: Contentious Politics, Enforcement, and the State*. New York: Oxford University Press.
INEI. 2018. *Análisis de la estructura empreserial de Lima Metropolitana*. Lima: Instituto Nacional de Estadística Informática.
Inglehart, Ronald. 1977. *The Silent Revolution: Changing Values and Political Styles among Western Publics*. Princeton, NJ: Princeton University Press.
Inglehart, Ronald. 1990. *Culture Shift in Advanced Industrial Society*. Princeton, NJ: Princeton University Press.
International Development Research Centre. Undated. *Reducción de la vulnerabilidad física y de riesgos frente a desastres en la Margen Izquierda del Río Rimac*. Ottawa: Canada.
Ioris, Antonio Augusto Rossotto. 2012. "The Neoliberalization of Water in Lima, Peru." *Political Geography* 31 (5): 266–78.
Jachimowicz, Maia. 2006. "Argentina: A New Era of Migration and Migration Policy." *Migration Information Source*. Washington, D.C.: Migration Policy Institute.

Jansen, Stef. 2001. "The Streets of Beograd: Urban Space and Protest Identities in Serbia." *Political Geography* 20 (1): 35–55.
Jaskoski, Maiah. 2014. "Environmental Licensing and Conflict in Peru's Mining Sector: A Path-Dependent Analysis." *World Development* 64: 873–83.
Jaskoski, Maiah. 2020. "Participatory Institutions as a Focal Point for Mobilizing: Prior Consultation and Indigenous Conflict in Colombia's Extractive Industries." *Comparative Politics* 52 (4): 537–56.
Jaskoski, Maiah. 2022. *The Politics of Extraction: Territorial Rights, Participatory Institutions, and Conflict in Latin America*. New York: Oxford University Press.
JICA. 2003. *Plan de acción estratégico (PAE) para la gestión ambiental sustentable de una area urbano-industrial a escala completa*. Tokyo: Japan International Cooperation Agency.
Joshi, Anuradha. 2017. "Legal Empowerment and Social Accountability: Complementary Strategies toward Rights-Based Development in Health?" *World Development* 99 (Supplement C): 160–72.
Joshi, Anuradha, and Mick Moore. 2004. "Institutionalised Co-Production: Unorthodox Public Service Delivery in Challenging Environments." *Journal of Development Studies* 40 (4): 31–49.
Juárez Soto, Henry. 2012. "Contaminación del Río Rímac por metales pesados y efecto en la agricultura en el Cono Este de Lima, Metropolitana." Master's thesis, Universidad Nacional Agraria la Molina, IDRC Canada, 1–87.
Kaiser, Susana. 2015. "Argentina's Trials: New Ways of Writing Memory." *Latin American Perspectives* 42 (3): 193–206.
Kapiszewski, Diana. 2012. *High Courts and Economic Governance in Argentina and Brazil*. New York: Cambridge University Press.
Karl, Terry Lynn. 1997. *The Paradox of Plenty: Oil Booms and Petro-States*. Berkeley: University of California Press.
Kashwan, Prakash. 2017. *Democracy in the Woods: Environmental Conservation and Social Justice in India, Tanzania, and Mexico*. New York: Oxford University Press.
Kauffman, Craig M., and Pamela L. Martin. 2014. "Scaling Up Buen Vivir: Globalizing Local Environmental Governance from Ecuador." *Global Environmental Politics* 14 (1): 40–58.
Keck, Margaret E. 2002. "Water, Water, Everywhere, nor Any Drop to Drink: Land Use and Water Policy in São Paulo, Brazil." In *Livable Cities: Urban Struggles for Livelihood and Sustainability*, edited by Peter B. Evans. Berkeley: University of California Press, 162–94.
Klein, Peter Taylor. 2022. *Flooded: Development, Democracy, and Brazil's Belo Monte Dam*. New Brunswick, NJ: Rutgers University Press.
Kopinak, Kathryn, and Ma Del Rocio Barajas. 2002. "Too Close for Comfort? The Proximity of Industrial Hazardous Wastes to Local Populations in Tijuana, Baja California." *Journal of Environment & Development* 11 (3): 215–46.
Krook, Mona Lena. 2010. *Quotas for Women in Politics: Gender and Candidate Selection Reform Worldwide*. New York: Oxford University Press.
Kummu, Matti, Hans De Moel, Philip J. Ward, and Olli Varis. 2011. "How Close Do We Live to Water? A Global Analysis of Population Distance to Freshwater Bodies." *PLoS One* 6 (6): e20578.

Lamprea, Everaldo. 2016. "Daño ambiental y sentencias de reforma estructural: El caso del Río Bogotá." In *Nuevas tendencias del derecho administrativo*, edited by Helena Alviar García. Bogotá: Universidad de Los Andes, 283–306.

Landrigan, Philip J., Richard Fuller, Nereus J. Acosta, Olusoji Adeyi, Robert Arnold, Niladri Basu, et al. 2017. "The Lancet Commission on Pollution and Health." 391 (10019): 462–512.

Lee, Chris. 2012. "The FARC and the Colombian Left: Time for a Political Solution?" *Latin American Perspectives* 39 (1): 28–42.

Leguizamón, Amalia. 2020. *Seeds of Power: Environmental Injustice and Genetically Modified Soybeans in Argentina*. Durham, NC: Duke University Press.

Lessa, Francesca. 2010. *Juicio y castigo: Nestor Kirchner and Accountability for Past Human Rights Violations in Argentina*. London: LSE Ideas.

Lessing, Benjamin. 2021. "Conceptualizing Criminal Governance." *Perspectives on Politics*, 19 (3): 854–73.

Levi, Margaret. 1996. "Social and Unsocial Capital: A Review Essay of Robert Putnam's Making Democracy Work." *Politics & Society* 24 (1): 45–55.

Levine, Adeline Gordon. 1982. "Love Canal: Science, Politics, and People." Lexington, MA: D.C. Health & Company.

Levitsky, Steven, and Maria Victoria Murillo. 2008. "Argentina: From Kirchner to Kirchner." *Journal of Democracy* 19 (2): 16–30.

Levitsky, Steven, and María Victoria Murillo. 2009. "Variation in Institutional Strength." *Annual Review of Political Science* 12 (1): 115–33.

Lewis, Paul. 2002. *Guerillas and Generals: The "Dirty War" in Argentina*. Westport, CT: Praeger.

Lijphart, Arend. 1975. "The Comparable-Cases Strategy in Comparative Research." *Comparative Political Studies* 8 (2): 158–77.

Lima Cómo Vamos. 2019. *Lima y Callao según sus ciudadanos: Décimo informe urbano de percepción sobre calidad de vida en la ciudad*. Lima: Lima Cómo Vamos Observatorio Ciudadano.

Lofrano, Giusy, and Jeanette Brown. 2010. "Wastewater Management through the Ages: A History of Mankind." *Science of the Total Environment* 408 (22): 5254–64.

Londoño, Beatriz. 2006. "Evolución legal y jurisprudencial de las acciones constitucionales en material ambiental." In *15 años de la constitución ecológica de Colombia*, edited by Beatriz Londoño. Bogotá: Universidad Externado de Colombia, 463–510.

Londoño, Beatriz, and Arturo Carrillo, eds. 2010. *Acciones de grupo y de clase en casos de graves vulneraciones a derechos humanos*. Bogotá: Defensoría del Pueblo de Colombia, George Washington University Law School, and University of Rosario.

Londoño Toro, Beatriz. 2008. "Las organizaciones no gubernamentales ambientales Colombianas y su ejercicio de las herramientas de participación institucionalizada." In *Gobernabilidad, instituciones y medio ambiente en Colombia*, edited by Manuel Rodríguez Becerra. Bogotá: Foro Nacional Ambiental, 523–49.

Lora-Wainwright, Anna. 2017. *Resigned Activism: Living with Pollution in Rural China*. Cambridge, MA: MIT Press.

Lubovich, Kelley. 2007. "The Coming Crisis: Water Insecurity in Peru." Falls Church, VA: USAID FESS Issue Brief.

Matthews, Peter, and Annette Hastings. 2013. "Middle-Class Political Activism and Middle-Class Advantage in Relation to Public Services: A Realist Synthesis of the Evidence Base." *Social Policy & Administration* 47 (1): 72–92.

Mayka, Lindsay. 2019. *Building Participatory Institutions in Latin America: Reform Coalitions and Institutional Change*. New York: Cambridge University Press.
Mayka, Lindsay. 2021. "The Power of Human Rights Frames in Urban Security: Lessons from Bogotá." *Comparative Politics* 54 (1): 1–25.
McClintock, Cynthia. 1984. "Why Peasants Rebel: The Case of Peru's Sendero Luminoso." *World Politics* 37 (1): 48–84.
McFarlane, Colin. 2008. "Governing the Contaminated City: Infrastructure and Sanitation in Colonial and Post-Colonial Bombay." *International Journal of Urban and Regional Research* 32 (2): 415–35.
McGranahan, Gordon. 2015. "Realizing the Right to Sanitation in Deprived Urban Communities: Meeting the Challenges of Collective Action, Coproduction, Affordability, and Housing Tenure." *World Development* 68 (April): 242–53.
Melosi, Martin. 2008. *The Sanitary City: Urban Infrastructure in America from Colonial Times to the Present*. Abridged edition. Pittsburgh, PA: University of Pittsburgh Press.
Merlinsky, Gabriela. 2013. *Política, derechos y justicia ambiental: El conflicto del Riachuelo*. Buenos Aires: Fondo de Cultura Económica.
Merlinsky, Gabriela, and Melina Tobías. 2016. "Inundaciones y construcción social del riesgo en Buenos Aires: Acciones colectivas, controversias y escenarios del futuro." *Cuadernos del Cendes* 33 (91): 45–63.
Mertha, Andrew. 2008. *China's Water Warriors: Citizen Action and Policy Change*. Ithaca, NY: Cornell University Press.
Meyer, David S., and Debra C. Minkoff. 2004. "Conceptualizing Political Opportunity." *Social Forces* 82 (4): 1457–92.
Milmanda, Belén Fernández, and Candelaria Garay. 2019. "Subnational Variation in Forest Protection in the Argentine Chaco." *World Development* 118: 79–90.
Milmanda, Belén Fernández, and Candelaria Garay. 2020. "The Multilevel Politics of Enforcement: Environmental Institutions in Argentina." *Politics & Society* 48 (1): 3–26.
Minambiente. 2015. Avanza recuperación ambiental, social, cultural y económica del Río Bogotá. Bogotá: Ministerio de Ambiente y Desarrollo Sostenible. https://archivo.mina mbiente.gov.co/index.php/noticias-minambiente/1782-avanza.
Ministerio de Ambiente. 2009. *Identificación de fuentes de contaminación en la Cuenca de Río Rimac resumen ejecutivo*. Lima: Ministerio de Ambiente.
Ministerio de Ambiente. 2018. *Distribución nacional de los rellenos sanitarios municipales 2018*. Dirección General de Educación, Ciudadanía, e Información Ambiental. Lima: Ministerio de Ambiente.
Ministerio del Ambiente. 2016. *Historia ambiental del Perú: Siglos XVIII y XIX*. Lima: Ministerio de Ambiente.
Misión de Observación Electoral. 2012. *Mecanismos de participación ciudadana en Colombia: 20 años de ilusiones*. Bogotá: Misión de Observación Electoral.
Mitlin, Diana. 2008. "With and beyond the State—Co-Production as a Route to Political Influence, Power and Transformation for Grassroots Organizations." *Environment and Urbanization* 20 (2): 339–60.
Moncada, Eduardo. 2016. *Cities, Business, and the Politics of Urban Violence in Latin America*. Stanford, CA: Stanford University Press.
Muñoz, Paula. 2019. "Political Violence and the Defeat of the Left." In *Politics after Violence: Legacies of the Shining Path Conflict in Peru*, edited by Hillel Soifer and Alberto Vergara. Austin: University of Texas Press, 202–25.

Murillo, Maria Victoria, and Carmen Le Foulon. 2006. "Crisis and Policymaking in Latin America: The Case of Chile's 1998–99 Electricity Crisis." *World Development* 34 (9): 1580–96.

Murungi, Caroline, and Meine Pieter van Dijk. 2014. "Emptying, Transportation and Disposal of Feacal Sludge in Informal Settlements of Kampala Uganda: The Economics of Sanitation." *Habitat International* 42 (April): 69–75.

Nápoli, Andrés. 2009. "Una Politica de Estado Para El Riachuelo." Buenos Aires: Fundación Ambiente y Recursos Naturales (FARN).

Nelson, Kara L., and Ashley Murray. 2008. "Sanitation for Unserved Populations: Technologies, Implementation Challenges, and Opportunities." *Annual Review of Environment and Resources* 33: 119–51.

Newell, Joshua P., and Laura A. Henry. 2016. "The State of Environmental Protection in the Russian Federation: A Review of the Post-Soviet Era." *Eurasian Geography and Economics* 57 (6): 779–801.

Nicholls, Walter J. 2008. "The Urban Question Revisited: The Importance of Cities for Social Movements." *International Journal of Urban and Regional Research* 32 (4): 841–59.

Nixon, Rob. 2013. *Slow Violence and the Environmentalism of the Poor*. Cambridge, MA: Harvard University Press.

O'Brien, Philip J. 1995. "Participation and Sustainable Development in Colombia." *European Review of Latin American and Caribbean Studies* 59: 7–35.

Observatorio del Agua Chillón Rímac Lurín. 2019. *Diagnóstico inicial para el plan de gestión de recursos hídricos de las Cuencas Chillón, Rímac, Lurín y Chilca*. Lima: Observatorio del Agua Chillón Rímac Lurín.

OECD. 2014. *OECD Environmental Performance Reviews: Colombia*. Paris: OECD Publishing.

OECD. 2016. *Environmental Performance Reviews: PERU*. Paris: OECD Publishing.

OECD. 2021. *Water Governance in Peru: Annex C: The Chillón, Rímac and Lurín River Basins (Chirilú)*. Paris: OECD Publishing.

Offstein, Norman. 2003. "An Historical Review and Analysis of Colombian Guerrilla Movements: FARC, ELN and EPL." *Revista Desarrollo y Sociedad* 52 (September): 99–142.

Oliveira, Gustavo, and Susanna Hecht. 2016. "Sacred Groves, Sacrifice Zones and Soy Production: Globalization, Intensification and Neo-Nature in South America." *Journal of Peasant Studies* 43 (2): 251–85.

O'Rourke, Dara. 2002. "Community-Driven Regulation: Toward an Improved Model of Environmental Regulation in Vietnam." In *Livable Cities? Urban Struggles for Livelihood and Sustainability*, edited by Peter Evans. Berkeley: University of California Press, 95–131.

Ostrom, Elinor. 1996. "Crossing the Great Divide: Coproduction, Synergy, and Development." *World Development* 24 (6): 1073–87.

Owens, Peter B. 2013. "Precipitating Events and Flashpoints." *The Wiley-Blackwell Encyclopedia of Social and Political Movements*, edited by David A. Snow, Donatella Della Porta, Doug McAdam, and Bert Kandermans. Hoboken, NJ: Wiley-Blackwell Publishing, 1–3.

Page, Scott E. 2006. "Path Dependence." *Quarterly Journal of Political Science* 1 (1): 87–115.

Palacio, Dolly Cristiana. 2014. "Dinámicas de participación en la formación de lugares-patrimonio: Humedales y centro histórico en Bogotá." *Bienes, paisajes e itinerarios* 85 (April): 78–99.

Paller, Jeffrey W. 2015. "Informal Networks and Access to Power to Obtain Housing in Urban Slums in Ghana." *Africa Today* 62 (1): 31–55.

Paredes, Maritza. 2019. "Indigenous Activism and Human Rights NGOs in Peru: The Unexpected Consequences of Armed Conflict." In *Politics after Violence: Legacies of the Shining Path Conflict in Peru*, edited by Hillel David Soifer and Alberto Vergara. Austin: University of Texas Press, 176–201.

Pasotti, Eleonora. 2020. *Resisting Redevelopment: Protest in Aspiring Global Cities.* New York: Cambridge University Press.

Pastore, Maria Chiara. 2015. "Reworking the Relation between Sanitation and the City in Dar Es Salaam, Tanzania." *Environment and Urbanization* 27 (2): 473–88.

Pegram, Thomas. 2008. "Accountability in Hostile Times: The Case of the Peruvian Human Rights Ombudsman 1996–2001." *Journal of Latin American Studies* 40 (1): 51–82.

Pérez Preciado, Alfonso. 1993. *El problema del Río Bogotá:* Bogotá: Estudio para la estrategia de saneamiento del Río Bogotá, CAR.

Perrow, Charles. 1997. "Organizing for Environmental Destruction." *Organization & Environment* 10 (1): 66–72.

Peruzzotti, Enrique. 2012. "The Societalization of Horizontal Accountability: Rights Advocacy and the Defensor del Pueblo de La Nacion in Argentina." In *Human Rights, State Compliance, and Social Change: Assessing National Human Rights Institutions*, edited by Ryan Goodman and Thomas Pegram. Cambridge: Cambridge University Press, 243–69.

Philip, George. 1984. "The Fall of the Argentine Military." *Third World Quarterly* 6 (3): 624–37.

Pierson, Paul. 2004. *Politics in Time: History, Institutions, and Social Analysis.* Princeton, NJ: Princeton University Press.

Polsby, Nelson W. 1958. "The Sociology of Community Power: A Reassessment." *Social Forces* 37: 232.

Ponce, Aldo F., and Cynthia McClintock. 2014. "The Explosive Combination of Inefficient Local Bureaucracies and Mining Production: Evidence from Localized Societal Protests in Peru." *Latin American Politics and Society* 56 (3): 118–40.

Portes, Alejandro. 1989. "Latin American Urbanization during the Years of the Crisis." *Latin American Research Review* 24 (3): 7–44.

Portes, Alejandro. 1998. "Social Capital: Its Origins and Applications in Modern Sociology." *Annual Review of Sociology* 24 (1): 1–24.

Post, Alison E. 2018. "Cities and Politics in the Developing World." *Annual Review of Political Science* 21: 115–33.

Procuraduría General de la Nación de Colombia. n.d. "Documento Orientador de La Ley 850 de 2003, Modulo 10." Bogotá: Red Institucional de Apoyo a las Veedurías Ciudadanas. Procuraduría General de la Nación de Colombia.

PRODUCE. n.d. *Gestión ambiental de las empresas industriales manufactureras.* Lima: Ministerio de la Producción: Gestión ambiental de las empresas industriales manufactureras.

Prüss-Ustün, A., J. Wolf, C. Corvalán, R. Bos, and M. Neira. 2016. "Preventing Disease through Healthy Environments: A Global Assessment of the Burden of Disease from Environmental Risks." Geneva: World Health Organization.

Pulgar Vidal, Manuel. 2006. "Constitución política del Perú de 1993: Un proceso algo accidentado." In *15 Anos de la constitución ecológica de Colombia*, edited by Beatriz Londoño. Bogotá: Universidad Externado de Colombia, 135–60.
Putnam, Robert D. 2000. *Bowling Alone: The Collapse and Revival of American Community*. New York: Simon and Schuster.
Putnam, Robert D., Robert Leonardi, and Raffaella Nanetti. 1993. *Making Democracy Work: Civic Traditions in Modern Italy*. Princeton, NJ: Princeton University Press.
Ramírez, Sandra. 2010. *Procesos participativos en la Cuenca Río Tunjuelo*. Report in possession of author.
Rauws, W. S., and Gert de Roo. 2011. "Exploring Transitions in the Peri-Urban Area." *Planning Theory & Practice* 12 (2): 269–84.
Reboratti, Carlos. 2008. "Environmental Justice and Environmental Conflicts in Argentina." In *Environmental Justice in Latin America: Problems, Promise, and Practice*, edited by David V. Carruthers. Cambridge, MA: MIT Press, 101–18.
Reif, Linda C. 2004. *The Ombudsman, Good Governance, and the International Human Rights System*. New York: Springer.
Rich, Jessica. 2019. *State-Sponsored Activism: Bureaucrats and Social Movements in Democratic Brazil*. New York: Cambridge University Press.
Riofrancos, Thea. 2020. *Resource Radicals: From Petro-Nationalism to Post-Extractivism in Ecuador*. Durham, NC: Duke University Press.
Rithmire, Meg E. 2015. *Land Bargains and Chinese Capitalism: The Politics of Property Rights under Reform*. New York: Cambridge University Press.
Rochlin, James F. 2007. *Social Forces and the Revolution in Military Affairs: The Cases of Colombia and Mexico*. New York: Palgrave Macmillan.
Rodriguez Becerra. 1994. *Crisis ambiental y relaciones internacionales: Hacia un estrategia colombiana*. Bogotá: Coordinación editorial: CEREC.
Rodríguez Gómez, Juan Camillo. n.d. "Acueducto de Bogotá, 1887–1914: Entre Público y Privado." Bogotá: Red Cultural del Banco de la República en Colombia (Banrepcultural).
Rodríguez-Garavito, César, and Diana Rodríguez-Franco. 2015. *Radical Deprivation on Trial: The Impact of Judicial Activism on Socioeconomic Rights in the Global South*. New York: Cambridge University Press.
Rodríguez-Vignoli, Jorge, and Francisco Rowe. 2018. "How Is Internal Migration Reshaping Metropolitan Populations in Latin America? A New Method and New Evidence." *Population Studies* 72 (2): 253–73.
Romanin, Enrique Andriotti. 2012. "From the Resistance to the Integration: The Transformations of the Mothers of Plaza de Mayo in the 'Age Kirchner.'" *Estudios Políticos*, no. 41: 36–56.
Root, Rebecca K. 2009. "Through the Window of Opportunity: The Transitional Justice Network in Peru." *Human Rights Quarterly* 31 (2): 452–73.
Root, Rebecca K. 2012. *Transitional Justice in Peru*. New York: Palgrave Macmillan.
Rosenqvist, Tanja, Cynthia Mitchell, and Juliet Willetts. 2016. "A Short History of How We Think and Talk about Sanitation Services and Why It Matters." *Journal of Water Sanitation and Hygiene for Development* 6 (2): 298–312.
Ross, Michael L. 2004. "How Do Natural Resources Influence Civil War? Evidence from Thirteen Cases." *International Organization* 58 (1): 35–67.
Rowen, Jami. 2017. *Searching for Truth in the Transitional Justice Movement*. New York: Cambridge University Press.

Ryan, Daniel. 2004. "Ciudadanía y control de gobierno en la Cuenca Matanza Riachhuelo." Center for Latin American Social Policy, University of Texas at Austin, September.

Sánchez-Triana, Ernesto, Kulsum Ahmed, and Yewande Awe. 2007. *Environmental Priorities and Poverty Reduction, A Country Environmental Analysis for Colombia*. Washington, D.C.: World Bank.

Scott, James C. 1985. *Weapons of the Weak: Everyday Forms of Peasant Resistance*. New Haven, CT: Yale University Press.

Se presentan comon terceros. 2006. *Se presentan como terceros. demandan por daño ambiental colectivo. Ofrecen Prueba*. Buenos Aires: CSJN.

Seawright, Jason, and John Gerring. 2008. "Case Selection Techniques in Case Study Research: A Menu of Qualitative and Quantitative Options." *Political Research Quarterly* 61 (2): 294–308.

Secretaría Distrital de Ambiente. 2021. *Informe consolidado del avance en el cumplimiento de las ordenes de la sentencia del Río Bogotá a cargo de la Secretaría Distrital Del Ambiente*. Bogotá: Secretará Distrital de Ambiente.

Sigal, Martin, Julieta Rossi, and Diego Morales. 2017. "Argentina: Implementation of Collective Cases." In *Social Rights Judgments and the Politics of Compliance: Making It Stick*, edited by Malcolm Langford, César Rodríguez-Garavito, and Julieta Rossi. New York: Cambridge University Press, 140–76.

Sikkink, Kathryn. 2008. "From Pariah State to Global Protagonist: Argentina and the Struggle for International Human Rights." *Latin American Politics and Society* 50 (1): 1–29.

Simmons, Erica S. 2016. *Meaningful Resistance: Market Reforms and the Roots of Social Protest in Latin America*. New York: Cambridge University Press.

Simon, David. 2008. "Urban Environments: Issues on the Peri-Urban Fringe." *Annual Review of Environment and Resources* 33: 167–85.

Smulovitz, Catalina. 2010. "Judicialization in Argentina: Legal Culture or Opportunities and Support Structures?" In *Cultures of Legality: Judicialization and Political Activism in Latin America*, edited by Javier A. Couso, Alexandra Huneeus, and Rachel Sieder. New York: Cambridge University Press, 234–53.

Soifer, Hillel, and Alberto Vergara. 2019. "Leaving the Path Behind." In *Politics after Violence: Legacies of the Shining Path Conflict in Peru*, edited by Hillel Soifer and Alberto Vergara. Austin: University of Texas Press, 1–16.

Solomon, Steven. 2011. *Water: The Epic Struggle for Wealth, Power, and Civilization*. New York: Harper Perennial.

Starn, Orin. 1995. "Maoism in the Andes: The Communist Party of Peru—Shining Path and the Refusal of History." *Journal of Latin American Studies* 27 (2): 399–421.

Stern, Rachel E. 2011. "From Dispute to Decision: Suing Polluters in China." *China Quarterly* 206: 294–312.

Stern, Rachel E. 2013. *Environmental Litigation in China: A Study in Political Ambivalence*. New York: Cambridge University Press.

Stern, Rachel E. 2014. "The Political Logic of China's New Environmental Courts." *China Journal* 72: 53–74.

Stokes, Susan C. 1995. *Cultures in Conflict: Social Movements and the State in Peru*. Berkeley: University of California Press.

Subgerencia de Defensa Civil. 2013. *Monitoreo de los sectores críticos de La Cuenca del Río Rímac y la reducción de riesgos en el ámbito del gobierno metropolitano*. Informe N° 048-2013/MML/SGDC/RHQM. Lima: Municiplidad Metropolitana de Lima/SGDC.

Svampa, Maristella. 2019. *Neo-Extractivism in Latin America: Socio-Environmental Conflicts, the Territorial Turn, and New Political Narratives.* Cambridge Elements. Cambridge: Cambridge University Press.

Tang, Ching-Ping, Shui-Yan Tang, and Chung-Yuan Chiu. 2011. "Inclusion, Identity, and Environmental Justice in New Democracies: The Politics of Pollution Remediation in Taiwan." *Comparative Politics* 43 (3): 333–50.

Tarr, Joel A. 1996. *Search for the Ultimate Sink.* Akron, OH: University of Akron Press.

Tate, Winifred. 2007. *Counting the Dead: The Culture and Politics of Human Rights Activism in Colombia.* Berkeley: Univerity of California Press.

Taylor, Dorceta E. 2000. "The Rise of the Environmental Justice Paradigm: Injustice Framing and the Social Construction of Environmental Discourses." *American Behavioral Scientist* 43 (4): 508–80.

Taylor, Dorceta E. 2014. *Toxic Communities: Environmental Racism, Industrial Pollution, and Residential Mobility.* New York: NYU Press.

Taylor, Whitney K. 2020. "On the Social Construction of Legal Grievances: Evidence from Colombia and South Africa." *Comparative Political Studies* 53 (8): 1326–56.

Teets, Jessica. 2018. "The Power of Policy Networks in Authoritarian Regimes: Changing Environmental Policy in China." *Governance* 31 (1): 125–41.

Thorp, Rosemary. 1977. "The Post-Import Substitution Era: The Case of Peru." *World Development* 5 (1–2): 125–36.

Tilly, Charles, and Sidney Tarrow. 2015. *Contentious Politics.* 2nd edition. Oxford University Press.

Tobasura Acuña, Isaías. 2003. "El Movimiento Ambiental Colombiano, Una Aproximación a Su Historia Reciente." *Debates Ambientales* 26: 107–19.

Tranter, Bruce, and Mark Western. 2009. "The Influence of Green Parties on Postmaterialist Values." *The British Journal of Sociology* 60 (1): 145–67.

Tribunal Administrativo de Cundinamarca. 2004. *Sección Cuarta, Subsección "B," Acción Popular Núm. 01-479.* Magistrada ponente: Nelly Yolanda Villamizar. Bogotá, Colombia.

UNEP. 2016. *A Snapshot of the World's Water Quality: Towards a Global Assessment.* Nairobi: United National Environment Program.

UNESCO. 2017. *Wastewater: The Untapped Resource.* Paris: United Nations World Water Development Report.

United Cities and Local Governments. 2008. *Decentralization and Local Democracy in the World: First Global Report by United Cities and Local Governments 2008.* Washington, D.C: World Bank Publications.

United Nations. 2018a. *World Urbanization Prospects: The 2018 Revision.* New York: United Nations Department of Economic and Social Affairs.

United Nations. 2018b. *The World's Cities in 2018 Data Booklet.* New York: United Nations Department of Economic and Social Affairs.

Urkidi, Leire, and Mariana Walter. 2011. "Dimensions of Environmental Justice in Anti-Gold Mining Movements in Latin America." *Geoforum* 42 (6): 683–95.

Van Cott, Donna Lee. 2008. *Radical Democracy in the Andes.* New York: Cambridge University Press.

Van Rooij, Benjamin. 2010. "The People vs. Pollution: Understanding Citizen Action against Pollution in China." *Journal of Contemporary China* 19 (63): 55–77.

Van Rooij, Benjamin, Rachel E. Stern, and Kathinka Fürst. 2016. "The Authoritarian Logic of Regulatory Pluralism: Understanding China's New Environmental Actors." *Regulation & Governance* 10 (1): 3–13.

Vélez Pardo, Martín. 2015. *El Reflejo Del Gigante En El Agua: Una Historia Ambiental Del Río Bogotá, 1950-2003*. Bogotá: Universidad de los Andes.

Vergara, Alberto, and Daniel Encinas. 2019. "From a Partisan Right to the Conservative Archipelago: Political Violence and the Transformation of the Right-Wing Spectrum in Contemporary Peru." In *Politics after Violence: Legacies of the Shining Path Conflict in Peru*, edited by Hillel David Soifer and Alberto Vergara, 226–49. Austin: University of Texas Press.

Véron, René. 2006. "Remaking Urban Environments: The Political Ecology of Air Pollution in Delhi." *Environment and Planning A* 38 (11): 2093–2109.

Vörösmarty, Charles J., Peter B. McIntyre, Mark O. Gessner, David Dudgeon, Alexander Prusevich, Pamela Green, Stanley Glidden, Stuart E. Bunn, Caroline A. Sullivan, and C. Reidy Liermann. 2010. "Global Threats to Human Water Security and River Biodiversity." *Nature* 467 (7315): 555.

Waddington, David P., Karen Jones, and Chas Critcher. 1989. *Flashpoints: Studies in Public Disorder*. Routledge London.

Wallace, Jeremy. 2014. *Cities and Stability: Urbanization, Redistribution, and Regime Survival in China*. New York: Oxford University Press.

Wapner, Paul. 1995. "Politics Beyond the State: Environmental Activism and World Civic Politics." *World Politics* 47 (3): 311–40.

Weisman, Steven R. 2007. "Democrats Divided as House Passes Peru Trade Bill." *New York Times*, November 8.

Wilson, Bruce. 2009. "Institutional Reform and Rights Revolutions in Latin America: The Cases of Costa Rica and Colombia." *Journal of Politics in Latin America* 1 (2): 59–85.

Winters, Matthew S., Abdul Gaffar Karim, and Berly Martawardaya. 2014. "Public Provision under Conditions of Insufficient Citizen Demand: Insights from the Urban Sanitation Sector in Indonesia." *World Development* (60): 31–42.

World Bank. 2006. *Republic of Peru Environmental Sustainability: A Key to Poverty Reduction in Peru Country Environmental Analysis*. Country Environmental Analysis. Washington, D.C.: World Bank.

World Bank. 2009a. *Program Document for a Proposed Environmental Development Policy Loan in the Amount of US$330 Million to the Republic of Peru*. Washington, D.C.: World Bank.

World Bank. 2009b. *Project Appraisal Document on a Proposed Adaptable Program Loan; Matanza Riachuelo Basin Development Program Phase 1*. Washington, D.C.: World Bank.

World Bank. 2010. "Informe No. 54311-CO: Proyecto de adecuación hidráulica y recuperación ambiental del Río Bogotá." Washington, D.C.: World Bank.

World Bank. 2014. *International Bank for Reconstruction and Development Project Paper on a Proposed Additional Loan in the Amount of US$55 Million to the Republic of Peru*. Washington, D.C.: World Bank Group.

Wu, Fengshi, and Ellie Martus. 2021. "Contested Environmentalism: The Politics of Waste in China and Russia." *Environmental Politics* 30 (4): 493–512.

Yashar, Deborah J. 2005. *Contesting Citizenship in Latin America: The Rise of Indigenous Movements and the Postliberal Challenge*. New York: Cambridge University Press.

Youngers, Coletta. 2003. *Violencia política y sociedad civil en el Perú: Historia de la Coordinadora Nacional De Derechos Humanos*. Lima: Instituto de Estudios Peruanos.

Zhang, Yue. 2021. "Rightful Squatting: Housing Movements, Citizenship, and the 'Right to the City' in Brazil." *Journal of Urban Affairs* 43 (10): 1405–22.

Interviews

Argentina

1. Belli, Leandro Vera. Researcher at Centro de Estudios Legales y Sociales (CELS), March 30, 2016. Buenos Aires.
2. Urbiztondo, Santiago. Researcher at Fundación de Investigaciones Económicas Latinoamericanas, March 30, 2016. Buenos Aires.
3. Napoli, Andres. Director of Fundación Ambiente y Recursos Naturales (FARN), March 31, 2016. Buenos Aires.
4. Alberti, Alfredo. President of Asociación de Vecinos de la Boca, April 1, 2016. Buenos Aires.
5. Reese, Eduardo. Director of Economic, Social, and Cultural Rights, Centro de Estudios Legales y Sociales (CELS), April 1, 2016. Buenos Aires.
6. Engineer. Agua y Saneamiento Argentinos S.A., April 1, 2016. Buenos Aires.
7. Urbiztondo, Javier. Former director of Obras Publicas de Gran Buenos Aires, April 4, 2016. La Plata.
8. Merlinksy. Gabriela. Professor at Universidad de Buenos Aires, Estudios Urbanos del Instituto Gino Germani, April 5, 2016. Buenos Aires.
9. Tobias, Melina. PhD student, professor at Universidad de Buenos Aires, Estudios Urbanos del Instituto Gino Germani, April 5, 2016. Buenos Aires.
10. Researcher. April 5, 2016. Buenos Aires.
11. Fins, Cristina. Member of Asociación de Vecinos de la Boca, April 6, 2016. Buenos Aires.
12. Attorney. Public Defender's Office of Buenos Aires, April 6, 2016. Buenos Aires.
13. Morales, Diego. Director of Litigation and Legal Defense, Centro de Estudios Legales y Sociales (CELS). April 6, 2016. Buenos Aires.
14. Aizen, Marina. Clarín newspaper, journalist, April 6, 2016. Buenos Aires.
15. Engineer A. Agua y Saneamiento Argentinos S.A., April 6, 2016. Buenos Aires.
16. Engineer B. Agua y Saneamiento Argentinos S.A., April 7, 2016. Buenos Aires.
17. Engineer C. Agua y Saneamiento Argentinos S.A., April 7, 2016. Tigre.
18. Engineer D. Agua y Saneamiento Argentinos S.A., April 8, 2016. Tigre.
19. Engineer E. Agua y Saneamiento Argentinos S.A., April 8, 2016. Buenos Aires.
20. Mingo, Leonel. Cuerpo Colegiado Representative at Greenpeace, April 8, 2016. Buenos Aires.
21. Estrada Oyuela, Raul. Member of Asociación de Vecinos de la Boca, April 8, 2016. Buenos Aires.
22. Koutsovitis, Eva. Member of Foro Hídrico de Lomas de Zamora, April 10, 2016. Buenos Aires.
23. Garcia Silva, Leandro. Attorney with Defensor del Pueblo de la Nación, April 11, 2016. Buenos Aires.
24. Garcia Espil, Javier. Attorney with Defensor del Pueblo de la Nación, April 11, 2016. Buenos Aires.

25. Esber, Horacio. Attorney with Defensor del Pueblo de la Nación, April 11, 2016. Buenos Aires.
26. Alzari, Maria Jose. Attorney with Consejo Empresario Argentino para el Desarrollo Sustentable (CEADS), April 11, 2016. Buenos Aires.
27. Magallanes, Antolin. Former director of ACUMAR, La Autoridad de Cuenca Matanza Riachuelo (ACUMAR), April 11, 2016. Buenos Aires.
28. Sallaberry, Daniel. Attorney for Causa Mendoza, April 12, 2016. Buenos Aires.
29. Engineer for Special Projects. World Bank Division, April 13, 2016. Buenos Aires.
30. Engineer F. Agua y Saneamiento Argentinos S.A., April 13, 2016. Buenos Aires.
31. Engineer G. Agua y Saneamiento Argentinos S.A., April 14, 2016. Buenos Aires.
32. Federovisky, Sergio. Member of Board of Directors of La Autoridad de Cuenca Matanza Riachuelo (ACUMAR), April 14, 2016. Buenos Aires.
33. Garone, Noelia. Attorney at Asociación Civil por la Igualdad y la Justicia (ACIJ), April 14, 2016. Buenos Aires.
34. Falbo, Guadelupe. Employee at Asociación Civil por la Igualdad y la Justicia (ACIJ), April 14, 2016. Buenos Aires.
35. Rossi, Julieta. Former researcher at Centro de Estudios Legales y Sociales (CELS), April 14, 2016. Buenos Aires.
36. Garcia Elorrio, Javier. Division head, Dirección de Limpieza for CABA, April 15, 2016. Buenos Aires.
37. Suarez, Lorena. Employee at La Autoridad de Cuenca Matanza Riachuelo (ACUMAR), April 15, 2016. Buenos Aires.
38. Employee. La Autoridad de Cuenca Matanza Riachuelo (ACUMAR), April 18, 2016. Buenos Aires.
39. Lanzetta, Maximo. Director of Environmental Division of Almirante Brown Municipality, April 18, 2016. Buenos Aires.
40. Arauz, Mora. Co-founder of Fundación Ciudad, April 18, 2016. Buenos Aires.
41. Caraballo, Andreina. President of Fundación Ciudad, April 18, 2016. Buenos Aires.
42. Engineer. Agua y Saneamiento Argentinos S.A., April 19, 2016. Buenos Aires.
43. Ciancio, Carolina. Member of Asociación Ciudadana de Derechos Humanos (ACDH), April 19, 2016. Buenos Aires.
44. Pujo, Lorena. Former employee, Greenpeace Argentina, April 19, 2016. Buenos Aires.
45. Inspector A. La Autoridad de Cuenca Matanza Riachuelo (ACUMAR), April 20, 2016. Buenos Aires.
46. Inspector B. La Autoridad de Cuenca Matanza Riachuelo (ACUMAR), April 20, 2016. Buenos Aires.
47. Inspector C. La Autoridad de Cuenca Matanza Riachuelo (ACUMAR), April 20, 2016. Buenos Aires.
48. Inspector D. La Autoridad de Cuenca Matanza Riachuelo (ACUMAR), April 20, 2016. Buenos Aires.
49. Employee. Unión de Industriales para Saneamiento Cuencas Matanza Riachuelo y Reconquista (UISCUMARR), April 20, 2016. Buenos Aires.
50. Esposito, Aldo. Director of Unión de Industriales para Saneamiento Cuencas Matanza Riachuelo y Reconquista (UISCUMARR), April 20, 2016. Buenos Aires.
51. Garcia Elorrio, Javier. Division head of Dirección de Limpieza for CABA, April 22, 2016. Buenos Aires.
52. Resident A. Villa 21-24, April 22, 2016. Buenos Aires.
53. Resident B. Villa 21-24, April 22, 2016. Buenos Aires.

REFERENCES 241

54. Demoy, Belon. Instituto de Viviendas de la Ciudad de Buenos Aires, April 22, 2016. Buenos Aires.
55. Garcia Silva, Leandro. Attorney with Defensor del Pueblo de la Nación, March 7, 2017. Buenos Aires.
56. Garcia Elorrio, Javier. Division head for Dirección de Limpieza for CABA, March 8, 2017. Buenos Aires.
57. Armella, Luis. Judge overseeing Beatriz Mendoza Case (2008–12), magistrate in Quilmes, March 9, 2017. Quilmes, GBA.
58. Napoli, Andres. Director of Fundación Ambiente y Recursos Naturales (FARN), March 9, 2017. Buenos Aires.
59. Farnstein, Carolina. Researcher at Centro de Estudios Legales y Sociales (CELS), March 9, 2017. Buenos Aires.
60. Division head. La Autoridad de Cuenca Matanza Riachuelo (ACUMAR), March 10, 2017. Buenos Aires.
61. Viales, Enrique. Environmental Attorney. March 10, 2017. Buenos Aires.
62. Rocha, Laura. Journalist at La Nación. March 10, 2017. Buenos Aires.
63. Celia. Member of Vecinos Autoconvocados de González Catan contra CEAMSE, González Catan, La Matanza. March 11, 2017. Gonzalez Catan, La Matanza.
64. Graciela. Member of Vecinos Autoconvocados de González Catán contra CEAMSE, González Catán, La Matanza. March 11, 2017. González Catan, La Matanza.
65. Domingo. Member of Vecinos Autoconvocados de González Catán contra CEAMSE, González Catán, La Matanza. March 11, 2017. González Catán, La Matanza.
66. Ana. Member of Vecinos Autoconvocados de González Catán contra CEAMSE, González Catán, La Matanza. March 11, 2017. González Catán, La Matanza.
67. Anibal. Member of Vecinos Autoconvocados de González Catán contra CEAMSE, González Catán, La Matanza. March 11, 2017. González Catán, La Matanza.
68. Rodriguez, Patricia. Member of Pilmayquen NGO, March 13, 2017. Phone.
69. Inspector D. La Autoridad de Cuenca Matanza Riachuelo (ACUMAR), March 13, 2017. Lanus, GBA.
70. Inspector E. La Autoridad de Cuenca Matanza Riachuelo (ACUMAR), March 13, 2017. Lanus, GBA.
71. Manager. Jordano Leather, March 13, 2017. Lanus, GBA.
72. Manager. Curtiembres Torres Hermanos, March 13, 2017. Lanus, GBA.
73. Employee. Jordano Leather, March 13, 2017. Lanus, GBA.
74. Manager. Curtiembres Torres Hermanos, March 13, 2017. Lanus, GBA.
75. Tedechi, Sebastian. Attorney with Defensoría General de la Nación, Coordinador de Programa de Derechos Económicos, Sociales y Culturales, March 14, 2017. Buenos Aires.
76. Gutierrez, Mariano. Attorney with Defensoría General de la Nación, Coordinador del Equipo de Abordaje Territorial de la Causa Riachuelo March 14, 2017. Buenos Aires.
77. Acosta, Mariel. Attorney with Defensoria General de la Nacion, Secretaria del Equipo de Riachuelo, March 14, 2017. Buenos Aires.
78. Farina, Martin. Member of Colectivo Ecologica Unidos por la Laguna de Rocha, March 14, 2017. Buenos Aires.
79. Steinberg, Agusta. Employee, Asociación Civil por la Igualdad y la Justicia (ACIJ), March 15, 2017. Buenos Aires.
80. Zulma. Villa Inflamable, Dock Sud, Avellaneda. March 15, 2017. Avellaneda, GBA.
81. Resident A. Villa Inflamable, Dock Sud, Avellaneda. March 15, 2017. Avellaneda, GBA.

82. Resident B. Villa Inflamable, Dock Sud, Avellaneda. March 15, 2017. Avellaneda, GBA.
83. Claudia. Villa Inflamable, Dock Sud, Avellaneda. March 15, 2017. Avellaneda, GBA.
84. Kiki. Villa Inflamable, Dock Sud, Avellaneda. March 15, 2017. Avellaneda, GBA.
85. Rocio. Villa Inflamable, Dock Sud, Avellaneda. March 15, 2017. Avellaneda, GBA.
86. Miguel. Villa Inflamable, Dock Sud, Avellaneda. March 15, 2017. Avellaneda, GBA.
87. Moramarco, Barbara. Attorney for Secretaria, Juzgado de Moron (Secretaria 5, Directora de la Causa Matanza Riachuelo), March 16, 2017. Buenos Aires.
88. Calvi, Ignacio. Attorney for Secretaria, Juzgado de Moron (Secretaria 5, Directora de la Causa Matanza Riachuelo), March 16, 2017. Buenos Aires.
89. Mendoza, Beatriz. Former healthcare worker and claimant for litigation Causa Mendoza, March 16, 2017. Avellaneda, GBA.
90. di Piero, Pedro. Director of Fundación Metropolitana, March 16, 2017. Buenos Aires.
91. Cafferatta, Nestor. Head of Secretario de Juicio Ambientales, Corte Suprema de Justicia de la Nación March 17, 2017, Buenos Aires.
92. Owner. Electroplating Firm, March 17, 2017. Buenos Aires.
93. Head engineer. BINKA S.A. (chemical company), March 17, 2017. Buenos Aires.

Colombia

94. Lamprea, Everaldo. Professor, Facultad de Derecho, Universidad de los Andes, July 14, 2016. Bogotá.
95. Pardo, Tatiano. Journalist, *El Tiempo*, July 14, 2016. Bogotá.
96. Member A. Asociación de Usuarios de los Recursos Naturales Renovables y Defensa Ambiental de la Cuenca del Rio Bogotá (ASURIO), July 15, 2016. Bogotá.
97. Member B. Asociación de Usuarios de los Recursos Naturales Renovables y Defensa Ambiental de la Cuenca del Rio Bogotá (ASURIO), July 15, 2016. Bogotá.
98. Member C. Asociación de Usuarios de los Recursos Naturales Renovables y Defensa Ambiental de la Cuenca del Rio Bogotá (ASURIO), July 15, 2016. Bogotá.
99. Member D. Asociación de Usuarios de los Recursos Naturales Renovables y Defensa Ambiental de la Cuenca del Rio Bogotá (ASURIO), July 15, 2016. Bogotá.
100. Reyes, Lucila. Former employee, Secretaria Distrital del Ambiente, Dirección Jurídica, Ciudad de Bogotá, July 17, 2016. Bogotá.
101. Vasquez, Fernando. Director, Fundación al Verde Vivo, July 18, 2016. Bogotá.
102. Franco, Freddy. Professor, Universidad Nacional de Colombia, Sede Manizales. Bogotá.
103. Galindo, Medardo. Member of Fundación Humedal de la Conejera, July 19, 2016. Bogotá.
104. Member. Red de Veedurías del Rio Bogotá, July 21, 2016. Bogotá.
105. Member E. Asociación de Usuarios de los Recursos Naturales Renovables y Defensa Ambiental de la Cuenca del Rio Bogotá (ASURIO) July 19, 2016. Bogotá.
106. Assistant to City Council member. Concejo de Bogotá, Partido Liberal. July 22, 2016. Bogotá.
107. Member. Fundación Humedal de la Conejera, July 22, 2016. Bogotá.
108. Sanchez, Alvaro. Empoyee, Dirección Desarrollo Regional, Secretaria de Planeación de Cundimarca, July 22, 2016. Bogotá.
109. Gonzalez, Roberto. Director, Desarrollo Regional Gobernación de Cundinamarca, July 22, 2016. Bogotá.

110. Sguerra, Sandra. Former director of Division, Secretaria Distrital del Ambiente, Dirección Jurídica, Ciudad de Bogotá July 22, 2016. Bogotá.
111. Member B. Asociación de Usuarios de los Recursos Naturales Renovables y Defensa Ambiental de la Cuenca del Rio Bogotá (ASURIO), July 24, 2016. Mesitas del Colegio, El Colegio, Cundinamarca.
112. Member D. Asociación de Usuarios de los Recursos Naturales Renovables y Defensa Ambiental de la Cuenca del Rio Bogotá (ASURIO), July 24, 2016. Mesitas del Colegio, El Colegio, Cundinamarca.
113. Claudia. Member of Veeduria. July 24, 2016. Mesitas del Colegio, El Colegio, Cundinamarca.
114. Jorge A. Member of Veeduria. July 24, 2016. Mesitas del Colegio, El Colegio, Cundinamarca.
115. Jorge B. Member of Veeduria. July 24, 2016. Mesitas del Colegio, El Colegio, Cundinamarca.
116. Jose. Member of Veeduria. July 24, 2016. Mesitas del Colegio, El Colegio, Cundinamarca.
117. Jairo. Member of Veeduria. July 24, 2016. Mesitas del Colegio, El Colegio, Cundinamarca.
118. Flor. Member of Veeduria. July 24, 2016. Mesitas del Colegio, El Colegio, Cundinamarca.
119. Sanchez, Arturo. Co-founder of Corporación Madre Tierra, July 25, 2016. Bogotá.
120. Vargas, Maria Victoria. City Council member, Liberal Party, July 26, 2016. Bogotá.
121. Assistant to City Council member, Liberal Party, July 26, 2016. Bogotá.
122. Sanz, Monica. President of INPRESEC, July 25, 2016. Bogotá.
123. Muhamed, Susana. Former Secretaria del Medio Ambiente, Gustavo Petro Administration, Bogotá July 26, 2016. Bogotá.
124. Engineer. Empresa de Acueducto, Alcantarillado y Aseo de Bogotá, E.S.P. (EAAB), July 27, 2016. Bogotá.
125. Velilla Moreno, Marco Antonio. Head magistrate, Consejo del Estado, July 28, 2016. Bogotá.
126. Castillo, Jorge. Procuraduría General de La Nación, July 29, 2016. Bogotá.
127. Moreno, Juan Andres. Member of Cantoalagua, July 29, 2016. Bogotá.
128. Buiprago, Hector. Co-founder of Cantoalagua, July 29, 2016. Bogotá.
129. Lopez, Sofia. Member of Recuperación Quebrada de Delicias, July 31, 2016. Bogotá.
130. Sguerra, Sandra. Employee, Secretaria Distrital del Ambiente, Dirección Jurídica, Ciudad de Bogotá July 31, 2016. Bogotá.
131. Pablo. Member of Recuperación Quebrada de Delicias, July 31, 2016. Bogotá.
132. Danilo. Member of Recuperación Quebrada de Delicias, July 31, 2016. Bogotá.
133. Bravo, Diego. Former director of Corporación Autónoma Regional de Cundinamarca, August 1, 2016. Bogotá.
134. O'Campo, Walter. Asociación de Empresarios de Sibaté, Soacha, y el Sur de Bogota (Asomuña), August 1, 2016. Bogotá.
135. Franco, Nestor. Director of Corporación Autónoma Regional (CAR) de Cundinamarca, August 1, 2016. Bogotá.
136. Luque, Marta. Division head at Contraloría General de la República August 2, 2016. Bogotá.
137. Acosta, Anibal. Division head at Corporación Autónoma Regional (CAR) de Cundinamarca, August 2, 2016. Bogotá.

138. Galindo, Medardo. Member of Fundación Humedal de la Conejera, August 2, 2016. Bogotá.
139. Torres, Alejandro. Environmental activist, August 2, 2016. Bogotá.
140. Galindo, German. Founding member of Fundación Humedal de la Conejera, August 3, 2016. Bogotá.
141. Former employee. Corporación Autónoma Regional de Cundinamarca, August 3, 2016. Bogotá.
142. Morales, Aydee. August 3, 2016. Phone.
143. Silva, Tatiana. Member of SIE Corporacón, August 3, 2016. Bogotá.
144. Fernandez, Jose Luis. Director, Dirección de Agropecuario y Sustentabilidad, Villapinzon, August 4, 2016. Villapinzón, Cundinamarca.
145. Gonzalez, Vidal. Guide, Dirección de Agropecuario y Sostenibilidad, Villapinzon August 4, 2016. Villapinzón, Cundinamarca.
146. Tannery owner A. August 4, 2016. Villapinzón, Cundinamarca.
147. Tannery owner B. August 4, 2016. Villapinzón, Cundinamarca.
148. Melo Garnica, Gildardo. Mayor of Villapinzón, August 4, 2016. Villapinzón, Cundinamarca. Phone.
149. Employee. Corporación Autónoma Regional de Cundinamarca, August 5, 2016. Bogotá.
150. Resident. August 5, 2016. La Moscera, Bogotá.
151. Tannery owner C. August 5, 2016. Bogotá.
152. Villamizar. Nelly. Magistrate, Tribunal Administrativo de Cundinamarca, August 5, 2016. Bogotá.
153. Mining company manager. August 8, 2016. Bogotá.
154. Employee. Corporación Autónoma Regional (CAR) de Cundinamarca, August 9, 2016. Phone.

Peru

155. Vasquez Vega, Jose Luis. Researcher at Ministerio del Medio Ambiente (MINAM). April 20, 2017. Phone.
156. Division head. OEFA, April 27, 2017. Lima.
157. Coral, Milagro. Employee at Ministerio del Medio Ambiente (MINAM). April 28, 2017. Lima.
158. Vasquez Vega, Jose Luis. Researcher at Ministerio del Medio Ambiente (MINAM). April 28, 2017. Lima.
159. Castro Vega, Juan Carlos. Subdirector, Autoridad Nacional del Agua (ANA), April 28, 2017. Lima.
160. Employee. Autoridad Nacional del Agua (ANA), May 2, 2017. Lima.
161. Roncal, Fausto. Ministerio de Vivienda, Construcción, y Saneamiento, May 2, 2017. Lima.
162. Huamani Olivo, Giselle. Division head, Defensoria del Pueblo, May 3, 2017. Lima.
163. Alburqueque, Fabiola. Researcher at Defensoria del Pueblo, May 3, 2017. Lima.
164. Diaz, Alejandro. Researcher at Defensoria del Pueblo, May 3, 2017. Lima.
165. Prieto, Jorge. Division head, Ministerio de Salud (DIGESA), May 3, 2017. Lima.
166. Rojas, Jaime. Division head, Ministerio de Salud (DIGESA), May 3, 2017. Lima.
167. Attorney. Ministerio del Medio Ambiente (MINAM), May 3, 2017. Lima.
168. Mora, Carol. Researcher at Sociedad Peruana de Derecho Ambiental (SPDA), May 4, 2017. Lima.

169. Sanchez Guerra, Mariella. Director at AquaFondo (Inversion en Agua para Lima), May 4, 2017. Lima.
170. Garcia, Francisco. Director at Organización de Evaluación y Fiscalizacíon Ambiental (OEFA), May 4, 2017. Lima.
171. Employee A. Organización de Evaluación y Fiscalizacíon Ambiental (OEFA), May 4, 2017. Lima.
172. Employee B. Organización de Evaluación y Fiscalizacíon Ambiental (OEFA), May 4, 2017. Lima.
173. Nunez, Hernan. City Council, Fuerza Social, May 4, 2017. Lima.
174. Guevara, Fanel. Consultant, May 5, 2017. Lima.
175. Vasquez Osorio, Miriam. Servicio de Agua Potalbe y Saneamiento (SEDAPAL). May 5, 2017. Lima.
176. Calle, Isabel. Division head, Sociedad Peruana de Derecho Ambiental (SPDA), May 5, 2017. Lima.
177. Guevara, Fanel. Consultant, May 11, 2017. Phone.

Index

For the benefit of digital users, indexed terms that span two pages (e.g., 52–53) may, on occasion, appear on only one of those pages.

Tables and figures are indicated by *t* and *f* following the page number

acción de tutela (to protect fundamental rights), in Colombia, 115–16, 130, 153
acciones populares (individual or group lawsuits), in Colombia, 115–16, 116n.7, 130–31, 131nn.33–34, 153
ACDH (Citizen Association for Human Rights, Asociacíon Ciudadana por los Derechos Humanos), 24, 87–88, 92*t*, 98, 99
ACIJ (Civil Association for Equality and Justice, Asociación Civil por la Igualdad y la Justicia), Argentina, 91–97, 92*t*, 95n.38
activist public officials
  Bogotá River, 24–25, 130–31, 132–33, 154, 155
  as bridges, 17, 27*t*
  Matanza Riachuelo River, 89–91
  Rímac River and, 175
ACUMAR (Matanza Riachuelo River Basin Authority, Autoridad de la Cuenca Matanza Riachuelo), 97, 99–100, 101–5, 101n.61, 103n.68, 103n.70, 106–7, 107n.89, 146
Administrative Court, Colombia. *See* Council of State (Consejo del Estado)
agricultural areas, 28–29, 54–55, 56–57, 179
Aguas Argentina (private water utility), 80n.12
air pollution or toxins, 1, 4–5, 37–38
Alfonsín, Raúl, 73n.4
Alsogaray, María Julia, 47–50, 72
amicus curiae (friend of the court), 86–87, 109–10
amparos (writs of protection for individual rights)
  in Argentina, 72–73, 109–10
  in Peru, 175–76, 176n.36, 194–95
ANA (National Water Authority), Peru, 185, 189, 190–91
Argentina. *See also* Buenos Aires; Matanza Riachuelo River
  constitutional reforms, 72–73, 72n.3, 73n.4, 98
  Dirty War, 84–85, 85n.20
  economy of, 87
  environmental institutions' history, 71–74
  environmental laws in, 72–73
  expansive policy shift in, 23–24, 25, 32
  human rights groups or movements, 24, 70, 86, 87–88, 87n.25
  ISI (Import Substitution Industrialization) in, 46
  judicial institutions in, 23–24, 70, 71, 86–87, 90
  slow harms awareness in, 70
armed conflict. *See also* Dirty War, Argentina; military
  in Colombia, 55, 117, 126–27, 129, 129n.28
  grassroots mobilization and, 28–29
  guerrilla, human rights movements and, 6
  guerrilla, in Colombia, 24–25, 113, 114, 129n.27
  guerrilla, in Peru, 25–26, 170–71
  guerrilla, presidential partisanship and, 19
  human rights violations, Colombia, 126–27, 128, 129n.28
  human rights violations, Peru, 172n.29, 173, 173n.30
  paramilitary, in Colombia, 126–29, 127n.25, 129n.28
  paramilitary, in Peru, 170–71, 171n.27
  in Peru, 157, 158, 170–71, 171n.27, 193

248 INDEX

Asdoas House (Corporación Casa Asdoas), 119*t*, 123–24
ASURIO (User Association for Renewable Natural Resources and the Defense of the Bogotá River Basin, Asociación de Usuarios de los Recursos Naturales Renovables y Defensa Ambiental de la Cuenca del Río Bogotá), 134*t*, 136–37, 142n.59
authoritarianism
  in Argentina, 84–85, 85n.20, 85–86n.21
  in China, 208–10
  in Latin America, 206–7
  in Peru, 160, 171, 171n.28, 172, 178
  in post-Soviet countries, 32, 208–9
AYSA (public water utility), Argentina, 80n.12, 87, 90, 102

Barrios Altos massacre, Peru, 171
Belaúnde Terry, Fernando, 170n.26
biodiversity loss, 37, 52–53, 54–55
Boca Neighborhood Association (Asociación de Vecinos de la Boca), Argentina, 74–78, 76*t*, 79*f*, 89–90, 96, 98–99, 109, 204
bodily harms. *See also* temporal proximity to bodily harm
  concentrated, 35*t*, 36–37, 198
  dispersed, 35*t*, 36–38, 198
  geographical proximity to, 34, 35*t*, 36–37, 40–41, 68–69, 198
  gradual, 35*t*, 198
  imminent, 35*t*, 38–39, 198
  incremental, 35–36
  spectrum of, 34–35
Bogotá (city). *See also* Bogotá River; Colombia
  Bogotá River development by, 51–52
  characteristics, 30–31, 67*t*
  city council, 58
  environmental NGOs, 114, 129, 133–36, 136n.45, 139–40, 145, 155
  Environmental Secretariat, 146n.70, 148n.76
  grassroots activism, 113–14, 117–25, 119*t*
  industrial growth in, 53–55
  mayors, 152–53, 193–94
  migration to, 55

slow-harms remediation in, 5–6, 20–21, 22, 22*t*, 24–25, 145–46
toxins polluting, 2, 56, 67*t*
wastewater management, 52, 53n.28, 56, 58, 102, 102n.65, 102–3n.67, 147, 148, 154–55
weak human rights organizations in, 6
wetlands, 121–22, 122*f*, 142n.60
Bogotá River. *See also* Bogotá (city); Colombia
  alternative policy reform explanations for, 150–54
  bonding mobilization for, 119*t*, 124–25
  bridging mobilization for, 125–26, 133, 134*t*, 154
  characteristics, 51–52, 66, 67*t*
  citizen oversight, 143–44, 146–47
  death of, 52, 53n.28
  financial investments, 22, 22*t*, 147
  flood origin myth, 53n.27
  grassroots activism, 113–14, 119*t*, 124–25
  informal settlements on, 90–91, 108–9
  litigation, 130–32, 131nn.33–34
  map, 118*f*
  media on, 56–57, 58, 149, 154
  mining, 54–55, 56, 67*t*, 148, 201
  NGOs and, 24–25, 129, 133–39, 134*t*, 145–46
  photographs, 54*f*–56*f*, 122*f*, 137*f*
  pollution of, 52–53, 53n.28, 56–57, 57n.31, 67*t*
  slow harms on, 51–58, 200
  state-level bridges and, 130–33
Bogotá Wetlands Network (Red de Humedales de la Sabana de Bogotá), 134*t*, 138–39, 151–52
Bolívar, Simon, 115n.4
bonding mobilization. *See also* grassroots activism or organizations
  Bogotá River and, 24–25, 117–25
  in case study cities, 25–26, 27*t*, 193, 199
  definition, 13–15
  as grassroots pressure about perceived harms, 74
  Matanza Riachuelo River and, 23–24, 70, 71, 74–84
  Rímac River and, 26, 163–69, 192, 197
bonds. *See* bonding mobilization; grassroots activism or organizations

INDEX   249

bridges. *See* bridging mobilization or activism; enabling conditions
bridging mobilization or activism. *See also* activist public officials
  actors, 16–17, 18n.13
  Bogotá River and, within state institutions, 130–33, 156
  Bogotá River and, NGOs, 133–40, 134*t*
  Bogotá River monitoring capacity, 140–45
  in case study cities, 23*t*, 27*t*, 199
  definition, 15
  enabling conditions for, 17–18
  human rights strength and messaging and, 18, 112
  Matanza Riachuelo River and, within state institutions, 89–91
  Matanza Riachuelo River and, NGOs, 24, 91–98, 92*t*
  Matanza Riachuelo River monitoring capacity, 98–100
  policy shifts and, 6, 13
  Rímac River and, within state institutions, 178–80
  Rímac River and, NGOs, 26, 180–83
Brite, Maria Carmen, 89–90
brown bodies or communities, 9–10, 36–37, 69. *See also* indigenous communities; marginalized communities
Buenos Aires. *See also* Argentina; Matanza Riachuelo River
  characteristics, 30–31, 67*t*
  grassroots activism, 7–10, 76*t*
  human rights organizations, 92*t*
  industrial growth in, 46
  Matanza Riachuelo River development by, 42–43
  migration to, 44–46, 108–9
  Plata River, 42–43
  Public Defender's Office, 89–91, 96–97, 96n.42, 106, 205–6
  slow-harms remediation in, 5–6, 20–21, 22, 22*t*, 101–2, 104
  toxins polluting, 46, 67*t*
  wastewater lagoons in, 3*f*
  wastewater management, 1, 79–80, 80*f*, 102

Cantoalagua (A Song for Water), Colombia, 134*t*, 137*f*, 137, 139n.51
CARs (Autonomous Regional Corporations, Corporaciónes Autonomas,
  Corporación Autonoma de Cundinamarca), Colombia, 56–57, 58, 115, 116–17, 137, 146, 147–48, 147n.73, 148n.76, 149–50
case study cities. *See also* Bogotá; Buenos Aires; Lima
  most similar comparative method of, 30
  similar characteristics of, 30–31
  slow harms in, 13, 32
  strength of bridges in, 23*t*
  variation in independent variables for, 27*t*
Castañeda Lossio, Luis, 167n.19
Center for Legal and Social Studies (CELS), Argentina, 85, 86–88, 89–90, 91–97, 92*t*, 95n.38, 98, 99
Cerro de Pasco, Peru, 66
chemicals, pollution and, 41–42, 53–54
China, 17, 32, 37–38, 40, 208–9, 210
Chinese Communist Party (CCP), 208–9, 210
cities. *See also* peri-urban fringe; urban renewal; urbanization
  as concentrated spatial forms, 203–4, 203–4n.3
  disruption and bridging in, 32, 202–6
  environmental injustice, 9–10
  environmental mobilization, 28–29, 194–95
  pollution and, 5, 42
  as relational incubators, 203
citizen action. *See* bonding mobilization; bridging mobilization; grassroots activism or organizations; human rights groups or movements
Citizen's Power (Poder Ciudadano), Argentina, 86–87, 89–90, 92*t*, 94–95, 96, 98n.52
City Foundation (Fundación Ciudad), Argentina, 89–90, 91–98, 92*t*, 98n.52
civil society. *See also* bonding mobilization; bridging mobilization or activism; grassroots activism or organizations; human rights groups or movements; nongovernmental organizations
  China's environmental policymaking and, 209
  environmental policymaking and, 207–8
  Global South regulatory regimes and, 211
  impacted by Argentine Dirty War, 84–85
  impacted by Colombian armed conflict, 129

civil society (*cont.*)
  impacted by Peruvian armed conflict, 174
  shut out of Bogotá River
    governance, 153–54
  shut out of Rímac River
    governance, 190–91
class
  bodily harm and, 37–38, 39–40
  Bogotá River and, 121, 151–52
  and cities, 9
  and environmental mobilization, 12, 28, 37–38
  Matanza Riachuelo River and, 42–43, 46–47, 81–83, 108
  Rímac River and, 166–69
climate change, 27–28, 150–51, 160, 168–69, 195–96
collaborative oversight arenas, 99. *See also* judicial advisory committee
collective construction, risk as, 11–12
collective issue identification, 13–14
Colombia. *See also* Bogotá River; Bogotá (city)
  armed conflict in, 55, 117, 126–27, 129, 129n.28
  constitutional reforms, 115–16, 116n.6, 130, 131n.32, 131n.33, 195
  environmental laws in, 115n.4
  Foreign Direct Investment in mineral extractives of, 129
  human rights groups in, 24–25, 114, 126–29, 129n.28, 139–40
  ISI (Import Substitution Industrialization) in, 53–54
  judicial institutions in, 114, 130–32, 131n.33, 153
  mining in, 54–55, 56, 67t, 129, 148
  stagnated policy shifts in, 32, 114, 145–50
common pool
  resources, 21–22, 198–99
Communist Party
  Argentina, 85n.20
  Colombia, 127–28
  Peru, 170–71
Comptroller's Office
  Argentina, 17
  bridging and, 205–6
  Colombia, 58, 130, 132–33, 132n.39, 136n.43, 143, 147n.73, 200
  Peru, 180n.52

Conejera Wetlands Foundation (Fundación Humedal de la Conejera), Colombia, 119t, 121–22, 122f, 124, 136, 138–39, 140–41, 142n.59, 142n.60, 153, 205
constitutions
  Argentina, 72–73, 72n.3, 73n.4, 98
  Colombia, 115–16, 116n.6, 130, 131n.32, 131n.33, 195
  Peru, 160, 175–76, 175n.35, 176n.36
consultancy projects, Peru, 180n.53, 181–82, 184
consultas previas (prior consultations), 115–16, 174, 176, 183
Coordinadora Nacional de Derechos Humanos (National Human Rights Coordinator), Peru, 171, 172, 174, 187, 196–97
co-production, definition, 18n.13
Córdova, Eduarda, 157
Council of State (Administrative High Court of Colombia, or Consejo del Estado), 131–32, 131n.33, 142n.60, 153–54
Cundinamarca Administrative Court, Colombia, 130–31. *See also* Villamizar, Nelly
Cundinamarca Secretariat of the Environment, Colombia, 146n.70

Day of Remembrance for Truth and Justice, Argentina, 86
democratic institutions. *See also* constitutions; judges or judiciary; legal institutions
  and environmentalism, 206–7, 210–12
  right to dissent, 201–2, 206–10
DIGESA (General Directorate for Environmental Health), Peru, 159, 185, 190
Dirty War, Argentina, 84–85, 85n.20
disappeared, 85n.20, 171, 171n.27
dissent, right to, 32, 201–2
drinking water
  Bogotá River and, 52–53
  Latin American rivers and, 42
  for Lima-Callao Metropolitan region, 59, 63, 157–58, 179, 184–85, 195–96
  Matanza Riachuelo River and, 34
  river pollution and, 33–34
Duque, Iván, 128–29

EAAB (Empresa de Acueducto y Alcantarillado de Bogotá), 53–54, 58, 121–22, 147, 148n.76
earthquakes, 59–60
Ecobus (education hub), Bogotá, 121–22, 203
Ecological Civilization, China's, 209
economic crises, 9, 27–28, 87
Ecuador, 36–37, 40
enabling conditions
  in Argentina, 27t, 84–88
  causes vs., 20n.14
  class and, 28
  in Colombia, 27t, 126–29
  human rights movements and, 18, 20
  in Peru, 27t, 158, 170–75, 192, 196
  political opportunities and, 18n.13
  presidential partisanship and, 19–20
  scope of, 17–18
Environment and Natural Resources Foundation. *See* FARN
environmental conservation
  in Argentina, 71
  in Colombia, 24–25, 133, 139, 200
  in Peru, 180–81, 181nn.54–55
environmental degradation, harms, hazards, or disasters. *See also* rapid harms; slow harms
  and citizen-led regulation of, 7, 17n.11, 201–2, 208, 210–12
  economic disparities and, 9–10
  as global phenomenon, 8, 198
  and global public health, 4–5, 41–42
  and impediments to citizen action, 34–40
  racial disparities and, 9–10
  typology of environmental harms, 35t
environmental justice. *See also* environmental rights protections
  in Argentina, 95–96
  claims, 18, 205–6
  in Colombia, 152–53
  environmental racism and, 9–10, 10n.5
  framing and, 18, 95–96, 152–53
  grassroots pressure and, 15, 207
  human rights and, 6–7, 18
  indigenous groups and, 9–10
  in Peru, 177–78, 183
environmental laws. *See* laws, environmental
environmental policy. *See also* policy change
  Argentina, 71–74
  China and post-Soviet countries, 32

Colombia, 115–17
Peru, 159–63
Russia, 208, 210
environmental rights protections. *See also* laws, environmental
  in Argentina, 72–73, 72n.3, 90, 95–96
  in Colombia, 113, 115–17, 152
  in Peru, 161, 162–63, 176
environmentalism of the poor, 28–29, 36–37, 39–40
ethnic disparities, 9, 10
ethnic ties, 14
expansive policy shift, 22, 23–24, 23t, 25, 32. *See also* Matanza Riachuelo River
expertise, 16–17, 91–97, 99–100, 110
export-oriented development, 24–26, 27t, 60, 114
external shocks, 27–28
extractives industry. *See also* export-oriented development; mining
  Argentina, 84–85
  Colombia, 129
  foreign, conservative presidential administrations and, 158
  Peru, 25–26, 158, 161, 173–74, 196, 201
  rural opposition to, 202

factories, 11, 40, 166–67. *See also* industrial parks or pollutants; industrialization
FARN (Environment and Natural Resources Foundation, Fundación Ambiente y Recursos Naturales), Argentina, 81–83, 86–87, 89–90, 91–99, 92t, 95n.38, 96n.42
faster-moving harms, 68–69, 157–58, 179–80. *See also* rapid harms
Fernández, Alberto, 88
floods or flooding. *See also* informal housing settlements
  as alternative explanation, 107–10, 150–54, 192–95
  Argentina, 44–46, 79–80, 107–8
  coastal, 37–38
  Colombia, 53n.27, 123–24, 150–51
  informal housing settlements and, 46–47, 69, 79–80
  Peru, 166, 168–69, 186, 192–93
  social mobilization and, 151
  of South American rivers, 27–28
  wastewater contamination and, 42
  water utility privatizing and, 80n.12

foundations, 16–17, 23–24. *See also* nongovernmental organizations
framing, 18, 27*t*, 94–96, 96n.42, 128
frentes or *Frentes de Defensa*, Peru, 162
Fucha River (Bogotá River tributary), 55
Fujimori, Alberto, 160, 171, 171n.28, 172, 178
Fujimorismo (Peruvian political movement), 172–73
Fundación Metropolitana. *See* Metropolitan Foundation

garbage. *See* waste, solid
García, Alan, 160–61, 170–71, 172–73
Garré, Nilda, 86
geographical proximity to bodily harms, 34, 35*t*, 36–37, 40–41, 68–69, 198
González Catán, La Matanza, Argentina, 1, 2*f*, 81, 82*f*, 109, 204
Gorbachev, Mikhail, 208
government officials or agencies
 in Argentina, 70, 89–91, 104–5
 in Colombia, 58, 140, 145–46, 149–50
 in Global South, 211
 in Peru, 158, 162–63, 167, 169–70, 184, 189, 190–91
 policy paralysis and, 69
 Rímac River and, 65–66, 186, 195–96
grassroots activism or organizations. *See also* bonding mobilization
 Argentina, 23–24, 70–71, 74, 111–12
 bonding mobilization and, 15, 119*t*, 124
 class and, 28
 Colombia, 25, 113, 117, 123, 124–25, 151–52
 environmental governance and, 7, 32, 161–62, 210–11
 interviews with, 31–32
 legal institutions and, 194–95
 Peru, 157–58, 183–84, 190–92
 slow harms policy shifts and, 13, 155
 slow-harms pollution policy and, 6
 South America, 27–28
Green Living Foundation (Fundación al Verde Vivo), Colombia, 134*t*, 136, 137, 140–41
Greenpeace Argentina, 90n.31, 91–94, 92*t*, 95n.38, 96–97, 97n.46, 98, 99
grievance articulation, 13–14
guerrillas. *See* armed conflict
Guzmán, Abimael, 170–71

hazardous environments, 11, 12, 14n.9. *See also* pollution
health impacts. *See also* illnesses, identified
 Bogotá River, 56–57
 contaminated water and, 69
 government interventions, 105
 Matanza Riachuelo River, 50, 52n.25
 Rímac River, 63, 163, 185
 unmanaged wastewater and, 41–42
heavy metals
 in Bogotá River, 56, 67*t*
 and illness, 79–80
 from industry, 46
 in Matanza Riachuelo River, 67*t*
 from mines, 65–66
 in Rímac River, 65, 67*t*, 197
housing. *See* informal housing settlements
Humala, Ollanta, 173, 173n.30, 176, 186–87
human rights. *See also* human rights groups or movements
 and environmentalism, 1, 6, 19
 and framing, 18, 94–95, 96n.41
human rights groups or movements. *See also* nongovernmental organizations
 Argentina, 24, 70, 86, 87–88, 87n.25
 Argentina's Dirty War and, 84–85, 85n.20, 85–86n.21
 bridging activism by, 6, 199–200
 Colombia, 24–25, 114, 126–29, 129n.28, 139–40
 enabling conditions and, 18
 environmental claims making and, 18, 112
 left-of-center presidential administrations and, 19, 24, 88, 112
 Peru, 25–26, 158, 170–75, 192, 200–1
 strength of bridging mobilization and, 23
hydroelectric power and hydrodams, 17, 38–39, 63. *See also* Muña Dam, Bogotá River Basin

illnesses, identified
 Bogotá River, 2–4, 56–57, 67*t*, 121
 documenting, 74
 informal housing settlement residents and, 46–47
 Matanza Riachuelo River, 1, 67*t*, 81
 Rímac River, 65–66, 67*t*
 World Health Organization on, 41–42
immigrants. *See* migrants
incinerators, objections to siting of, 38–39

indigenous communities. *See also* brown bodies or communities; marginalized communities
   in Colombia, 52–53, 115–16, 116n.5, 123, 124n.21
   environmental inequities for, 10n.5
   internal migration patterns and, 9–10
   in Peru, 166, 167–68, 170, 172, 172n.29, 188
industrial parks or pollutants. *See also specific industries*
   Matanza Riachuelo and, 46, 46n.9, 102–4, 103n.68, 103n.70
   pollution and, 10n.5, 33, 69
industrialization
   Bogotá River, 53–54, 60–61, 67*t*
   Matanza Riachuelo River, 48*f*, 60–61, 67*t*
   in peri-urban fringe, 8–9
   pollution from, 8, 42, 69
   Rímac River, 60–61, 63–64, 67*t*
informal housing settlements. *See also* floods or flooding; MIRR; urban settlements; urbanization; Villa Inflamable, Avellaneda, Buenos Aires
   on Bogotá River, 90–91, 108–9
   excluded from participation, 105–6
   flooding in, 79–80, 80n.12
   health risks in, 52n.25
   on Matanza Riachuelo River, 3*f*, 44–47, 47n.12, 47*f*
   natural disasters and, 192–93
   photograph, 3*f*
   political movements and, 60
   pollution and, 42
   relocation, 90–91, 94, 105, 149–50, 163, 167–68, 167n.19, 168*f*, 186, 197
   on Rímac River, 166–68
   in urbanized Latin American, 39–40
INPRESEC, Colombia, 134*t*, 136–37, 140–41
Inter-American Development Bank (IDB), 47–50, 72–73
InterBasin Space RRR (Espacio Intercuenca RRR), Argentina, 76*t*, 78, 203
Internally Displaced People, 55, 166
invisible harms, 5, 83–84, 198
ISI (Import Substitution Industrialization)
   in Argentina, 46
   in Colombia, 53–54
   in Peru, 60–61

Japanese Development Agency (JICA), 50
journalists/reporters, 31–32, 78, 104–5, 206, 206n.6
judges or judiciary. *See also* legal institutions
   in Argentina, 70, 71, 86–87
   bridging role of, 17, 200
   in Colombia, 114, 130
   in Peru, 25–26, 158, 200–1
   pollution-remediation policymaking by, 29, 207
judicial advisory committee
   Bogotá River and, 139–42, 141n.56, 142nn.58–59, 143n.62, 145–46, 147n.73, 148, 149–50, 154
   Matanza Riachuelo River and, 96n.42, 99, 104–5, 106–7, 111–12, 141–42

Kirchner, Cristina, 87, 88
Kirchner, Néstor, 86–87, 86n.23, 88, 88n.27
Kuczynski, Pedro Pablo, 190
Kyoto Protocol on Climate Change, Conference of the Parties of, 73

Laguna de Rocha, Argentina, 81–83, 203, 204
landslides. *See also* waste, solid
   Peru, 66
   Rímac River, 163, 166, 168–69, 169*f*
Latin America. *See also* Argentina; Colombia; Peru
   and environmental problems, 8
   and environmental racism, 9–10, 10n.5
   and migration, 9
   and urban rivers, 69
   and urbanization, 7–8
laws, environmental
   role of, 29
   in Argentina, General Environmental Law (2002), 72–73
   in Colombia, Law 23, National Code for Renewable Natural Resources and Environmental Protection (1974), 115n.4
   in Peru, Code for Environment and Natural Resources, 159
   in Peru, Law 30230 (*paquetazo ambiental*), 176, 186–88, 189–90, 194
lead poisoning, 46–47, 66, 67*t*, 79–80
legal institutions. *See also* judges or judiciary
   in Argentina, 23–24, 90
   in China, 209–10

legal institutions (*cont.*)
  citizen advocacy and mobilization
    and, 195
  in Colombia, 130–32, 131n.33, 153
  in Peru, 157–58, 175–78, 194
Lima. *See also* MIRR; Peru; Rímac River
  basic services in, 61–62
  characteristics, 30–31, 59f, 61f, 65n.45, 67t
  drinking water, 63, 157–58, 184–85, 195–96
  environmental concerns, 197, 197n.96
  export-oriented oligarchs and, 60
  grassroots activism, 163–69
  human rights organizations in, 6, 171
  industrial growth in, 60–61, 63–64
  international NGOs and, 181n.56
  migration to, 60
  Rímac development by, 65n.45
  slow-harms remediation in, 20–21, 22, 22t, 23–24, 25–26
  toxins polluting, 65, 67t
local governments, Peru, 161–62, 167–68, 167n.19, 168f
Lomas de Zamora, Argentina, 79–80, 81–83, 107–8, 109
Lorenzetti, Ricardo, 109–10
low-income communities. *See also* class; informal housing settlements
  in Argentina, 44–46, 50, 52n.25, 74, 108
  in Colombia, 56–57, 121, 123–24
  environmentalism of, grassroots activism and, 28–29
  in Peru, 158–59, 192–93
  on riverine land, 56–57, 69, 79–80, 149–50, 166, 195–96
  slow targeted harms in Latin America and, 39–40
  social organizing around slow harms and, 108–9
  U.S., concentrated bodily harms and, 36–37

Macri, Mauricio, 102–3n.67
Las Madres de la Plaza de Mayo (Mothers of the Plaza de Mayo), Argentina, 85, 85–86n.21, 87–88
Mao Zedong, 170–71, 170n.25
marches, 38–39, 71, 79n.11, 81, 207. *See also* protests
marginalized communities, 9–10, 10n.5, 39–40. *See also* indigenous communities; low-income communities

Matanza Riachuelo River. *See also* ACUMAR; Buenos Aires; *Mendoza* case, Argentina
  alternative policy reform explanations for, 107–10
  bonding mobilization for, 23–24, 70, 71, 74–84
  bridging mobilization for, 91–98
  characteristics, 66, 67t
  citizen oversight, 76t, 83–84, 98–100
  death of, 50–52
  financial investments, 22, 22t, 47–50, 72–73, 91–94, 95n.38, 100–1, 102
  government officials' promises on, 46–50, 49f, 51f
  grassroots activism and, 76t, 78, 83–84, 111–12
  informal settlements on, 3f, 43–47, 47n.12, 50, 52n.25, 79–80, 81–83, 104, 105–6, 108–9, 193
  institutional innovation for, 101–2
  litigation and, 70, 90, 90n.33, 97, 97n.47
  map, 75f
  media on, 43–44, 49f, 50, 51f, 53f, 70, 71, 81
  NGOs and, 23–24, 70, 91–96, 92t, 95n.38, 96n.42, 104–5
  photographs, 44f–53f
  policy shifts and, 23–24, 100–7
  pollution of, 1, 3f, 47–52, 47f, 51f, 67t
  regulatory capacity improvements, 98–100, 102–4, 110
  slow harms on, 42–50
  state-level bridges and, 89–91
material resources
  Argentina, 91–94
  bridging role, 6, 16–17, 26, 199
  Colombia, 114, 133–36
  local mobilization leaders and, 14
  Peru, 180–83, 196
mayors
  in Colombia, 144–45, 146, 148–49, 152, 193–94
  in Peru, 178–79
media. *See also* journalists/reporters
  on Bogotá River pollution, 56–57, 58, 149, 154
  as bridges, 12, 15
  on environmental degradation and policymaking, 161, 208

on Matanza Riachuelo pollution, 43–44,
    49f, 50, 51f, 53f, 70, 71, 81, 95–96
  for precipitating events, 27–28
  on Rimac River pollution, 197
  on urban presence, 206
Mendoza, Beatriz, 70, 90, 111
Mendoza case, Argentina (2008)
  advocacy network and, 111–12
  basis for, 90n.33
  Cuerpo Colegiado (judicial advisory
    committee), 96n.42, 99, 104–5, 106–7,
    111–12, 141–42
  federal judges overseeing, 97n.47
  Matanza Riachuelo remediation
    and, 70, 90
  monitoring capacity after, 98–100, 110
  online accountability platform
    and, 97
  visibility of issues and, 111
Menem, Carlos, 71–72, 73, 73n.4, 86–87
Metropolitan Foundation (Fundación
  Metropolitana), Argentina, 90n.31, 91–
  94, 92t, 96–97, 98n.52
migrants
  to Bogotá, 55
  to Buenos Aires, 42–43, 44–46, 108–9
  in the Global South, 8, 9
  with indigenous backgrounds, 9–10
  to Lima, 60
  rural-to-urban, 9, 55, 60, 69, 158–59
military. *See also* armed conflict
  Argentina, 27t, 71–72, 85n.20, 86
  Colombia, 27t, 114, 128
  human rights movements and, 6, 18
  paramilitary, in Colombia, 126–29,
    127n.25, 129n.28
  paramilitary, in Peru, 170–71, 171n.27
  Peru, 19, 27t, 60–61, 158, 170, 173,
    173n.30, 173n.31, 196–97
MINAM (Environmental Ministry), Peru,
  160–61, 175–78, 182, 185, 190, 195–96
mining. *See also* extractives industry
  Bogotá River and, 54–55, 56, 67t, 148
  in Colombia, 129
  contaminated water and, 69
  Matanza Riachuelo River and, 67t
  objections to siting of, 38–39
  in Peru, 24, 26, 63, 66n.48, 67t, 160, 161–
    62, 163, 169–70, 179–80, 183, 184–85,
    187, 196

Rímac River and, 63–66, 66n.48, 67t,
  157, 163
San Mateo, Peru, 163–65, 165f, 183–84
as slow targeted harm, 39–40
Ministry of Mines and Energy,
  Colombia, 148
Ministry of the Environment
  Argentina, 71–72
  Colombia, 116
  Peru, 159
MIRR (La Margen Izquierda, Rímac
  River settlement), 166–68,
  167n.19, 168f
monitoring capacity. *See* regulatory
  monitoring capacity
Mother Earth Corporation
  (Corporación Madre Tierra),
  Colombia, 134t, 136, 138f, 140–41
Moya Ángel, Gustavo, 131n.34
mudslides, 192–93. *See also* floods or
  flooding; landslides
multinational firms, 19, 24–25. *See also*
  extractives industry
Muña Dam, Bogotá River Basin, 2–4, 4f, 57,
  130–31, 131n.32, 148, 154, 204–5

National Code for Renewable Natural
  Resources and Environmental
  Protection (1974), Colombia,
  115, 115n.4
National Commission on the Disappearance
  of Persons (CONADEP), Argentina,
  85, 86n.22
National Environmental Law (Ley
  General del Ambiente 25675),
  Argentina, 91n.35
National Environmental Licensing
  Authority, Colombia, 116
National Environmental Secretariat,
  Argentina, 71–72
National Environmental System,
  Colombia, 116
National Forest Reserve, Colombia, 115n.4
National Liberation Army, Colombia,
  129n.27
National Office of Evaluation of Natural
  Resources (ONERN), Peru, 159
National Public Defender's Office
  (Defensoría General de la Nación),
  Argentina, 90–91, 106

natural disasters, 168–69, 186, 192–93. *See also* floods or flooding; landslides; mudslides
Neighbors Autonomously Organized against the CEAMSE in González Catán (Vecinos Autoconvocados contra la CEAMSE de González Catán), Argentina, 76*t*, 81, 82*f*, 90, 204
Neighbors in Defense of Santa Catalina (Vecinos en Defensa de Santa Catalina), Argentina, 76*t*, 81–83, 203
NIMBY (Not in my backyard) movements, 38–39, 74, 84, 147, 199–200
nongovernmental organizations (NGOs). *See also* human rights groups or movements
  Argentina, 73, 91–98, 96n.42
  Bogotá River and, 24–25, 129, 133, 134*t*, 145–46
  as bridges, 16, 27*t*, 199–200, 204–5
  China, 209
  Colombia, 114, 124–25, 127–28, 133–40, 136n.45, 155
  Global South, 37
  human rights movements and, 18
  Matanza Riachuelo and, 23–24, 70, 92*t*, 104–5
  Mendoza ruling and, 98–100, 99n.54, 110, 111–12
  Peru, 25–26, 172–73, 174, 180–83, 181n.56, 196–97, 200
  Rímac River and, 157–58, 195–96
  Russia, 208
non-point-source pollution, 20–21. *See also* pollution

OEFA (Agency for Environmental Assessment and Enforcement), Peru, 161, 176, 185, 186–90
oil drilling, 129. *See also* extractives industry
Ombudsman's Office (Defensor del Pueblo de la Nación), Argentina
  bridging role, 17, 23–24, 89–90, 96–98, 199–200
  environmental litigation and, 97, 106, 205–6
  Mendoza ruling and, 99, 99n.54, 110
  no elected Ombudsman since 2009 for, 99–100, 100n.58, 106n.87

Ombudsman's Office (Defensoría del Pueblo), Colombia, 116n.7, 137, 143n.62, 205–6
Ombudsman's Office (Defensoría del Pueblo), Peru, 25–26, 172, 174, 188, 190–91, 205–6
  no bridging within, 157–58, 178–80, 194–95, 196–97, 200–1
La Oroya, Peru, 66, 160–61

Paniagua, Valentín, 172
paramilitary
  armed conflict in Colombia and, 126–29, 127n.25, 129n.28
  armed conflict in Peru and, 170–71, 171n.27
participatory institutions. *See* judicial advisory committee; *veedurias*
peri-urban fringe, 8–9, 28–29. *See also* informal housing settlements
Permanent Assembly for Human Rights, Argentina, 85–86n.21
Perón, Juan, 71–72
Peru. *See also* Lima; Rímac River
  armed conflict in, 157, 158, 170–71, 171n.27, 193
  citizen participation kept at arm's length in, 190–92
  constitutional reforms, 160, 175–76, 175n.35, 176n.36
  environmental institutions' history, 159–63
  environmental laws in, 159, 176, 186–88, 189–90, 194
  environmental NGOs in, 180–81, 181nn.54–55
  Foreign Direct Investment in mineral extractives of, 173–74
  hostile enabling conditions in, 170–75
  human rights groups in, 25–26, 158, 170–75, 192, 200–1
  ISI (Import Substitution Industrialization) in, 60–61
  judicial institutions in, 25–26, 157–58, 175–78, 194, 200–1
  mining in, 24, 26, 63, 66n.48, 67*t*, 160, 161–62, 163, 169–70, 179–80, 183, 184–85, 187, 196

INDEX   257

natural resources and armed conflict in, 157
policy shift uninitiated in, 32
socioenvironmental conflicts, 162, 162n.7, 178–79
Peruvian Agency for International Cooperation (APCI), 180–81, 180n.53
Petro, Gustavo, 152–53, 193–94
petrochemical refineries, 1, 46, 50, 78, 79n.11, 89–90, 105
Plata River, Buenos Aires, 78
Platform for the Defense of the Upper Basin of the Rímac River (Plataforma por la Defensa y Promoción del Medio Ambiente en la Cuenca Alta del Río Rímac), 165, 183–84, 191–92
policy change (shifts)
    in Argentina, 22, 22t, 23–24, 27t, 70, 100–10
    citizen action against slow harms and, 5
    collective issue identification and, 13–14
    in Colombia, 22, 22t, 24–25, 27t, 32, 113–14, 145–54, 200
    definition, 21
    financial commitments and, 21
    in Global South, 158–59
    in Peru, 22, 22t, 25–26, 27t, 169–70, 184–86, 195
    regulatory monitoring capacity and, 21–22
    strength of bonds or bridges and, 2n.3, 23t
political parties
    in Argentina, 109
    bridging opportunities and, 17–18, 18n.13
    in Colombia, 152
    environmental harms activism and, 28
    in Global South, 7–8
    Latin American environmental concerns and, 193–94
    in Peru, 170–71, 170n.25, 180n.53, 193–94
political will
    in Argentina, 71–72, 102
    in Colombia, 117, 148
    in Peru, 186
    regulatory monitoring capacity and, 21–22, 58, 73

pollution, 4–5, 21. *See also* environmental degradation and harms, non-point-source pollution; wastewater
post-Soviet countries, 32, 207–8
potable water. *See* drinking water
presidential partisanship
    Argentina, 24, 70–71, 88, 112
    bridging mobilization strength and, 23
    Colombia, 24–25, 114, 128–29, 129n.27, 152, 200
    external resourced actors and, 26
    grassroots mobilization and, 28–29
    Peru, 25–26, 158, 170–75, 196, 200–1
    slow-harms bridging and, 19–20, 27t
private-sector interests. *See also* industrial parks or pollutants; mining
    in Argentina, 1, 46, 50, 78, 79n.11, 89–90, 105
    in Colombia, 147–48
    in Peru, 169–70, 189
    regulatory monitoring and, 21–22
Process of National Reorganization (Proceso), Argentina *See* Dirty War
process tracing, 31–32, 201–2
protests. *See also* marches
    in Argentina, 71, 78, 79–80, 80f, 81–83, 204
    in China, 40, 209
    in Colombia, 125f
    demonstrations/rallies, 38–39, 71, 78, 79–80, 166–67, 203–4n.3, 207
    in Peru, 166–67, 168f
    by urban activists, 203–4
PTAR Salitre, Bogotá, 126f, 147
public officials. *See* government officials or agencies
Public Prosecutor's Office
    Colombia, 140–41, 143n.62, 144–45, 147n.73, 205–6
    Peru, 25–26, 200–1, 205–6
Putin, Vladimir, 208

racial disparities or racism, 9–10, 18
Ramsar Convention on Wetlands, 121–22
rapid harms
    diluted, 35t, 37–38
    targeted, 35t, 38–39, 162, 179
Reconquista River, Argentina, 78
Red Muqui, Peru, 183–84, 191–92

regulation. *See also* regulatory monitoring capacity
  as citizen-led process, 7, 17n.11, 201–2, 208, 210–12
  definition, 21, 211
  Weberian bureaucracy, 7, 211
regulatory authorities. *See* government officials or agencies
regulatory monitoring capacity. *See also* environmental laws or regulations
  Argentina, 98–100, 102–3, 103n.68
  changes, as policy shift measure, 21–22
  civil collective action and, 211–12
  Colombia, 53–54, 113–14, 144–45, 147–49, 154–55
  compared, in case study cities, 22
  Peru, 169–70, 176, 188
relocations
  Argentina, 94, 105–6, 149–50, 167–68, 167n.19, 168*f*
  Colombia, 149–50
  Peru, 163, 186, 197
reporters/journalists, 31–32, 78, 104–5, 206, 206n.6
resignation, slow-moving harms and, 5, 40–41, 202
Riachuelo River. *See* Matanza Riachuelo River
Rímac River. *See also* Lima; Peru
  alternative policy reform explanations for, 195
  bonding mobilization for, 157–58, 163–69
  bridging mobilization for, 157–58, 169–70, 178–80
  characteristics, 59, 66, 67*t*, 158–59
  citizen oversight, 190–92
  drinking water from, 63, 157, 184–85, 195–96
  financial investments, 22, 22*t*, 185, 186, 186n.72
  government data on water quality of, 64, 66n.48
  grassroots activism and, 163–69
  informal settlements on, 166–68
  map, 164*f*
  media on, 161
  mining, 63–66, 66n.48, 67*t*, 157, 162, 163, 165
  natural disasters and, 166, 168–69, 169*f*, 186, 192–93
  NGOs and, 157–58, 180–84, 195–96
  photographs, 59*f*–62*f*, 165*f*, 169*f*
  policy shifts uninitiated, 25–26, 65, 158–59, 184–90, 186n.72
  pollution of, 60–66, 67*t*, 166–68, 166n.13
  resignation to contamination, 195–97
  slow harms on, 59–66, 200–1
  Vía Parque Rímac and, 193–94
Rio Conference (1992), on Environment and Development, 116n.5, 160, 207
risk perception, 11, 28. *See also* slow harms
river basin councils
  Bogotá River, 134*t*, 136–37, 142n.59
  Matanza Riachuelo River, 99–100, 101–2, 101n.61, 104–5, 146
  Rímac River, 190–92
rivers
  early Latin American development of, 42
  in Global South, 41
  multijurisdictional, 21–22, 29–30, 31, 47–50
  slow-harms accumulation and, 42
Rocha Collective (Colectivo Ecológica Unidos por la Laguna de Rocha), Argentina, 76*t*, 81–83, 83*f*, 203, 205
Rodrigo Franco Command, Peru, 170–71, 171n.27
RRR (InterBasin Space), Argentina, 76*t*, 78, 203
rural environmental degradation, 8, 202
Russia, environmental policymaking in, 208, 210

Salitre River, Colombia, 55
sanitation. *See* wastewater
Santos, Juan Manual, 128–29
SEDAPAL (Peru's water and sanitation utility), 183, 185
self-built housing. *See* informal housing settlements
sewage. *See* wastewater
sewage canals, rivers as, 33–34, 61–62
shantytowns. *See* informal housing settlements
Shell petrochemical processing plant, 1, 46, 50, 78, 79n.11, 89–90, 105
Shining Path (Sendero), 170–71, 170nn.25–26
SIE Environmental Corporation (SIE Corporación Ambiental), Colombia, 119*t*, 123–24, 140–41

siting conflicts, 38–39, 162, 202
slow diluted harms, 35t, 37
slow harms. *See also* Bogotá; Buenos
    Aires; Lima
  Bogotá River, 51–58
  bridging activism and, 6, 23t
  in case study cities, 13, 32
  community mobilizing around, 13
  in Global South, 23
  invisible development of, 33, 112
  Matanza Riachuelo River, 42–50
  Rímac River, 59–66
  temporal proximity to bodily harm and,
    68–69, 198
  in typology of harms, 35t
slow targeted harms, 35t, 39–41, 198–99
sludge facilities, 38–40, 41
slums, Latin American, 40–41. *See also*
    informal housing settlements
smoke signals, 13–14, 70, 117–25
social capital, 14, 14n.10, 15, 28
social justice, 94–96. *See also* human rights
social mobilization. *See* bonding
    mobilization; bridging mobilization
    or activism; grassroots activism or
    organizations; human rights groups or
    movements
Soviet Union. *See* post-Soviet countries
SPDA (Sociedad Peruana de Derecho
    Ambiental), Peru, 177–78, 180–82,
    183, 194–95
stagnated policy shifts, 2n.3, 22, 23t, 24–25,
    32, 114, 145–50
Suba, Bogotá, Colombia, 2, 113, 121, 203
Supreme Court
  Argentina, 70, 86–87, 90–91, 91n.35, 95–
    96, 96n.42, 98n.52, 104–5
  Colombia, 131n.33, 194
  Peru, 176

Talking River. *See* Rímac River
Tamboraque mine, Peru, 65–66, 163, 165f
tanneries
  Bogotá River and, 53–54, 148–49
  Matanza Riachuelo River and, 46, 47–50,
    102–3, 103n.70
  Rímac River and, 63–64
targeted rapid harms. *See* rapid harms
temporal proximity to bodily harm
  acceleration, 35n.2

citizen collective action and, 198–99
  duration, 34–36, 35n.2, 40–41
  as environmental harm, 34, 35n.2, 198
  impediments to citizen action and, 34
  individual strategies based on, 68–69
  social behaviors surrounding, 35–36
  tempo, 35n.2
  timing, 35n.2
  in typology of harms, 35t
terrorism, in Peru, 170–71, 184n.69, 190
ties, strong and weak types, 14, 14n.9, 15
Toledo, Alejandro, 172
toxic exposure, 10, 12, 35–36. *See also*
    slow harms
toxic uncertainty, 11, 166
toxic waiting, 5
trash. *See* waste, solid
trust in expert systems, 11, 176–77
Truth Commissions (after armed conflict)
  Argentina (CONADEP), 85, 86n.22
  Colombia (SIRJVNR, established after
    2016), 130n.29
  Peru (CVR), 172–73
Tunjuelo, Bogotá, 123–24, 125f, 193
Tunjuelo River, 55, 123, 151
Tunjuelo Southern Assembly (Asamblea Sur
    de la Cuenca Tunjuelo), 119t, 123, 124
Turbay Quintero, Julio Cesar, 132n.39

uninitiated policy shifts, 22, 23t, 32. *See also*
    Rímac River
United States, 12, 18, 36–37, 160–61,
    203–4
Universal Declaration of Human Rights, 172
universities or university professors, 16–17,
    23–24, 78, 79–80, 104–5, 204–5
urbanization, 7, 9, 30–31, 33–34, 55, 60, 160.
    See also informal housing settlements;
    migrants
urban peripheries/ fringe, 8–9, 28–29. *See
    also* informal housing settlements
urban renewal, 74
urban settlements, 8–9. *See also* informal
    housing settlements
Uribe, Alvaro, 128–29

Vecinos de Lomas de Zamora, 98n.51
Veeduria Network for the Bogotá River
    (Veeduria Ciudadania Nuestro Rio
    Bogotá), 133

veedurias (citizen fiscal watchdog groups), Colombia, 132–33, 132n.39, 140–41, 142–44, 144n.67, 204–5
Velasco, Juan, 170n.26
Vía Parque Rímac (transit line), Lima, 167–68, 167n.19, 193–94
Videla, Jorge, 85n.20
Vietnam, 211
Villa Inflamable, Avellaneda, Buenos Aires, 3f, 43–44, 50, 52n.25, 108–9, 193
Villamizar, Nelly, 130–32, 139, 140–41, 142–43, 142n.61, 153
Villarán, Susana, 167n.19, 193–94
violence (political violence)
 Argentina, 27t, 71–72, 85n.20, 129
 citizen action against, 6, 210–11
 Colombia, 113, 117, 126–27, 129, 129n.28
 environmentalism and, 7, 32
 Peru, 157, 178, 196, 201
 presidential partisanship and, 19
 slow, environmental harms as, 34
 social, faster-moving harms and, 179–80
vulnerability, exposure to physical harm and, 36–37

waste, solid
 Argentina, 44–46, 101–2, 104, 105
 Colombia, 52, 53n.28, 55, 56, 58, 113, 147
 industrial, 1, 46, 56
 landfills, 1, 38–40, 44–46, 63–64, 74, 81, 105, 166–67
 livestock, 2–4, 4f, 47–50, 53–54, 56–57, 179
 management, services, or disposal, 41, 74, 104, 105, 195–96
 Peru, 61–62, 63–64, 167
 slow-harms accumulation and, 42, 69
wastewater. *See also* sanitation
 in Africa, 7, 41
 Argentina lagoons, 3f
 Argentina sewers, 1, 79–80, 80f, 102
 Bogotá River and, 52, 53n.28, 56, 147, 148
 in case study cities, 30–31
 Colombia sewers, 56
 global health impacts or deaths from, 4–5, 29–30, 33–34
 healthy cities and, 41
 household pollution and, 4–5
 management, 41
 Matanza Riachuelo River and, 1, 42–44, 45f, 50, 52n.25
 one-sector, many places approach and, 29–30
 Rímac River and, 61–62, 166–67, 179, 186
 slow harms and, 4f, 32, 33, 33n.1, 34, 39–40, 69
 treatment plants, 58, 102, 102n.65, 102–3n.67, 154–55
We Are the Bogotá River (Somos Río Bogotá), 119t, 122–23, 124, 133
weather events, extreme, 161. *See also* floods or flooding
wetlands, 74, 81–83, 121–22, 203
working-class groups, 42–43, 44–46, 123, 151–52
working sessions or tables (*mesas de trabajo* or *de dialogo*) or groups
 Argentina, 79–80, 89–91, 110
 Colombia, 123, 130–31, 139
 Peru, 167–68, 177–78, 179, 190
 pollution-remediation policymaking and, 207
 on rapid targeted harms, 38–39
World Bank, 102, 147, 150–51, 160–61, 161n.5, 186
World Health Organization, 4–5, 41–42